VAHAGN VARDANYAN

NATIONAL IDENTITY, DIASPORA, AND SPACE OF BELONGING

AN ARMENIAN PERSPECTIVE

Ψ

Gomidas Institute
London

Vahagn Vardanyan was born in Armenia and has lived in East/South-East Asia for nearly two decades. He has a PhD in political geography and an active interest in national identity and homeland-diaspora relations. He currently teaches at Han Academy in Hong Kong.

Published by Gomidas Institute

ISBN 978-1-909382-69-5

05 04 03 02 01

For comments and more information please contact:
Gomidas Institute
42 Blythe Rd
London W14 0HA
United Kingdom
Email: *info@gomidas.org*
Web: *www.gomidas.org*

To my daughter

Anna, cherish your heritage!

ACKNOWLEDGEMENTS AND THANKS

I wish to thank all the people whose assistance was a milestone in the completion of this work, in particular,

Associate Professor Victor R. Savage, Dr. Carl Grundy-Warr, and Professor Tim Bunnell of the National University of Singapore for their professional advice in the research process;

Hranush Hakobyan, Minister of Diaspora of the Republic of Armenia (2008-2018), and Anahit Zohrabyan, (then) head of a division in the Ministry, for providing materials for the work;

My research 'gatekeepers' for assistance in the fieldwork in Australia and all my interviewees;

His Eminence Archbishop Haigazoun Najarian, the Primate of Australia and New Zealand of the Armenian Apostolic Church, for his insightful thoughts shared in our discussions;

Professor Gagik Gurzadyan, Derenik Margaryan, Domenica Piantedosi, Ghevond Barikyan, Kristine Alagulyan, and the late Asya Khachatryan for encouragement and advice, and to Ara Sarafian for the valuable help provided in the final stage of preparing this book;

Poghos Varzhapetyan, Lusine Davtyan, Hripsime Simonyan, Vahan Hovhannisyan, Karen Tamazyan, and Armen Papazyan for kindly providing photographs for this work;

My daughter Anna for her substantial contribution as a language editor and, finally, my parents Roland and Tamara, for helping me shape and live my Armenian identity.

TABLE OF CONTENTS

NATIONAL IDENTITY, DIASPORA, AND SPACE OF BELONGING

AN ARMENIAN PERSPECTIVE

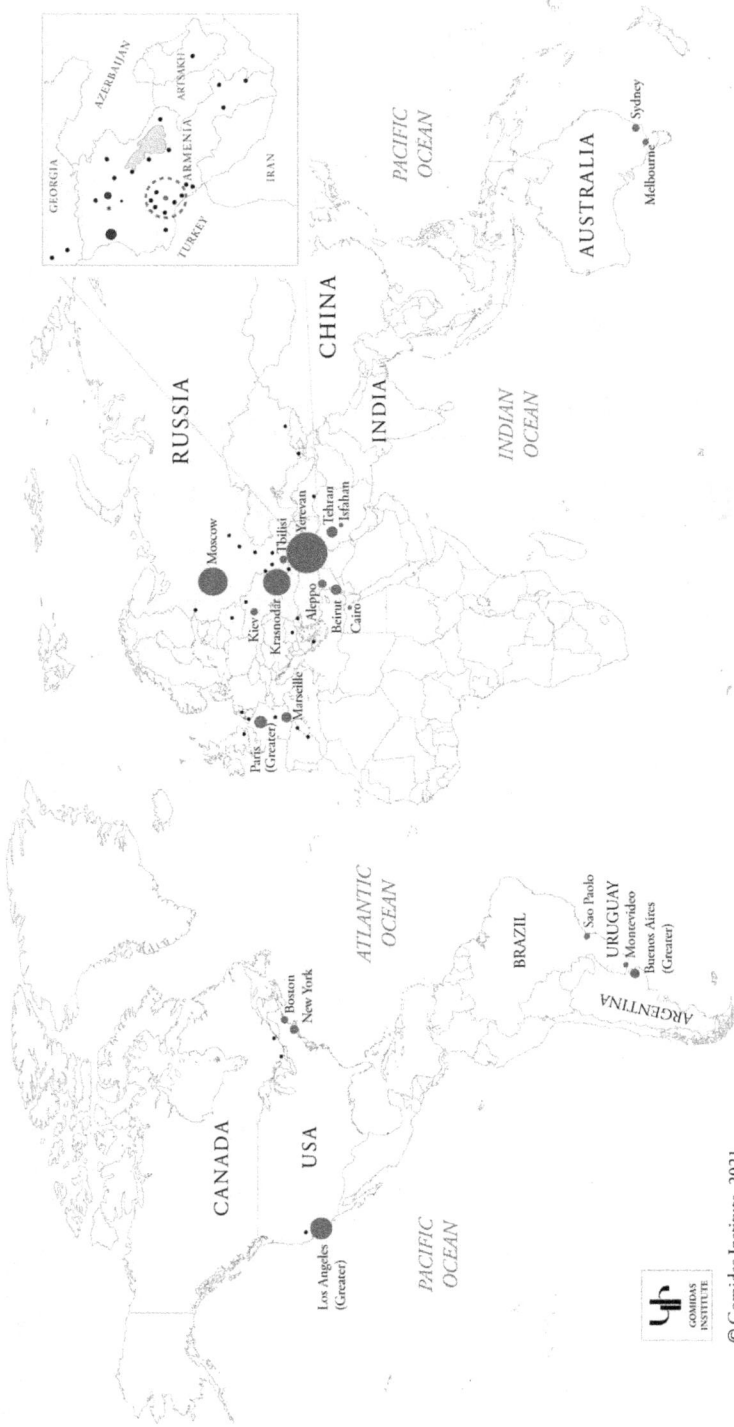

MAJOR URBAN-ARMENIAN COMMUNITIES OF THE WORLD

Armenian communities of 10,000 people and above, as detailed in this study, pp. 96-100

© Gomidas Institute, 2021

"Place is security, space is freedom; we are attached to the one and long for the other."

— Yi-Fu Tuan

PREFACE

"Geography is destiny." It is rumored that Emperor Napoleon said this before his Russian campaign of 1812. History has witnessed rises and falls of nations and empires, predetermined by their location, terrain, and climate. Geography makes countries attractive for invasion, but also for cooperation; for destruction, but also integration. Countries have left their colonies and have acquired new territories driven by geography. "Geography," as Tim Marshall points out, "is clearly a fundamental part of the 'why' as well as the 'what'" in politics (Marshall, 2019: viii). The Armenian people, throughout their history, 'blessed' by geography, have failed to develop survival skills and maintain their national identity in their territory, on the Armenian Highlands, in order to stay immune to the threat of annihilation and destruction. The lack of pragmatism, particularly, in nation-building, has arguably shaped the existing geopolitical trap for the Armenian nation-state and, through it, for the Armenian people. The need to find a way for survival and progress has become second to none for Armenians.

This work was mostly completed when early morning on Sunday, September 27, 2020, I, as all Armenians worldwide, received shattering news. War in Artsakh! After nearly three decades, since the collapse of the Soviet Union, as a result of unsuccessful diplomatic attempts by Azerbaijan to gain control over the Armenian-populated Republic of Artsakh (formerly known as Nagorno-Karabakh), Azerbaijan unleashed a military campaign and broke the UN-mandated OSCE-mediated negotiation process.[*]

With sovereignty proclaimed through a referendum, though internationally unrecognized, the Armenian-populated Republic of Artsakh[†] was attacked by the Republic of Azerbaijan with the massive

---

[*] Organization for Security and Co-operation in Europe.
[†] The Republic of Artsakh is located between the Republic of Armenia (as it is recognized internationally) and the Republic of Azerbaijan.

1

support of Turkey and the involvement of international terrorists.* The war, later known as the 44-Day War or the Second Artsakh War, ended on November 9, 2020, by signing a declaration between President Putin of Russia (as the mediator), Prime Minister Pashinyan of Armenia, and President Aliyev of Azerbaijan. The war became a turning point in the modern history of Armenia-Artsakh and the Armenian people. Moral depression, economic downturn, territorial losses, and, on top of these, the loss of thousands of lives, mainly young military servicemen, have been the outcomes of this war. Never a part of independent Azerbaijan, Artsakh exercised its right to sovereignty when it left the Soviet Union in December 1991 by following a legally-sanctioned path. However, its independence is not recognized by any UN member-state. Since the early-1990s, for nearly three decades, the parties to the conflict and the mediators repeatedly and consistently stressed the importance of peaceful resolution of the conflict and rejection of a military solution. The borders of Artsakh were established as a result of the counter-offensive by Artsakh against the undeclared military campaign by Azerbaijan, known as the First Artsakh War, which resulted in the 1994 cease-fire. The premeditated war unleashed by Azerbaijan in September 2020, therefore, became an attack on Artsakh's territorial integrity and an illegal attempt to occupy it. The war also demonstrated unprecedented support and mobilization of the global Armenian diaspora to support Artsakh.

* * *

Diaspora studies have become increasingly popular over the past two to three decades. This has happened, in part, because of the increased mobility of people over the past decades and the stronger impact diasporan communities have had on their homelands' political, economic, and social life. Seeing diaspora communities as bridging tools with the rest of the world is another factor which motivates homelands' inclusive policies toward their diasporas. Diasporas, in this sense, are seen as bodies that can "serve to strengthen rather than undermine nation states" (Kenny, 2013: 107).

It is essential to identify what preserves diasporic identities such as the Armenian diaspora across the world, in order to understand the extent of

---

* President Macron of France openly accused Turkey of sending Syrian jihadists to Nagorno-Karabakh (Reuters, 01.10.2020)

the engagement of diasporas in pan-national processes. What are the factors and conditions affecting the relationship between this diaspora and its homeland nation-state? Does the size of diaspora communities matter? Have the inclusive policies of their nation-state (Armenia) shaped diaspora communities? Is the Armenian diaspora, with its institutions, capable of promoting national identity as it did before the independence of the Armenian Republic? Addressing these questions will contribute to meeting the objectives of this book and further broaden the framework of diaspora studies.

This book views the homeland-diaspora relations and their connections to national identity within the framework of the foundational political geography concepts of 'space' and 'place.' It attempts to advance our understanding of relations between the diaspora and its homeland, particularly after the latter obtained political sovereignty (i.e., the establishment of a nation-state). In the book, the relations between the two parts of the nation are viewed through the prism of three dimensions: the role of institutions which link the diaspora with the homeland; the phenomenon of 'permanent return' as a process of reaching the homeland through spaces; and the formation or development of diasporans' sense of belonging to their historical or cultural homeland.

Through an empirical study of the Armenian diaspora, which offers a framework for the study of diaspora-state relationships, this book focuses on two geographically remote-from-homeland Armenian communities in the same country – in Sydney and Melbourne in Australia. Thus, and more specifically, the following main objectives are undertaken on the basis of this work:

- To understand how the post-independence homeland relates to the diaspora and people in diaspora communities to their homeland;
- To identify the role diaspora institutions play in the relations between diaspora communities and their homeland, as perceived by diasporans. The particular focus will be on the role of religious, educational, and social institutions.
- To examine the political and cultural geographic dimensions of the inclusion of a multi-sited non-territorial diaspora in relation to the territorial nation-state (homeland), and to identify the extent to which the latter influences ideas about the national identity of diasporans.

The inclusion of the diaspora in the homeland is not a smooth process and, as argued later in the book, faces a problem of contested leadership between the two sides. Arguably, this can be one of the reasons why nation-states sometimes even choose to apply specific exclusionary policy measures, as was the case in Armenia in the mid-1990s, when various segments of the diaspora, in particular the Armenian Revolutionary Federation (ARF), one of the oldest Armenian political institutions was excluded from the country's political life (Herzig and Kurkchiyan, 2005: 233).

The selection of the two cities – Sydney and Melbourne – has been based on the following factors: first of all, Australia is home to the two largest Armenian communities in the whole Asia-Australia region, with about 40,000 community members in Sydney and about 10,000 in Melbourne (ANC Australia, *Armenian-Australian Community*),[*] while in the whole of Asia, from the Middle East to the Far East (i.e., east of Iran and excluding the former Central Asian Soviet republics), there cannot be more than a couple of thousand Armenians found.[†] The two cities selected for the study are the largest in Australia by population[‡] and have significantly larger ethnic Armenian populations compared to other cities in the country.

Studies of classical diasporas, including of the Armenian diaspora, have been conducted worldwide. However, in terms of the identification of relations between the diaspora and Armenia, and the implications of this relationship on the national identity of diasporans, the diaspora remains understudied. This study is an attempt to fill the gap, to a certain extent, by examining diaspora-Armenia relations from the perspective of geographically remote communities, in particular, regarding a nation that has achieved political sovereignty while already having an established diaspora.

Our approach to understanding the diaspora, as outlined, can be relevant to other diasporic nations as well, and it can serve as a framework for further study by other scholars of the field. Apart from on-site data

---

[*] Numbers vary from source to source, while being comparable at some level.

[†] These estimates are based on Ayvazyan, H. and Sargsyan, A., *Encyclopedia of the Armenian Diaspora* (in Armenian), Armenian Encyclopedia, 2003, pp. 173, 357, 387, 458.

[‡] 5,600,000 people in Sydney and over 4,500,000 in Melbourne (Population Australia, *Australia Population 2018*).

collection in the selected two cities, data from other communities in Australia and beyond have also been used. A significant part of the information used in this work has been collected in Armenia, particularly in its capital city of Yerevan, which has a high concentration of political, cultural, and economic pan-Armenian institutions.[*]

This book covers a wide spectrum of 'diaspora' as a category, from its theoretical framework down to real-life cases of particular diasporic communities. Set within the framework of fundamental political-geography concepts of 'nation,' 'space' and 'place,' with specific emphasis on 'national identity' and 'diaspora,' our framework leads through the theory of what scholars have written about 'nation' and 'national identity,' followed by the coverage of 'diaspora' and 'diaspora return.' The connection between 'space' and 'identity' is presented with coverage of what shapes the relationship between the diaspora and its homeland.

Based on the above conceptual framework, this book introduces the Armenian diaspora by providing an in-depth coverage of Armenian national identity, as perceived by diasporans in our chosen communities. A brief introduction of the overall distribution of Armenian communities in the world is followed by the study of two communities in Australia, conducted mainly through on-site interviews with local Armenians, as well as through observations made in the communities. As an essential beginning of the study of the two communities is an identification of the 'roots' and 'routes' of Armenians in both cities. Such an argument is presented by historian Kevin Kenny, who emphasizes "movements and connections" rather than origin when discussing diasporas, and that "in the language of cultural studies, it deals more with 'routes' than with 'roots' (Kenny, 2013: 108). A similar approach is proposed by Elizabeth Mavroudi, who states that traditionally diasporas have been studied in terms of "roots and the homeland," though new approaches "are based on ideas of fluidity, movement, routes and the destabilization of (potentially) homogenizing boundaries (cf identity, community, and the nation-state" (Mavroudi, 2007: 2). The discussion of the 'roots' and 'routes' of communities assumes a logical continuation of identification of what the

---

[*] One of such institutions is the Armenian Apostolic Church, the Seat of which – the Holy See of Etchmiadzin – is located in the town of Vagharshapat, about 30 km to the west of the Armenian capital, Yerevan (The Armenian Church, *Mother See*).

studied sample group identifies as its space of belonging. We have attempted to dig into the perception diasporans have of their historical homeland (Armenia, in this particular case), as well as their understanding of their own national identity. The latter, being affected by many determinants, can be subject to transformation (strengthening or weakening) from time to time and space to space. The study of national identity has, thus, been complemented by a discussion of the transformation of such an identity over the decades. The study of any diaspora community becomes more comprehensive not only by understanding the diasporans' own roots and their sense of belonging but also by their perception of the homeland. Diasporans, first of all, are 'ethnies,' if we apply Anthony Smith's term in this context (Smith, 1991; 1995: 5), who are in "permanent return" (Vardanyan, 2016: 76). As such, one can assume that they have an active awareness of their roots, and it is essential to understand the level of their engagement in their host space [hostlands], within their communities, as well as with the homeland. Engagement within the community can take various forms, and this book covers the framework of such engagement, as well as engagement with the homeland. Specifically, their connection to Armenia is examined from the perspective of both cultural and physical connections, i.e., to what extent the diasporans' physical presence, through their life experience in or visits to the homeland, has influenced their national identity.

Diaspora-homeland relations involve the engagement of individuals as community members or diasporans who interact with other community members and are in the process of diaspora return, in its various forms, with their homeland. Interaction can take place at an individual level. Still, the role of diaspora institutions is instrumental since these institutions help (or are there to help) diasporans maintain and strengthen their national identity and serve as networks in the whole communication process. This study does not attempt to provide an analysis of the activities of each diaspora institution but to present an overall perception of and engagement in such institutions by diasporans. These are social, political, educational, and religious institutions in the (Australian) Armenian communities. The role of the Armenian Apostolic Church has been studied, in particular, since it has been recognized by many diasporans, and commonly by the wider Armenian public, as one of the most important, if not the most important, carriers of Armenian identity over the past centuries. Thus, discussions of the role Armenian diaspora institutions play and are expected to play in the selected two communities, in the diasporans' viewpoint, demonstrate an ongoing transformation process that is taking place in the studied communities. It is widely argued for and against whether the size of the community matters for the community to be more effective as a space where diaspora identity can be preserved and strengthened.

In the end, this book provides an extensive overview of primary challenges in relations between the contemporary Armenian diaspora and Armenia. The analysis of problems has been conducted on the basis of information provided by the diasporans involved in the research and through observations and numerous conversations that reflect diasporans' views on the ongoing transformation of diaspora-homeland relations, in particular, as viewed through the prism of the problem of contested leadership between the two sides of the nation.

This book is written primarily because of the author's strong intellectual curiosity about the nature of diaspora-homeland relations and perspectives of national identity within diasporic communities. In a sense, it is an outcome of personal political-geography encounters. Being involved in this area of study through the personal first-hand life experience in Armenia, before and after it became a sovereign nation-state, I have witnessed the geopolitical transformation of Armenia into a small nation-state with a large diaspora and thought about the perception of Armenia in the diaspora. Throughout the past decades, by living in the diaspora in different countries and cities in Asia, I have developed a keen interest in issues of ethnic, national, and transnational identity, as well as the role of identity in promoting cultures, the relationship between the two parts of a nation, diaspora and the homeland nation-state. An experience acquired through a wide range of diaspora events, which particularly relates to Armenian institutional activities overseas, as well as events inside Armenia, has become another asset for the study.

My overall personal scope of dealing with diaspora-related processes and events includes living in and visiting countries where the Armenian diaspora is found, an experience of communication with diaspora communities in various regions, involvement in many local diaspora community events, and meetings of pan-Armenian and diaspora- related events in different countries. My interdisciplinary educational background and international work experience in academia and beyond (banking) have provided significant support in pursuing this endeavor. As the author, my position of an insider, who has lived the experience (in Armenia and diaspora), developed language skills and gained exposure to a broad range of cultures has enabled me to enjoy direct access to pertinent literature in English, Russian, and Armenian, in both of its dialects, Eastern and Western.

When conducting this study, my positionality has been an important factor, mainly as one for establishing effective connections with diasporic communities and their members. This work is an attempt to bring diasporans' views on national identity, narrative short stories told by the interviewees on their space of belonging, perception of the historical and cultural homeland, and the connections maintained with the homeland. As conceptual-analytical support to the study, the book provides coverage of what 'diaspora' is as an extraterritorial body.

The two largest Armenian diaspora community in Asia-Australia selected for the study are remote from the homeland, and diverse in terms of diasporic roots. Also, they have been understudied. Besides the communities in the selected two cities (Sydney and Melbourne), I have also visited other cities with Armenian diaspora communities (Singapore, Hong Kong, Perth, Kolkata, Yangon), and during the process of writing this work, travelled to Armenia more than 20 times.

This study assumes a cross-disciplinary approach, particularly as the notions of nation and national identity vary so much across time and space (Sidaway and Grundy-Warr, 2016: 118), with 'national identity' as a phenomenon viewed from a geographical perspective, in particular, by focusing on people in multi-sites of the diaspora. Two distinctive elements – extraterritorial aspects of the nation and the relevance of homeland as a territorial space – are views related to ideas of the diaspora's existence through notions of permanent return. Another dimension concerns the 'emotional significance' (Knight, 1982: 514) of places in the homeland for diasporans. The whole work has been an intensely personal story for the researcher. My position – an Armenian who spent his childhood in the Soviet Union, then the largest country in the world by landmass, in Soviet Armenia (the Union's smallest republic by landmass), who voted for its independence from the Union, who then spent many years studying and working outside of Armenia – in the United States, the largest economic power in the world, in China, the largest country by population, in Singapore, the smallest country in its region and one of the few city-states in the world, and, more recently in Hong Kong, a special territorial formation within a larger country (China) – definitely assumes that the book cannot be written without reference to my own experiences and knowledge of 'being Armenian' within and outside the homeland. Thus, it is time to reveal something of that history and the research conducted throughout the years of this study, much of which has been done while juggling with private and work commitments.

PART I

Chapter 1

THE ROOTS OF THE STUDY

At the beginning of this research process, it was very difficult to know precisely where to begin with the topic of diaspora, particularly given its broad geography and multiple locations where Armenians reside globally. As a small nation, Armenia's relations with its global diaspora are seen essential in terms of the inclusion of the latter in the whole nation, as well as for the successful development of the country's progress and international reputation.

Yerevan, the capital of Armenia, is the city where I was born and lived three decades of my life, albeit with some travel to other countries. By 1991, when Armenia was still part of the USSR (Soviet Union), my travel was limited to Armenia and some regions (republics) of the Soviet Union. While traveling within Armenia. I was exposed to Armenian architecture and the cultural landscape by visiting numerous churches, museums, and other sites. After Armenia achieved its independence, any travel out of Armenia was already a journey abroad. During the Soviet times, it was not easy to travel abroad since special permission was required in order to leave the country. Soviet citizens in the USSR used their passports for internal travel. For travelling abroad, a special international passport was required.

In early-1988, an unprecedented event took place, which became the beginning of a new era for the Armenian nation. In February, the people in predominantly Armenian-populated Nagorno-Karabakh Autonomous Oblast (region) in Azerbaijan Soviet Socialist Republic applied to local and later central authorities in Moscow for a decision to join the Armenian SSR (BBC, *Nagorno-Karabakh Profile*). Mass political demonstrations to support Karabakh (or Artsakh, as a historical, and now official, name) took place in Yerevan and other regions of Armenia. The whole year was very dramatic. Soon after the development of the unification movement, the Soviet authorities decided to bring military troops to Yerevan. A curfew regime was imposed later that year. 1988 ended with the tragic earthquake on December 7th, which killed about one percent of Armenia's total population, left 19,000 people injured, 540,000 homeless, and "destroyed 21 towns and 302 villages" (Crippen, 2001), virtually the entire northern region of the country.

The period of 1989-91 was one of rapid economic and political transformation in the country; simultaneously, it was a time when the entire Soviet Union started showing signs of its end. 1991 was a very important turning point for me too. A referendum for Armenia's independence was organized on September 21, 1991, which became the first-ever referendum in Armenia (CSCE report, 1991: 1). It was also the first time I was able to exercise my voting right as a citizen of Armenia having turned 18 only a month prior to the event. Shortly after that, in mid-October, the first elections of the President of the Republic of Armenia took place, and, in only two months from then, in December, the USSR was dissolved and ceased its seven decades of existence in the world political arena.

In the early 1990s, as a result of major political and economic transformations, as well as an economic blockade initiated by Turkey against Armenia in solidarity with Azerbaijan in its war with Armenian-populated Nagorno-Karabakh (Artsakh), Armenia's economy nearly collapsed. Thus, the very early years of independence posed major challenges for the survival of the newly independent homeland-state for Armenians – the Republic of Armenia.

With a couple of short trips abroad, my first major travel was to the United States for graduate study. That time proved formative in relation to this book. It was during my travels in the United States when I met Armenian diaspora communities, visited churches, and participated in Armenian events. At the time, I had begun thinking about pursuing a study about national identity. Therefore, this book is an extension of a personal journey. It began with Armenia's independence, my experiences of living in the country under the Soviet Union, then, in a small (already) sovereign state, plus my travels abroad, which all led me to understand the significance of the diaspora. In a sense, as already mentioned above, the work is an outcome of my personal experiences, which also include living as a professional worker overseas. These experiences all affect the perception of one's own identity in diverse spaces.

As a geo-cultural pre-nation-state phenomenon, the Armenian diaspora has existed for centuries, mainly as a trade diaspora. However, as argued, over the 20th century (mainly after 1915), it has become a predominantly 'victim' diaspora.[*] The diaspora, as suggested, in its modern post-nation-state form, is more or less a phenomenon shaped in the post-Genocide era. While living in Soviet Armenia, we had a distant knowledge of the diaspora, and among its main representatives, the Armenian Revolutionary Federation - *Dashnaktsutiun* (ARF) and *Hay Dat*[†] abroad were perceived as probably its most active parts. However, the ARF was portrayed as a hostile organization to the USSR, particularly through Soviet propaganda. Things started to change, especially after the earthquake, which centered near the town of Spitak in Armenia in December 1988. The diaspora's involvement in helping the country after its north was severely damaged was extraordinary. By the late-1980s, in particular by 1988, when the Karabakh Movement had commenced, Armenia became the focal point for political news in the Soviet Union and drew serious attention in various parts of the world, and the diaspora, in particular. The year (1988), which was initiated with the Karabakh Movement and concluded with the devastating earthquake, became a critical moment in the history of Armenia. The diaspora, although still not efficiently engaged with Armenia, began to realize that the least that could be achieved in order to create a bridge to Armenia would be economic assistance.

Prior to the end of the 1980s, one of the most important (if not the main) collective memory moments for Armenians – the Armenian Genocide, as a legal concept, or the *Medz Yeghern*, as a more profound term – could not be openly discussed in the Soviet Union (outside of Soviet Armenia) because of the declared friendship of the peoples of the USSR, which included Azerbaijan.[‡] However, within Armenia, the

---

[*] For instance, the Jewish diaspora is an example of a 'victim' diaspora; the Greek diaspora has trade in its origin, while the Armenian diaspora, initially being trade-based, became predominantly a 'victim' diaspora at the end-19th and early 20th century (based on Robin Cohen's classification, in Cohen, 1997), as a result of the Hamidian Massacres of 1895-97, and especially, the Armenian Genocide – the *Medz Yeghern* – of 1915.

[†] *Hay Dat* refers to 'the Armenian Question', "i.e., it is centered on the concepts of recognition and retribution" (Zolian, Heinrich Boll Stiftung, *Remembering and Demanding*).

[‡] The population of Azerbaijan consists of nearly 92% ethnic Turkic people, often referred to as 'Azerbaijani' (The CIA World Factbook, *Azerbaijan*).

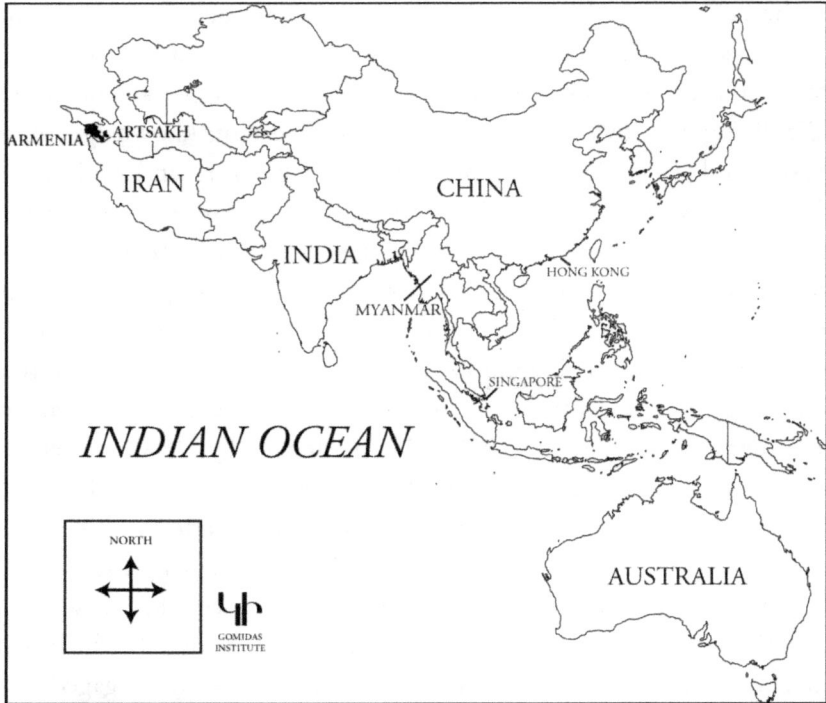

Map of South-East Asia and Australia, including
Armenia, Iran and India

Armenian Genocide was a tragedy the people remembered, and many visited the Genocide Memorial at Tsitsernakaberd on April 24 every year.[*]

At the end of the Soviet era, Armenia started more active engagement with the diaspora. During the early years of independence, Armenia even had ministers in the Armenian government from the diaspora,[†] including the first Minister of Foreign Affairs (1991-1992), although the links with

---

[*] The Armenian Genocide Memorial at Tsitsernakaberd in Yerevan is the main monument dedicated to the memory of the victims of the Genocide. It was completed in 1968, as construction works started, to commemorate the 50th anniversary of what was known as the official start of the tragedy (in 1915). The Memorial has been further developed into a museum and a research complex (Armenian National Institute at the Tsitsernakaberd Complex).

[†] Raffi K. Hovhannisyan (the first Minister of Foreign Affairs), Vardan Oskanian (Deputy Minister, then Minister of Foreign Affairs), Sebouh Tashjian (Minister of Energy), and Gerard J. Libaridian (senior adviser to the President and Secretary of the Security Council) were all from the diaspora (Payaslian, 2007: 201).

16

diasporic communities were geopolitically weak at that time. In its early years of independence, Armenia's political leadership did not favor the institute of dual or multiple citizenships. The main arguments against it, as it was commonly highlighted, were related to possible problems with mandatory military conscription in Armenia and the political engagement of diasporan citizens of Armenia. Thus, the diaspora (as well as local citizens) was deprived of an opportunity for dual citizenship (Panossian, 1998: 171).

A key aspect of Armenians' sense of nation relates to religion, and the central role of the Armenian Apostolic Church in Armenian culture cannot be overestimated. According to a recent study by Pew Research Centre on religious and national identity in Eastern Europe (Panarmenian.net, 2017), Armenia is one of the top nations (the 2nd) regarding the proportion of religious followers in the population (95%, second to Georgia to its north, with 99%). Most of these 95% percent (89% of the total) reveal their affiliation to the Orthodox churches (Eastern Orthodox), specifically the Armenian Apostolic Church in Armenia (Panarmenian.net, 2017). The attitude toward religion has not diminished over the years of Armenia's independence. Notwithstanding a large number of adherents, it is another point whether the people affiliating themselves to religion are actually religious or not. Thus, according to the same study, 45% of Armenia's population prays every day, and, as responded, only 9% attend a church on a regular basis – once a week (Panarmenian.net, 2017). Nevertheless, in a country that hosts hundreds of churches (buildings), most of which have been standing for centuries, another hundred have been built throughout the past nearly three decades of independent Armenia (Hetq.am, 2017).

Before embarking on this study, as already mentioned above, I visited many Armenian churches and other cultural sites in different cities – Los Angeles and Moscow, Singapore and Hong Kong, Kolkata and Perth, Sydney and Melbourne, and indeed, in Armenia and Artsakh. Furthermore, over the years of living in the diaspora, I became more interested in ethnic, national, and transnational identity issues, the importance of identity in promoting cultures, and the relationship between the two parts of a nation – diaspora and nation-state. Over the years, my immersion in many diasporic events and activities enhanced my

Meeting Armenia's President (S. Sargsyan) in Singapore, March 2012

Liturgy at the Armenian Apostolic Church of St. Gregory
the Illuminator, Singapore, March 2011

experience. It included events overseas and in Armenia. For instance, in Singapore, a key event was the State Visit of the President of the Republic of Armenia in March 2012,[*] as well as the visit of a group of Armenian government officials earlier in January 2011, who arrived in the country for civil service training, organized by the Government of Singapore.[†]

In March 2011, one of the largest gatherings of Armenians took place in Singapore's history, many of whom arrived from overseas, to celebrate the 175th anniversary of the Armenian Church of St. Gregory the Illuminator. The liturgy service was conducted by Archbishop Aghan Baliozian, a long-serving head of the Far East and Australia Diocese of the Armenian Apostolic Church.

The visit of the head of the Armenian Church – His Holiness Garegin II, the Catholicos of All Armenians to Singapore in September 2014 was of particular importance, as, after his short stay, there was a well-represented trip to the Armenian Church in Yangon, Myanmar. While I was in Myanmar, I was astonished to find many assimilated Armenians, who were excited by the visit of the Catholicos and gathered for a meeting with him, attended a liturgy and child baptism services conducted by him during the tour.

Such events helped me shape my experience of Armenian community life in South and South-East Asia. From time to time, over these years, there have been visits by priests, in particular, His Eminence Bishop Vardan Navasardyan, Father Khoren and Father Arsen of Etchmiadzin, His Eminence Archbishop Aghan Baliozian and Archbishop Haigazoun Najarian of Sydney, the former and current Primates of the Armenian Apostolic Church of Australia and New Zealand, Father Zaven Yazichyan of Kolkata and, later, of Yangon. They all have conducted a liturgy service in the Armenian Church in Singapore. The visit of the *Armenia* ship in 2011, led by Zori Balayan, an Armenian writer and publicist, was another major event that triggered a gathering of the community. The boat was navigating around the world by visiting countries "where members of the Armenian diaspora have settled" (*Straits Times*, June 12: 2011). In South and South-East Asia, it stopped at cities and towns where there were Armenian churches, in particular, in India (Kolkata), Singapore, and Indonesia (Armenian Diaspora News Forum, "'*Armenia' ship arrives in Singapore.*")

---

[*]   The State Visit to Singapore by Serzh Sargsyan, the President of the Republic of Armenia was conducted on March 27-29, 2012, at the invitation of the President of the Republic of Singapore Tony Tan Keng Yam. It was "the first State Visit to Singapore from the Republic of Armenia" (Ministry of Foreign Affairs of Singapore, *Visit of the President of Armenia*).

[†]   Source: The Istana, *Toast by Singapore's President.*

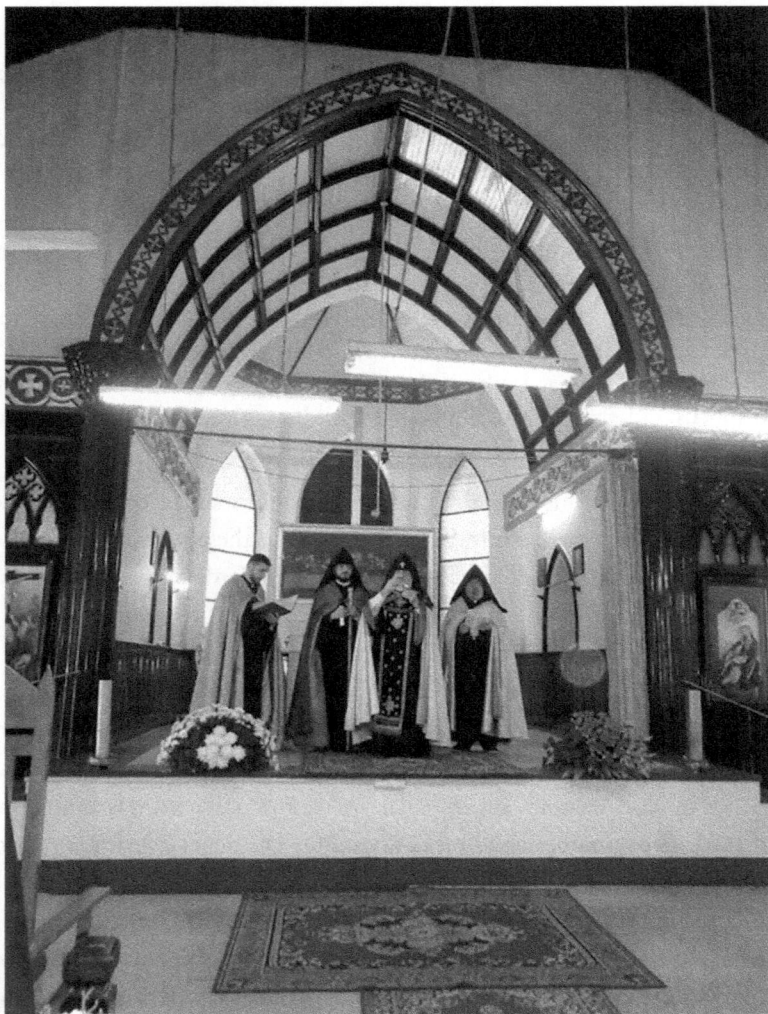

Liturgy served by His Holiness Garegin II, the Catholicos of
All Armenians, at the Armenian Apostolic Church of St. John
the Baptist, Yangon, Myanmar, September 2014

Other forms of participant observation have also shaped this study, including some in Armenia, in an official capacity. Among such were participation in a meeting of the State Committee on 100th Anniversary of the Armenian Genocide (May 2014), the Forums for Prevention of the Crime of Genocide (2015, 2016), a forum on national identity and diaspora organized jointly by the Ministry of Diaspora and the Diplomatic Academy of the Ministry of Foreign Affairs (July 2016). In addition, attendance at the liturgy service conducted by His Holiness Francis I, the Pope of Rome (June 2016), speeches delivered in universities (American University of Armenia, Russian-Armenian State University, Academy of Public Administration) and to the senior staff of the Ministry of Diaspora (February 2016), and interviews given on Armenia-diaspora relations and national identity, have all enriched my capacity for this study.

On September 21, 2016, the 25th anniversary of Armenia's independence, an open letter authored by me was sent to several institutions in Armenia and the diaspora. The letter touched on various issues relating to national identity preservation, the development of Armenia's 'brand,' and Armenia-diaspora relations (Vardanyan, 10/2016). Among the proposed measures was changing the name of the Republic of Nagorno-Karabakh to 'the Republic of Artsakh.' This change was eventually included in the constitutional amendments in December 2016 (Lenta.ru, 11/2016). A lecture to clergy members in the Holy See of Etchmiadzin (January 2017) was another unique experience of speaking on national identity and Armenia-diaspora relations in the center of the Armenian Church – as argued, the most connected and widespread Armenian institution across the world. Speaking at the Armenian Genocide commemoration evening organized by the AGBU Sydney Chapter (April 22, 2018) became another memorable event. Being geographically remote from Armenia, the audience was curious about the political processes in Armenia – events that led, on the following day (April 23, 2018), to the process later named 'the Armenian Velvet Revolution.'[*]

---

[*] On April 23, 2018, facing large-scale protests throughout the whole country, lasting for 10 days, Serzh Sargsyan, newly-appointed as Prime Minister of Armenia, who served as President of the country for two consecutive five-year terms immediately prior to April 2018, resigned. The news was welcomed by mass celebrations across the country until early morning on the following day, which was already the Armenian Genocide Commemoration Day (April 24).

Before September 2020 and afterward, in my writings, the Armenia-diaspora relations and the importance of strengthening, enduring and promoting Armenian national identity were discussed. In an extended article, the development philosophy of a small nation-state was analyzed (Vardanyan, Economics Scientific, 2019). Based on Singapore's example, it provided a comparative insight into the perspectives of Armenia's development. As notified by the publisher, the material provided information support for the official visit of Armenia's Prime Minister to Singapore.[*]

As mentioned above, September 2020 became another cornerstone of Armenia's and Artsakh's history. After 26 years of cease-fire in force, since May 1994, and commitments toward the peaceful resolution of the Artsakh (Nagorno-Karabakh) conflict, confirmed through repeated statements, including from Azerbaijan's side, the war initiated by the latter put an end (or, at least, paused for a while) to the established international negotiation process, as delegated by a mandate given by the United Nations to the Organization for Security and Co-operation in Europe (OSCE) and its *Minsk Group* (OSCE Minsk Group website).

Throughout my first-hand exposure to Armenian gatherings and events and my Armenian positionality, I identified the scope of related activities to conduct in the two selected cities – Sydney and Melbourne. I established relations with community leaders and representatives of diaspora institutions, government officials in Armenia, many Armenian diasporans in the selected and other cities of Australia and Asia with relatively large Armenian communities – Perth, Kolkata, Singapore, Kuala Lumpur, Beijing and Hong Kong. Additionally, the Ministry of Diaspora of Armenia was helpful in its support by providing materials and information for the study.

Understanding Diaspora: On-site Visits

My first visit to Australia was in 2008 for a professional development workshop. The trip was for three days only, yet its very first day already created a diasporic short story. On an Australian autumn day in April 2008, together with two of my colleagues, an American of Jewish ancestry and Canadian with Portuguese roots, we settled down in a hotel in North Sydney. As it was already late evening, we found only one open restaurant

---

[*] The visit of Prime Minister Pashinyan was paid on July 7-8, 2019 (Government of Armenia website).

in the area, called *El Capitano*. Soon after we entered, the waiter asked where I was from, and upon my reply, "I am Armenian," he responded, in Armenian, "Hay es?" ("Are you Armenian?"). We began conversing in Armenian, and he told me that the restaurant was their family business and that both his father and uncle were working there, both of whom emerged from the kitchen, and we spoke briefly. My two colleagues revealed to me how surprised they were. I was the first Armenian they had known by then, as they told me, and they could not imagine witnessing me speaking Armenian with the first stranger we met on our foreign trip, in a country so remote from Armenia. This was an emotional experience, another one, which further encouraged me to go deeper in my understanding of national identity and diaspora.

Years later, in December 2013, while in Sydney on a short visit, on one hot summer Sunday, I decided to go to the Armenian Church in North Sydney (in the Chatswood area). Arriving at Chatswood train station, but being unfamiliar with the area, I could not locate the Church. After walking back and forth, I noticed an old lady slowly walking toward the residential area from the closest mall. There was nobody else around there to approach, so I went to her and asked for the way to Macquarie Street. She looked at me and asked if I was looking for the Armenian Church. I did not expect such a response and replied, "Yes, are you Armenian?" to which she answered affirmatively. Eventually, I found the Church. A liturgy service (*badarag*) had already started when I arrived there, and I stayed until its end. The service was devoted to the memory of the victims of the 1988 Earthquake in Armenia, with about 200-250 people attending it, followed by a dinner reception. After the liturgy service was over, His Eminence Bishop Haigazoun Najarian, in his address to the people, when referring to Armenia, said, "…and in remote Armenia…" This was a very unusual phrase for me to hear, as back in Armenia, we perceived Australia and the community there as far and remote. It was a different perception of the 'Armenia space' for me. That gathering further enriched my understanding of community life in Sydney and the perception diasporans have on reaching Armenia and the Armenia geographic space.

In addition to Sydney and Melbourne, as already mentioned, I have conducted interviews in Kolkata (India), where a historically significant Armenian diaspora community has been living since the early 17th century (The Australian, *The last Armenians in Old Calcutta*). I spoke with members of the Armenian community there, which is one of the oldest Armenian communities in Asia and the world, outside Armenia. Besides visiting Kolkata, I have also visited Perth, Australia, where I met the small Armenian community at an event dedicated to the establishment of the 'First Republic' and delivered a talk relating to Armenian national identity.* The presence of His Eminence Bishop Haigazoun Najarian from Sydney stressed the symbolic importance of the event, which was devoted to the anniversary of the Day (28 of May). I was one of the two speakers, along with Mr. Nishan Basmajian from Sydney, who spoke about the Sardarabad-Bash-Aparan Battle and about its significance for preserving Armenian statehood and identity.† The event was conducted in a small hall, adjacent to a Catholic church in Perth.‡

The event was followed by a short discussion after the presentations, followed by the *badarag* the next morning. During the following small reception, the community members were actively discussing various issues of pan-Armenian importance, with the most recent one being the Four-Day War in Artsakh in early-April, 2016.** Undoubtedly, these events built upon particular ideas about the nation in relation to Armenians living overseas. However, they also led me to critically consider the relationship between homeland and diaspora in ways that are different from a territorial state-centered viewpoint.

---

* May 28, 1918, is the day the Armenian National Council declared Armenia's independence and the creation of the Republic of Armenia (News.am, *Armenia Marks First Republic Day*). The Republic was the first nation-state for Armenians in modern times and has been commonly referred to as the 'First Republic.' May 28 is a public holiday in Armenia and is a popular holiday in the diaspora, especially in the West. The significance of the day for diasporans is strengthened by the fact that throughout the two years of independent Republic of Armenia, the country was governed by the Armenian Revolutionary Federation – *Dashnaktsutiun* (ARF), one the most influential political institutions in the Armenian diaspora, then and nowadays.

† The Battle of Sardarabad-Bash-Aparan is widely considered the event that enabled the Armenians to prevent Turkish occupation of Armenia and, thus, to establish the Republic of Armenia in 1918 (The Armenian Weekly, *Remembering Bash Aparan*).

‡ There is no Armenian Apostolic Church premise in Perth.

** The 'Four-Day War' was the first large-scale clash between the Armenian (Karabakh) and Azerbaijani forces, the first after the Karabakh cease-fire in May 1994 (The Economist, *Nagorno-Karabakh's War: A Frozen Conflict Explodes*).

* * *

There have been various factors and conditions that have assisted me in the process of writing this book. First of all, the strong willingness and sincere attitude of all the participants, who voluntarily joined the study and provided their in-depth views on questions raised by me. Despite the consent provided by the interviewees to mention their real names, I decided to use pseudonyms to refer to them. In addition, the events that have taken place in the communities I visited provided me with invaluable experiences in terms of first-hand exposure to the day-to-day problems and challenges diasporans face. Another factor was the information support I received from various diaspora-related organizations, located overseas or in Armenia. Vital support was transportation, which was provided to me by several interviewees. As a result of this, my overall travel time in both Sydney and Melbourne was significantly saved and was used efficiently.

Geographer Stan Stevens emphasizes the kindness of strangers and their special contribution because of the "relationships established with people and places" through good rapport, and not only through specific data collection exercises, including interviews and observations. (Stevens, 2001: 68, 70). This study, therefore, has been a story, a journey of discovery that can become another approach to work with the diaspora and its different communities. Certainly, the work does not aim to understand all the possible problems and issues diasporans experience in their host countries. Neither is there an intention to cover all possible places of importance and all the institutions and diaspora organizations in this study. Instead, the main objective is to provide an insight into how diasporans perceive their own national identity within the context of diaspora-homeland relations, and in particular, the transformation of those relations following the creation of a sovereign Armenian homeland. The data collected through visits to diaspora communities became small stories and opinions consolidated in one study.

As in any study, the fieldwork "is the ultimate mode of geographical exploration" (Stevens, 2001: 66). Various conversations held in those cities have helped me to shape more comprehensive insights into the relations between the Armenian diaspora and Armenia, as well as on a broad range of issues relating to the formation and preservation of Armenian national identity. The interviews and conversations were rich and reflected upon a series of viewpoints, often complementing each other and reflecting the views of diaspora community members on a wide range of issues related to diasporic life. The interviewees represented different generations, from those in their 20s and up to a person in his late-80s. They also came from a broad range of occupations and experiences, among them teachers, retired community members, businesspeople, engineers and lawyers, even representatives of diaspora organizations.

The interviews focused on three aspects:

- The sense of identity and belonging,
- A broader perspective on diaspora-return and the relationship between the diaspora and the homeland, and
- The ongoing transformations, challenges, and expectations regarding the diaspora-homeland relationship.

The interviewees had to be of Armenian origin, with at least one grandparent being of Armenian descent,[*] and at least 21-years-old. Furthermore, they had to possess at least one non-Armenian citizenship and to have been living out of Armenia for at least two years prior to the interview. To reduce or eliminate any possible biases, only one person from the same family could be interviewed.

Almost all the interviewees could speak Armenian; however, many had problems in writing in the language. Nevertheless, a lack of knowledge of Armenian was not a barrier to participation, as all the interviews were conducted in English. It is essential to specify that, without exception, all the interviewees who participated in the study did so willingly and without hesitation, with no preliminary filtering or selection process. All the interviewees identified themselves as diasporans and their views have been considered as those of true representatives of their respective communities, and a sample for broader generalizations.

Throughout the whole process of conducting the interviews, three interviewees served as 'gatekeepers' as part of their contribution to this project, as Campbell classifies such contributors (Campbell et al., 2006: 97). They provided access, direct or indirect, to resources needed for the study, such as "logistical, human, institutional, or informational," as it could be specified for a 'gatekeeper' in any other similar study (Campbell et

---

[*] A similar standard is applied by the Government of Armenia with regard to recognizing ethnic Armenians, who are qualified to obtain the citizenship of the Republic of Armenia through a simplified process (Ministry of Foreign Affairs of Armenia, *Citizenship*).

al., 2006: 97). Their help included assistance in driving to an interview place, providing relevant information, referencing to other interviewees, and linking to them. It should be stated here that all the interviewees showed their strong willingness to share ideas with me and some even asked to be interviewed upon hearing about the study.

The Diasporan Representatives

Helen, whom I had known since I began this work, lived in Melbourne. She helped me by referring several other interviewees through direct and indirect contacts and kindly aided me with transportation in that vast city. Vahe linked me to a couple of other interviewees in Sydney, and Vartan introduced me to some other diasporans I interviewed. It can be strongly argued that all of the interviewed diasporans provided their independent responses since there was no third person present during any interviews. Moreover, the interviewed diasporans could not know the questions used in interviews and how other diasporans responded (even if they knew them).

I contacted Vahe while I was in Singapore. I was referred to him by an Armenian friend in Singapore, where I lived and worked then. We met for an interview on a Sunday morning, and Vahe suggested sitting somewhere in a nearby shopping mall, where we could talk before shoppers started crowding the mall's space. After the interview with Vahe, he suggested visiting the Armenian Church on Macquarie Street in Chatswood, about which I have briefly written previously. There was a liturgy service *(badarag)* going on, led, as in the previous time, by His Eminence Bishop (now Archbishop) Haigazoun Najarian. The Church was full of people. Among the community members who attended the service was Ms. Gladys Berejiklian, then Minister of Transport of New South Wales, who later, in January 2017, became the Premier of New South Wales and served in the position until October 2021 (Parliament of New South Wales, *Gladys Berejiklian*).

After the service, Vahe introduced me to several community members, and I asked two of them whether they would agree to an interview for this study, to which they kindly agreed. Vrej greeted me in his house, together with his wife and two little children. We sat under a large umbrella in the backyard and, after a brief chat, I began conducting the interview. The next interview was with Bedros, a diasporan originally from the Middle East. To find a convenient place for the interview, Bedros suggested driving to a suburb of Sydney, where we sat on a balcony of a plaza.

Holy Badarag (liturgy) service at the
Armenian Apostolic Church of Holy Resurrection
in Sydney, Australia, October 2014

In the Galstaun College, New South Wales (Sydney area),
Australia, October 2014

Following our conversation, we visited one of the only two Armenian day schools in Australia – the Galstaun College.[*]

During my visits to Australia, I met His Eminence Archbishop Haigazoun Najarian a number of times at the Armenian Church in Sydney. In the course of an hour-long, fruitful discussion, His Eminence shared his views on a broad range of pan-Armenian national issues and, most importantly, on the role the Armenian Apostolic Church had to perform to strengthen Armenian national identity in the modern world.

During one of my trips to Melbourne, I interviewed Helen, who introduced me to her friend Lily, a high school teacher. Lily was on her way to meet us, while Helen and I were waiting at a shopping mall for her. Then, something interesting happened while we were waiting. We noticed three women sitting at a table next to us, an older one and two in their 40's. They were having a conversation in Turkish. Nevertheless, I had a gut feeling that they were Armenian. Helen was quite sure about it too and initiated a conversation with them. It turned out that they were *Bolsahay* (Armenians from Istanbul); a mother in her 70s, along with her two daughters, who, as we were told, spoke Turkish as their first language. One of the daughters even told me about their brother, who, according to her, had a stronger sense of Armenian identity than they did. These ladies were examples of only Armenian 'ethnies' and not diasporans who, despite their ethnic roots, did not carry attributes of 'diaspora return.'[†]

In Melbourne, Helen showed me a little book titled, *My Beloved Armenia,* and told me that she bought two copies of it years earlier and treated them as something of particular emotional value. It was a touching moment for me to receive one of these copies as a gift from Helen. On another day, the two of us visited the Armenian Church in Melbourne together. The church building was bigger compared to the one in Sydney; the Armenian community purchased it in 1962.[‡] Quite spacious, it had an

---

[*] Hamazkayin Arshak and Sophie Galstaun School (College) is one of the two Armenian day schools in Australia (with the second being AGBU Alexander Primary School) (Hayern Aysor, *Interview with Australian-Armenian political scientist*).

[†] Under 'ethnie,' in the context of this work, only carriers of ethnic identity with no connection to the diasporic homeland are meant.

[‡] Source: The Armenian Apostolic Church of St. Mary, *The History of St. Mary Church in Melbourne.*

adjacent hall with a stage, so that theatre and other performances could be conducted there. Apart from the Armenians I met and spoke within the church and the hall, I noticed a gentleman sitting at a table in the corner. He appeared to be in his late 40s and did not look Armenian. I approached him. The man told me that he had never been to Armenia. He said that he was taking Armenian language lessons and added that he had been interested in Armenian for a long time. Was it pure curiosity? During our brief conversation, the man revealed that he had a tiny (1/16, as specified) portion of Armenian blood. This was a pure example of diaspora-return. A person with only a tenuous Armenian ethnic background maintained links to the community and one of its primary institutions – the Church. In addition, he made a great effort to learn the language of his Armenian ancestors, who lived at least a century ago, by spending a significant part of his time at weekends doing so. Since then, we have been in touch by email, and he continues to preserve his Armenian heritage. Luckily, that visit was on a Saturday, and I could see the weekend school in operation, as well as meet its principal and visit its classrooms.

Indeed, children attending a weekend school have comparatively limited opportunities to learn the language (Armenian, in our case) than those who study it at a full-day school, where the language is used in teaching on a more regular basis. However, such weekend schools play essential diasporic roles since students attending them are exposed to the Armenian language, meet other diasporans (children and teachers), and become a part of the diaspora space, surrounded by what Nigel Thrift calls, 'empirical constructions,' which will be discussed in more detail below (Thrift, 2003: 96-104). As in the case of the man taking Armenian language lessons every Saturday, the families who send their children to the Saturday school also aim at preserving the national (Armenian) identity in their child's mind. This takes place when many parents have to overcome an extra barrier, as their children, who are often primary to lower secondary school age, complain about why they should be studying while their non-Armenian day school classmates and friends are having a study-free day.

Each interview conducted during the visits to the selected cities was unique, complex and interesting. Despite the answers to the questions asked under the same overall diasporic umbrella, many responses actually matched. It was interesting to know the opinion of diasporans who had left their active career lives behind and retired. One of them was Michael

Bazikian, a retiree from Melbourne in his late 80s. Mr. Bazikian expressed his interest in participating in the study when he heard about it in a private conversation. The conversation with Mr. Bazikian took place informally, at a fast-food restaurant when I heard the story of a person who had lived his entire life as a diasporan, preserved his identity, yet only in his 80s made his first move to visit his diasporic homeland. As in the case of several other interviewees, I had another follow-up meeting with Mr. Bazikian during my next visit. Generally speaking, I found these conversations extremely useful since we already had a good rapport established by then, and the interviewees were even more open in expressing their ideas.

The experience Vartan from Sydney shared during the interview was probably the most geographically diverse. In particular, he spoke about his fascinating life experience at the monastery of the Mkhitarian (or Mkhitarist) Catholic Congregation on the Island of St. Lazarus in Venice, Italy, a place that played a significant role in the development of the Armenian language and identity (Seferian, 2017).[*] Having lived in Syria, Lebanon, Armenia, Sudan, Italy, and, later, in Australia, Vartan accumulated extensive experience in living among Armenians and being an active part of his local Armenian community, but in a very different cultural-social-religious environment, where the expectations to preserve national identity also differ.

Vartan was one of my 'gatekeepers.' He not only helped me with transportation but also referred to other interviewees and provided me with an insight into various aspects of diaspora life in general, beyond the very questions raised during the formal interviews. Together with Vartan, we visited one of the two Armenian day schools in Australia – AGBU Alexander Primary School, also situated in the Sydney area, similar to the other one visited with another interviewee earlier. It was an excellent opportunity to visit another diasporic institution in the city and to form a

---

[*]   The Mkhitarist Catholic Congregation was established in 1717 by Mkhitar from Sepasdia [Sebastia] (modern-day Sivas in Turkey) "had a profound effect on research, education, and publishing in Europe generally, and for the Armenian world in particular." The monastery is an important center for publishing books in Armenian, which it has done continuously over three centuries. Besides, the Congregation has schools in Beirut, Los Angeles, Buenos Aires and the most recently opened one in Yerevan. (Seferian, in World News, *The Armenian Island of Venice*).

Armenian Apostolic Church of St. Mary, Melbourne,
Australia, October 2014

Aginian Saturday school, Melbourbe, Australia, October 2014

comprehensive idea about the role of Armenian formal educational institutions in the Armenian community of Sydney. I met the school's staff and students and had an opportunity to enter classrooms and greet the children. The school was a small-scale institution on a small but beautiful and cozy campus. As I was told, despite the small number of Armenian day schools in the city (only two) they experienced a student number-related problem: the AGBU Alexander Primary School, at the time of the visit, had only 32 students in a community of about 30,000-35,000 people (in Sydney). Such a low number of school enrolment does not correspond to the total number of primary-school-age children in Armenian families in Sydney, which could be estimated at around 1,500. He regretfully added that the school was only eight students short of 40, which would have made it eligible for state funding.

During one of my visits to the Church in Sydney, I met Mr. Mavlian, a retired man from a small Armenian community in another Australian city – Perth. It was a matter of luck to meet him on that particular day because he only visited Sydney (and the Church) a couple of times a year. In Perth, he is one of the most active diasporans, and for more than a decade, he has been preparing and distributing a periodical newsletter on various issues relating to Armenia and pan-Armenian affairs. It was Mr. Mavlian who, in May 2016, invited me to speak at a community event in Perth on the occasion of the First Republic Day, as mentioned previously.

Levon and Maria, a young manager at a private company and a school teacher, respectively, were other diasporan Armenians I interviewed in Melbourne. They were introduced to me by Helen, one of my research 'gatekeepers.' I met both Levon and Maria (separately) in the Riverside area of downtown Melbourne, which they found convenient for interview. The conversation I had with Levon was during lunch, in one of the restaurants there, while the interview with Maria was in one of the shopping malls, where she arrived from work.

In Melbourne, I also met Mateos, as he introduced himself. He never disclosed his real name to me since his social environment knew him as a Turkish man. Mateos was a crypto-Armenian, or a hidden Armenian, born and raised in Istanbul, Turkey. He lived there until his migration to Australia several years ago. This became a unique experience for me. The conversation with Mateos was probably the most touching among all the interviews. During my earlier visit to Sydney, when I met Archbishop

Armenian Apostolic Church of Holy Resurrection in Sydney

Najarian (again), he gave me a souvenir – a forget-me-not flower badge, a symbol of the 100th anniversary of the Genocide. I was so touched by my conversation with Mateos that I decided to give the valuable gift to him so that he could possess a symbol of the national humiliation and, simultaneously, hope.

The main purpose of gathering information from various other cities and even countries, beyond the two cities selected as the focus of the study – Sydney and Melbourne, was to understand the broader picture. It became clear that views and responses shared by the diasporans engaged in this study, in many cases, were similar to each other.

During one of the visits to the Armenian Church in Melbourne for the liturgy service, I was introduced to a priest who had recently arrived from Armenia. The Church was not full this time; there were only about 20-25 people attending the service. A small reception was organized in the adjacent hall. During a discussion on various aspects of community life, one young Armenian, Garo, expressed his willingness to participate in my study, and we went to a quieter place for an interview.

My hours of observations, private conversations in different cities conducted over the years, lengthy formal interviews have also been complemented by follow-up talks during subsequent visits to Sydney and Melbourne. The interviews, being a core of primary data, were enriched by other visits and events, which helped me to further advance my experience and understanding of diaspora communities and diasporic return. My visit to Kolkata in June 2015 was a significant one. Generally speaking, Kolkata's role is considerable since, historically, it had been a destination for many Armenians who, mainly for trade reasons, migrated from Persia to seek their fortune in the East. According to the most prominent work that had been written about the Armenians in India (by Mesrovb J. Seth), Kolkata (Calcutta then) contained "by far the largest number of influential and well-to-do Armenians in India" (Seth, 1897: 172). During the trip there, my intention was to visit at least Armenian churches, the Armenian College, as well as to meet some Indian Armenians.[*]

In Kolkata, my contacts helped me reach several Armenians. I visited three churches within the city, an old but well-preserved Armenian cemetery located by one of the Armenians churches, and the Armenian College. I also managed to speak to several Armenians. When I met the students in the Armenian College, I even had an opportunity to conduct a lesson for them. I also attended a Sunday service celebrated by Father Zaven, the Director of the College and the Head of the Armenian Church in India. He told me that he was trying to conduct a liturgy service in a revolving manner so that all three churches in the city could stay active.

It was unusual to hear the Eastern Armenian dialect being spoken by diasporan Armenians, in Kolkata. Initially, I was surprised to hear it, until I realized that it was due to the education they received at the Armenian College there. The Armenians in Kolkata spoke fluent and pure (Eastern) Armenian. The Kolkatan Armenian community is unique among the other Armenian communities in the world since the maintenance of all the Armenian churches in its region and the College are under the financial support of a special community fund, created through a substantial contribution made by several philanthropists, among them – Sir Catchick Paul Chater. Sir Catchick Paul Chater was a prominent Armenian banker of Kolkatan origin and lived most of his life in Hong Kong (during the late 19th and early 20th centuries). His will was set to support the Armenian

---

[*] As told by Father Zaven Yazichyan, the Pastor of the Indian Armenians and Manager of the Armenian College and Philanthropic Academy in Kolkata, in a personal conversation, there are five Armenian Apostolic churches in Kolkata and the bigger West Bengal area, with three of them located in Kolkata proper. More details are in Rangan Data, *Armenian Churches*.

community of Kolkata and, in particular, the Armenian College and Philanthropic Academy (Hindustan Times, *The Case of Vanishing Armenians*). During my visit to Kolkata, I stayed at the Fairlawn Hotel – another Armenian landmark in the city, known for its exceptionally rich history and traditions. By the time of my visit, the hotel's long-time owner – Violet Smith, an Armenian who managed it for more than four decades – had passed away, aged 94.[*]

All such visits to Armenian communities and meetings with community members have provided me with insights into diasporan life and the problems experienced by Armenians concerning the diaspora-homeland relationship. The information I gathered helped me comprehend the sense of belonging and national identity in the selected diaspora communities within the context of diaspora-homeland relations and the transformation of these ties over the decades.

---

[*] Source: Post Magazine, *Fairlawn Hotel Changes Hands.*

Chapter 2

ARMENIA – A SMALL NATION-STATE WITH A GLOBAL DIASPORA

Armenia Before and After 1991

An ancient civilization, the Armenians lost their last kingdom during medieval times (Encyclopaedia Britannica, *Cilicia*). Although on a smaller territory than the medieval Armenian space of habitation, the Armenians (re)gained their state, a nation-state already in its contemporary form, in 1918.[*] It was a state on its national territory, with clearly set boundaries. This 'First Republic' had a short life of two years and it could not survive the hostility and aggression from post-Ottoman Turkish forces. As a result of the arrival of the Red (Soviet) Army in November 1920, Armenia lost its sovereignty and was later transformed into a Soviet republic, which existed until the breakdown of the Soviet Union in 1991.[†]

The Armenian ('Second') republic was the smallest among the fifteen republics of the Union by area,[‡] which, over nearly seven decades, experienced rapid industrial growth and continuous improvement of people's standard of living. The deterioration of the macroeconomic situation within the Soviet Union by the late 1980s and the political-social-economic restructuring in the USSR (*Perestroika*) (among other political, economic and social factors) led to a revival of independence movements in the whole of the Soviet Union. Months prior to the collapse of the Union in December 1991, on September 21, 1991,[**] 94% of the Armenian population (Khachikyan, 2010: 219) voted in a referendum, and only about 0.5% supported Armenia remaining in the Soviet Union.[††]

---

[*] Source: 100 Years-100 Facts, *The First Armenian Republic*.

[†] Source: BBC, *Timeline – Armenia*.

[‡] Source: Encyclopaedia Britannica, *Armenia*.

[**] September 21 is a public holiday in Armenia and is celebrated as Independence Day (100 Years – 100 Facts, *The Republic of Armenia declared its independence*).

[††] Source: Lenta.ru news portal. Getting Rid of the Colonial Yoke (in Russian) https://lenta.ru/articles/2019/09/21/araday

Following the collapse of the USSR, the 'Third Republic' in Armenia – the Republic of Armenia – was established.

The Post-WWII period witnessed over a hundred newly-established nation-states on the world political map. Many were formed after protracted independence movements. In many cases, new states' boundaries were "drawn" by former colonial powers to serve their own geopolitical interests rather than the interests of those new states. Thus, according to Foucher, as of 1991, 20% of world boundaries were determined by the British and 17% by the French (Foucher, in Kolossov, 1998: 25). The proportion changed in 1991, with 15 new sovereign nation-states entering the world geopolitical arena instead of one Soviet Union. In the Union, the boundaries were designed by the central authorities in Moscow. All fifteen republics were based on the ethnic criterion, and in each case, there was a titular or dominant ethnic group. However, in many cases, the boundaries of republics were drawn in a way to make these titular ethnic groups spread beyond their national republics. Thus, people of the same ethnic group also inhabited a republic or republics outside their ethnic one. Moreover, there were tiny ethnic enclaves (often at a village level) created within neighboring republics, which, as argued by some, "was done to raise a conflict between the two neighboring peoples" (Avagian, 1994: 25). Such an approach, as presented, was to strengthen the connections between the republics and the peoples in the Union. However, in fact, such practice led to more escalation during the late-USSR period when nationalist movements formed in different regions of that vast country. As argued by Vladimir Kolossov from the Institute of Geography of the Russian Academy of Sciences, the aim of nationalism was "to create a national identity that is based on state boundaries" (Kolossov, 1998: 6). During the last years of the Union's existence, in many of its republics, nationalist sentiments were heightened among both the dominant national groups and minorities. After achieving independence, some ethnic groups found themselves a minority within a foreign country. Such cases took place because of what James Hughes and Gwendolyn Sasses described as the "planned bounding of ethnicity in the Soviet Union," which appeared to be "crude, creating administrative units without regard to history, ethnicity or geography" (Hughes and Sasse, 2001: 18). An example of such cases was the Armenians in Nagorno-

Karabakh (Artsakh), which was an autonomous region in Soviet Azerbaijan.

Anthony Smith points out that "the idea of one nation, one state, one territory, has remained a cornerstone of the international community" and that few nations are "territorially compact" (Smith, 2002: 22). In a number of cases, such situations led to a revival and strengthening of the sense of national-ethnic identity, such as the movement in Nagorno-Karabakh (Artsakh) to unite with Armenia, which started in 1988.[*] Being anthropocentric, it was "the first-ever congress of democratic forces in the post-Soviet area," which led to the "first-ever alternative elections in the post-Soviet area and in Eastern Europe."[†] Nationalism, as one could argue, is a relative phenomenon, as any nationalistic approach is in relation to other nations. The collapse of the Soviet Union and the uncertainty created as a result of that major geopolitical transformation led the rest of the world to recognize all of the fifteen parts (republics) of the former Union within the boundaries of their Soviet era borders "in the interests of international order" (Hughes and Sasse, 2001: 18). Despite the recognition of the status quo, after the collapse of the Soviet Union, there were eight violent regional and ethnic conflicts in the former Union's territory (Hughes and Sasse, 2001: 21).

Each nation state develops specific political and economic pathways. By the end of the 1980s, the Armenian (Soviet Socialist) Republic was one of the most industrialized republics in the Union (Holding, 2014: 24). However, as a result of the collapse of the USSR, the economic situation in Armenia began its drastic deterioration. After the Union ceased to exist, it became impossible to maintain former industrial and trade links, and the whole manufacturing industry in Armenia faced the threat of collapse. However, changes in the former USSR were not only of economic nature.

---

[*] Karabakh, or Nagorno-Karabakh, or as officially renamed according to its historical name of Artsakh, is a territory inhabited mainly by Armenians, to the east of the Republic of Armenia. During the decades under Soviet rule, it was an autonomous region in the territory of Azerbaijan Soviet Socialist Republic. At the end of the 1980s, an armed conflict broke out between Azerbaijan and Armenian forces in Karabakh, which ended in a ceasefire in 1994 (President of Armenia [official website], *Nagorno Karabakh Republic*), (BBC, *Nagorno-Karabakh Profile*), (Council on Foreign Relations, *Nagorno-Karabakh Conflict*).

[†] A comment given by Ashot Manucharyan, one of the leaders of the Karabakh Movement in the late-1980s (Manucharyan, *Karabakh Movement*).

With rising independence movements and stronger national identity perception, by the end of the 1980s, various parts of the vast country had become less tolerant toward 'others' and more focused on the 'self,' which led to those eight conflicts, as mentioned above. These processes, escalated over time, ultimately became irreversible. The position of the Soviet central authorities was far from being considerate and was not well-focused on understanding the ethnic conflicts in the country. The center was merely providing situational solutions to already burning conflicts. The prevailing approach was to prevent the creation of any precedent that could spread to other parts of the multi-ethnic country. The government, by all means, was trying to use force for blocking and eliminating any attempt of organized nationalist movements. As a result, despite the absence of internal conflicts in Armenia, the central government in Moscow declared a curfew regime in Armenia on November 24, 1988 (Khachikyan, 2010: 214).

Armenia's initial conditions after it acquired independence became very complicated. Being of diverse nature, they affected the country's economy mostly negatively. There were geographic, political, economic, social, and cultural factors that shaped Armenia's post-independence history from the early 1990s to the present.

Geographic Conditions

The Republic of Armenia is a landlocked country with a territory similar to the size of Belgium, Albania, or Taiwan Island (The CIA World Factbook, *Armenia*). Regarding population density, Armenia is not inhabited proportionately well, and close to 40% of the country's population lives in the capital city of Yerevan (WorldPopulationReview.com, 2017). Moreover, among urban settlements, Yerevan has the largest concentration of ethnic Armenians in the world, with its total population of more than one million people (WorldPopulationReview.com, 2017). By 1992, Armenia was the most ethnically homogenous among all former Soviet republics, and currently, more than 98% of its population are ethnic Armenian who share a common language and culture (The CIA World Factbook, *Armenia*, 2019). The country is also home to about twenty ethnic minorities, with the main ones being Yazidis, Russians, Greeks, Assyrians, Ukrainians, Poles, Germans, Jews, Kurds, and Georgians (Asatryan and Arakelova, 2002: 2).

With regard to its area and population, Armenia is the smallest not only among its immediate neighbors, but also among its all second-degree (land) neighbors. A country of just about 2.5-3 million people,[*] located on the crossroad between Eastern Europe, Western Asia, and the Middle East, Armenia has a potential of utilizing its geographic position to link vast regions and markets. Thus, within only 2.5-3-hour air flight distance (which is considered relatively short by even low-cost airlines), the country can access EU-members Cyprus, Greece, Bulgaria, and Romania, as well as other Eastern European nations of Moldova, Ukraine, Russia, and Georgia. In Asia, countries within the mentioned distance are Turkey, Syria, Lebanon, Israel, Egypt, Jordan, Saudi Arabia, Kuwait, Iraq, Iran, and Azerbaijan (in the Middle East), as well as Kazakhstan, Uzbekistan, Turkmenistan, and Afghanistan (in Central Asia). Altogether, these countries, with a total population of over 500 million people,[†] create an enormous potential market for the Armenian economy and its businesses.

Armenia is mountainous, and in some of its parts, its borders with neighbors are natural ones (i.e., mountain chains or rivers). The country is located in a part of the geographic area known as the Armenian Highlands. Armenia has four immediate neighbors – Georgia to the north, Turkey to the west, Azerbaijan to the east and southwest, and Iran to the south. Armenia's longest borders are with Turkey and Azerbaijan, both of which are Turkic-speaking and predominantly Muslim-populated countries with long-standing unsolved political problems with Armenia.

Two of Armenia's other neighbors are quite distinct from each other. Leaning closer toward Europe, Georgia is Armenia's closest exit to the open sea through its Black Sea port. To the south, the border with Iran is incomparably shorter, with poor routes leading to it through mountains, often restricted during winter.

Regarding natural resources, Armenia is not well-blessed, in particular, with traditional energy sources. It is one of the few countries in the region without proven oil or natural gas reserves. The mountainous country's main natural resources are metals, such as aluminum, molybdenum, copper, and some deposits of gold (Global SPC, *Invest in Armenia*).

---

[*] The population number estimates vary. There has been mass emigration in several stages through the past three decades, resulting in a significant decline in the population.

[†] Source: The CIA World Factbook, *Country Comparison – Population*.

Armenia experiences difficulties in utilizing its potential advantages in international trade, to a certain extent, because of relatively scarce resources and its landlocked position. On the other hand, Armenia has abundant spring and mineral water resources (Global SPC, *Invest in Armenia*). The country's location within an active earthquake zone makes it vulnerable to natural hazards. As mentioned above, in December of 1988, while the curfew regime imposed in Armenia by the Soviet central government was in force, a devastating earthquake hit the country's north, which killed close to 1% of the country's population and affected the lives of about 17%, many of whom were deprived of shelter (Goenjian et al., 1997: 536). Overall, approximately 40% of the country's territory was in ruins (Khachikyan, 2010: 214).

Despite promises and official plans set by (then) the central government in Moscow to rebuild the damaged region, the area affected by the earthquake has not been fully recovered up to now, more than three decades after the tragedy. At the same time, it should be stressed that the earthquake became the first significant event that motivated the diaspora to be involved in Armenia. Indeed, this development was possible because of the more open political climate of that time.

Geopolitical Situation

As already mentioned, after centuries of foreign dominance, Armenia became an independent state in 1918. After Byzantium annexed the Cilician Armenian Kingdom in 1137 and the kingdom finally ceased to exist in 1375 (Tejirian and Simon, 2012: 31), the whole area of historical Armenia ended up partitioned between two empires – the Ottoman and the Persian, and since early-19th century, between these two and the Russian Empire, which entered the Armenian Highlands in Karabakh in 1813 and Armenia's current territory in 1828. Following the Treaty of Turkmenchay (1828) between the Russian Empire and the Persian Empire, Eastern Armenia (which included the regions of Yerevan and Nakhijevan) was given to the Russian Empire (Presidential Library of the Russian Federation.

After the Byzantine Empire fell to the Ottomans in 1453, a new era of existence with the Turks began for the Armenians. Thus, the Armenian Highlands, which was divided between the empires, became a unique region, where the people carrying that geographic name and inhabiting

that area, lived under the dominance of foreign cultures. Over time, as historian Edmund Herzig and sociologist Marina Kurkchiyan explain, the immigration of Muslims in traditionally Armenian areas of the Ottoman Empire (about two million people between 1862 and 1870) "often worsened Muslim-Armenian relations, as the newcomers were embittered against Christians" (Herzig and Kurkchiyan, 2005: 68-69).

Over the centuries, what was known as Armenia became smaller in size and found itself the smallest among its immediate neighbors and trapped within its geopolitical problems. Indeed, the 'sea-to-sea Armenia' of ancient times was not a political entity with its contemporary meaning. It was a territory inhabited by Armenians in ancient Armenian kingdoms and other (including vassal) states. Armenia since ancient times has been changed to a significant extent. In its modern form, Armenia is a nation-state recognized by the international community within the borders of Soviet Armenia.

Understanding the Armenian diaspora and its relations with the homeland firstly assumes understanding what 'homeland' as a concept means to Armenians. Diasporas, anthropologist Ulf Bjorklund specifies, are "transcend nations" (Bjorklund, 2003: 337). With regard to this, Armenians in both Armenia and the diaspora, as Bjorklund stresses, "tend to insist on a meaningful identification with an Armenian 'nation' spanning many countries" (Bjorklund, 2003: 337). 'Homeland' as a general term used by diasporans "became an object of nostalgia, desire, and identification, most viscerally so for those displaced and without a home of their own" (Gregory et al., 2009). The idea of a homeland is not exactly the same for all Armenians in the diaspora. Having the historical homeland lost as a result of the Armenian Genocide, the nostalgic dream for many Armenian diasporans is to recover the loss of land and, at the same time, associate (the Republic of) Armenia with their cultural roots and perceive it as a carrier of their ethnic and cultural identity.[*] The Republic of Armenia, as Sossie Kasbarian, a scholar of diaspora studies, states, is a "step-homeland" for many (old) diasporans, who negotiate the gap between it and their mythical homeland (Kasbarian, 2009: 358).

The Armenians have been an ethnic group or tribe that has had a continued existence since ancient times and inhabited the Armenian Highlands continuously and under different political entities (Badalyan, G., *Armenian Highland*). According to Hobsbawm, a nation "belongs exclusively to a particular, and historically recent, period" (Hobsbawm, 2012: 9). National identity, as a concept in its current understanding, is not something that has existed for centuries. However, one could argue that the sense of being Armenian, including having a common culture, language, and religion, has been a reality for an extended period of time. Being in a geopolitically complex region, Armenia has, for centuries, struggled to preserve these national attributes.

By the time of its independence (at the end of 1991), the political environment in Armenia had become euphoric, and there was widespread excitement for independence. It was a period of tremendous political consolidation and hope, as many people had positive expectations for

---

[*] The Armenian Genocide is referred to as "the atrocities committed against the Armenian people of the Ottoman Empire during WWI" when, as estimated, one and a half million Armenians perished between 1915 and 1923 (Armenian National Institute – ANI, *FAQ About the Armenian Genocide*).

Armenia's future.[*] Many Armenians who were part of the diaspora were particularly supportive of the country's political independence and sovereignty. As a relatively homogenous country in terms of its population's ethnic structure, Armenia did not experience internal ethnic or religious conflicts. However, external geopolitical conditions proved to be more challenging for Armenia. After standing against the Soviet government's position on the Nagorno-Karabakh (Artsakh) problem for several years, which finally led to a large-scale conflict between Armenia's neighbor Azerbaijan and the incomparably smaller Artsakh, Armenia faced severe pressure from Azerbaijan and its racial ally Turkey which, in 1992, initiated a political and economic blockade of Armenia that has continued until the present.[†]

In the USSR and after the dissolution of the Union, the Soviet/Russian army has been in charge of protecting Armenia's borders with the former USSR neighbors Turkey and Iran. Armenia, in turn, has been providing Russia with access to Iran and beyond in the Middle East, since the current geopolitical situation prevents Russia from relying on Georgia and, to an extent, on Azerbaijan for their support in this regard. Iran in its policy toward its neighbor Armenia has been cooperative by providing transportation links to the seas (Indian Ocean) and by maintaining a balanced position between geopolitically strong Turkey, as well as Azerbaijan, with which, to an extent, it shares the same religion (Shia Islam). Thus, caught up in a region where vectors of global geopolitics cross, Armenia has had no choice but to start nation-building with consideration of actual and potential threats to its existence. Armenia, consequently, has been compelled in its nation-building process to be

[*] 99% of votes were in the 1991 referendum were given in favor of independence. (Government of Armenia, *General Information*).

[†] Armenia supported the autonomy of Armenian-populated Nagorno (Mountainous) Karabakh, also known as Artsakh, in its stance for independence from the Soviet Union in the early 1990s. Nagorno-Karabakh Autonomous Region was created as an enclave within Soviet Azerbaijan, which existed until 1991. The struggle for Karabakh's independence (achieved in 1991, while still unrecognized) resulted in a conflict initiated by Azerbaijan. After years of fighting, by 1994, the Armenians of Karabagh proclaimed a de facto republic by establishing full control over their territory and opening a link with Armenia, even though it continued facing an uncertain future (Engelhart, *The Nagorno-Karabakh Republic*).

mindful of dominant geopolitical powers in the region, as well as other potential external threats to its existence. The presence of Armenian communities living in the territories of neighboring states has also affected Armenia's regional geopolitical codes.

To a large extent, Armenia's political orientation has been directed toward the West and Russia (by maneuvering between the two), while, in terms of social relations, it has continued to share common attributes of the Middle East. Thus, in parallel with obtaining independence, Armenia faces a problem of shaping a clear perception of its geographical and cultural affiliation – is it a European or an Asian/Middle Eastern nation? This uncertainty, arguably, has also affected post-independence developments of Armenian politics and the country's social-economic system.

Economic Conditions

By the end of the 1980s, several economic sectors were dominating in Armenia, particularly food processing, chemical production, machinery, textile and shoe manufacturing.[*] By 1991, Armenia had a relatively developed but aging infrastructure, which was in need of significant investments. The inherited Soviet-era industrial plants had been shut down, as they could neither secure centrally-planned production orders nor apply enough expertise to enter the world market and remain competitive.

As a country of high elevation above sea level, Armenia has limited transportation routes.[†] By 1992, the country's railway system had become the principal exit route to Georgia, as Turkey and Azerbaijan had already initiated an economic blockade against Armenia, as mentioned previously, which resulted in a massive energy crisis (Suny, 1996: 48). There is no railway connection to Iran, as the terrain makes it extremely difficult to construct one. Armenia's road system keeps all of the country's regions accessible; however, in many regional towns and the countryside, not all roads are of satisfactory quality. With a significant portion of country's population living in the capital city, its airport remains a vital gate to the outside world.

---

[*] Source: Nations Encyclopedia, *Armenia.*

[†] The highest peak in Armenia is Mount Aragats at 4,090 meters above sea level (Armenian Travel Bureau, *General Information*), the lowest level is 400m above sea level, the average altitude is 1,370m above sea level and only 10% of the country's land is under 1,000 meters. (Holding: 2014, 4).

In the early 1990s, Armenia was not subsistent in energy resources. Apart from generating thermal energy and relying on imported natural gas that lasted until the late 1980s, a significant portion of electricity was produced by a nuclear power plant, the only one in the region then. However, after the 1988 earthquake, the government made a critical decision to shut the power plant down, and it remained closed until the mid-1990s, when the plant was partly reopened (one of the two reactors). Consequently, after acquiring its independence, Armenia being deprived of a critical source of energy, as the country was already under the blockade by two of its four neighbors, continued supporting Artsakh in an unequal conflict with Azerbaijan as the guarantor of Artsakh's security, and had to build an independent nation-state.[*]

Social and Cultural Conditions

As already mentioned, Armenia's population is ethnically homogenous.[†] By the 1920-30s, Armenia (its 'Second Republic') had become a homeland for many ethnic Armenians who had fled from mass violence and persecution, most notably the Armenian Genocide (*Medz Yeghern*) of 1915. The homogenous ethnic environment in Armenia, arguably, limits an effective first-hand interaction of Armenians with other cultures and peoples. Apart from a possible positive aspect to this characteristic – an opportunity to preserve national identity and heritage, such a situation limits the interaction of Armenia's population with foreign cultures.[‡] Up to several years ago, even most of the tourists visiting Armenia (nearly 70%) were of Armenian origin.[**]

---

[*] Armenian-populated Karabakh in the early 1990s had an average population of 125-130 thousand people compared to about eight million in Azerbaijan (The National Statistical Service of Nagorno Karabakh, *Population*) and (The CIA World Factbook, *Azerbaijan*).

[†] Ethnic Armenians make 98.1% of Armenia's population, with the main minority groups being Kurds, Yazidis, Russians, Greeks (PoliAtlas, *Country Profile: Armenia*).

[‡] A Report on the Study on International Travel through Borders of the Republic of Armenia in 2013, (Ministry of Economy of the Republic of Armenia, 2014).

[**] As reported, there were 1,260,000 tourists in Armenia in 2016 (Steffens, Liliana, *Armenia Tourism, on the Rise*) and over 1.65 mln in 2018 (Panorama.am, The *Number of Tourists Visiting Armenia*).

Ancient Armenia was the first country that officially proclaimed Christianity as its state religion in 301 AD.[*] This was when the king of Armenia decided to convert the nation to Christianity, which "was a move towards a more centralized state, at the expense of increasingly powerful feudal houses" (Ayvazyan, 2015). Throughout the centuries, the Armenians, supported by the Armenian Apostolic Church, have struggled to preserve their identity, including language and culture, against assimilation. As a religious minority in the area "Armenians had to maintain a low public profile" for centuries and "experienced a complex interaction with Islam, the dominant force in the surrounding region." The Armenian Apostolic Church, thus, "became the only institution tolerated by the authorities" (Cowe, in Angold, 2014: 430-431).

Located in a region of continuous conflicts and wars, the role of the Church, arguably, had been dominant, especially as the nation lost its kingdoms centuries earlier. The struggle for identity preservation over the past couple of centuries made the perception of independence among the Armenians increasingly stronger, and, by the time it was achieved, expectations from independence were high. On the other hand, as argued, there was uncertainty regarding expectations toward the diaspora, mainly because there were no open and active connections with the diaspora during the decades of Soviet rule. Then, it was not evident yet that the people, who lived in a periphery of the vast empire, lacked interaction with the rest of the world and, in particular, with its diaspora.

By the time of independence, Armenia's population was slightly above 3.3 million people.[†] Worldwide, the number of ethnic Armenians, as estimated, is around 9 to 10 million people (Institute of Demography of the National Research University, 2019). At the time of Armenia's independence, the total number was estimated at seven and a half to nine million (Avagian, 1994: 77). After gaining independence, Armenia could have become an official state-representative of Armenian identity, even if it was home to only a third of ethnic Armenians in the world. It was then that, as argued, the Church could help overcome this limitation, as the

---

[*] Source: America: the Jesuit Review, *Pope Francis will visit Armenia.*
[†] Source: Institute of Demography of the National Research University, Higher School of Economics. *All-Union Census:* 2019.

Church continued to be the main religious institution underpinning Armenians worldwide.[*]

The Armenian diaspora is a phenomenon that has existed throughout centuries. Historian and anthropologist James Clifford argues that Armenian (as well as Jewish and Greek) diasporas can be considered "non-normative starting points for a discourse" of diaspora (Clifford, 1994: 306). Armenians, as British historian Christopher Walker specifies, "were used to traveling and settling abroad." However, attacks in the Ottoman Empire, in their homeland, gave the Armenians "a new impetus to the process of seeking a home and livelihood abroad" (Walker, 2014: 19). According to Walker, the later development of the diaspora was an outcome of "succeeding decades," which led to the massive enlargement of diaspora communities (Walker, 2014: 19). The diaspora in the late-1980s and early 1990s was dispersed on all continents. The cities with significant concentrations of Armenians were remote and distinct – Moscow, Los Angeles, Beirut, Tbilisi, Tehran, Paris, and Marseille (more details are provided later in this book). This network, to a certain extent, helped to create a unique opportunity for newly-independent Armenia for establishing effective political and economic relations with several global and regional powers.

Throughout the decades of Soviet rule, Armenia (the Soviet Socialist Republic) experienced rapid industrial growth. It had also achieved high levels of literacy and life expectancy. By the time Armenia became a sovereign nation-state, a strong sense of national identity and willingness to build an independent state prevailed in the country. On the other hand, deprived of opportunities to interact with the rest of the world for decades, the young state was caught unprepared for effective communication with the outside world and was uncertain in its attitude and policies toward the larger part of the nation – the Armenian diaspora.

---

[*] The official title of the head of Armenian Apostolic Church is Supreme Patriarch, the Catholicos of All Armenians (Armenian Apostolic Church, *Catholicos of All Armenians*).

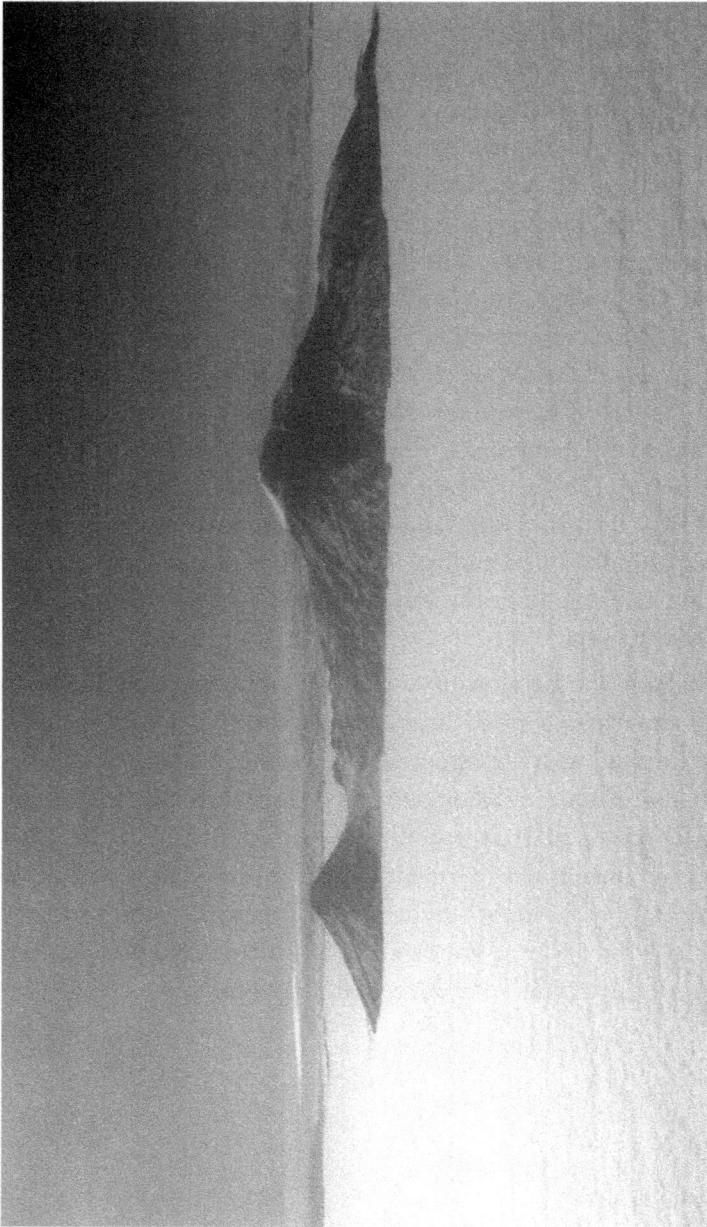

The Biblical Mt. Ararat peering over the clouds across Armenia (aerial photograph)

Chapter 3

DIASPORA AND THE HOMELAND: TOGETHER AND SEPARATE

National identity and diasporas have been subjects of study by scholars of a wide range of disciplines: history, economics, political science and international affairs, sociology and anthropology, development studies, and, within the framework of the concepts of 'space' and 'place,' most importantly, geography. The study of national identity in the diaspora is seen inseparable from the connection diasporans have with their homeland. Being diasporan assumes, as proposed here, being in permanent return, and the idea of connecting to the homeland and the homeland culture is what makes diasporans different from those who only carry an ethnic identity. The homeland's policy toward its diaspora can be inclusionary, but also entail separation or exclusion. This study looks at how diasporan Armenians see Armenia's policy and their connection to Armenia as the homeland. In order to have a complex view of the connection between a global nation and its diasporic nation-state, it is essential to go over the complexity of concepts and phenomena forming the study framework of the diaspora world, its geographic aspects, and identity perception. Here, the aim is to helps a reader first understand the nature of 'diaspora' and, in particular, the Armenian diaspora, within the framework of political geography – the key concepts of 'nation,' 'national identity,' 'space,' and 'place.'

Throughout the past centuries, migration of people has resulted in the formation of the phenomena of 'transnation' and 'diaspora.' The migrant transnation transforms the concept of 'nation' into a more conscious community than merely ethnicity and community "of people whose members are bound together by a sense of solidarity, a common culture, and an ethnic consciousness" (Uzelac, 2002: 37). Hence, diasporas can be geographically dispersed, but they are culturally more or less united. While for a long time, the Jewish diaspora fitted the category of 'diaspora,' over the last century, other 'classical' diasporas have been identified – the Armenians and Greeks, and, to some extent, the Chinese (Brubaker, 2005: 2). The migration of people from country to country opens new horizons for the study of the concept and critical analysis of its original and new meanings.

Kingsley Atkins of the Worldwide Ireland Fund refers to the Migration Policy Institute in Washington, D.C. and points out that 450 government institutions in over 55 countries are engaged with their diasporas (Atkins, 2014). He further states that, in 1999, 150 million people lived in a country other than the country of their birth, or about 2.5% of the global population at that time (The UN, *Population in 1999 and 2000*). Fifteen years later, in 2014, the number reached 240 million people (Atkins, 2014), or about 3% of the world population. Indeed, the study of diaspora as a phenomenon will be continuous, never-ending, and always relevant, especially considering that diasporas change and transform over time. They also transform the space they inhabit and have the potential to transform the homeland as well.

Diaspora as a Phenomenon

'Diaspora' as a category has been inflated over time (Dufoix, 2003: 1). Its use has been extended, particularly over the last several decades (Knott and McLoughlin, 2010: 19) by covering more than a few classical cases, such as the Armenian, Jewish, Greek, Palestinian, or Chinese diasporas. With more nations classified as diasporic, the literature of diaspora has also been enriched (Dufoix, 2003: 21-29). William Safran, a political scientist and diaspora scholar, argues that such enlargement of the concept empties "the authentic meaning of diaspora" and "that the concept of diaspora is losing its analytical utility" (Safran, in Alonso and Oiarzabal, 2010: 6). The increasingly inflated nature of 'diaspora', which is one of the problems of the contemporary use of the term, is also stressed by Rogers Brubaker, a sociologist, and Khachig Tölölyan, one of the founders of diaspora studies (Brubaker, 2005, Tölölyan, 2011). Diaspora is becoming a diluted category with more complex uses that cover a broader range of people who do not reside in the homeland of their ancestors. Arguably, one of the primary causes leading to the dilution of 'diaspora' is an increasingly larger-scale mobility of people – transnationals in all parts of the world, which, to a large extent, is due to an advancement of communication technologies and of transnational corporations in their global operations that search for skilled talent as part of this expansion.

Common history, with its traditions and culture, becomes the unifying element, even if a nation is geographically divided and its various parts are surrounded by different foreign cultures and peoples, such as the case of the Armenians split between the Ottoman, Persian and, later, Russian Empires for centuries. Interestingly, the relationship between the diaspora and the homeland transforms over time, and a significant shift takes place following major political events such as independence (establishment of a sovereign nation-state) of the homeland. The problem of contested leadership, as argued here, becomes more intense from both sides – the nation-state and the diaspora. For instance, from Armenia's standpoint, contested leadership can be related to the way Armenians perceive their country, independence, and relations with diaspora communities. It can be argued that contested leadership is a major barrier for an active and effective relationship between Armenia and its diaspora, and that barrier has been strengthened as an outcome of arguably the most significant change in the modern history of Armenia – acquisition of political independence (in 1991). The role of (trans)national institutions, arguably, also differs as a result of that change.

Understanding relations between diaspora and its homeland needs a thorough study of what each side expects from the other. On the one hand, being an entity within clearly defined territorial boundaries, the homeland nation-state deals with the extraterritorial space of its diaspora. With contacts and communication between the two, they are in the process of both engagement and separation. Engagement takes place based on common objectives and interests that drive both homeland and diaspora toward following and pursuing these interests. Separation, on the other hand, is caused by following objectives and interests which do not match those of the homeland. Such separation can take place, for instance, as a result of a particular host state's restrictive policy aiming to weaken the connection of its particular ethnic (diasporic) community to its homeland. It can also be an outcome of contested leadership demonstrated on either side of the diasporic nation – the homeland or the diaspora.

Geographer John Agnew stresses that modern political theory tends to understand geography entirely as territorial, based on the territorial expression of sovereignty (Agnew, 1994: 60). Territorialization is seen as a process of describing how nation-states produce geographies of power (Agnew, 1994: 60). More than two decades after Agnew's explanation of territorial limitations of geography, a nation's territory continues to be seen as "the most concrete feature of a nation for a management of nationhood as a whole," as geographers James Sidaway and Carl Grundy-Warr specify (Sideway and Grundy-Warr, in Daniels, Bradshaw, Shaw, and Sideway, 2008: 417). Nation-states' borders play a powerful role. Geographers Alexander Diener and Joshua Hagen justify the importance of borders by arguing that they are "most commonly associated with the idea of territory" and borders make the political, social, cultural and economic "meanings of one geographic space" separate from those of another (Diener and Hagen, 2012: 4). Does power extend beyond the territorial borders of the nation-state when it comes to reaching and engaging the national diaspora abroad? The territorial state, as Agnew metaphorically describes, "unthinkingly serves as the container of society" (Agnew, 1994: 71). When revisiting the territorial trap, he admits that "politics is not simply bottled up in territorial containers, state-based on place-based" and that it "can operate in networked ways across space" (Agnew, 1999: 47). This argument opens a new horizon for the study of diaspora, an extraterritorial space connected through a network of institutions and people. The 'territorial trap,' as Agnew uses the concept, even if it assumes a limit, can arguably become less important or weaker over time, considering the dynamic nature of diasporas and, especially, regarding nations with strong communal identities, such as the case of Armenians.

The discourse about the diaspora-homeland relations, including those between communities and the homeland, and the role homeland and diaspora institutions play in the relationship, is positioned within the framework of the communal identity, in our case, of the Armenians. It is a case of a nation with a strongly emphasized perception of communal identity, ahead of territorial or ideological identity. Historical sociologist Anthony Smith highlights this point by stating, "a sense of common Armenian identity has remained throughout their diaspora, and the forms of their antecedent culture, notably in the sphere of religion and language/script, have ensured a subjective attachment to their cultural identity and separation from their surroundings" (Smith, 1991: 26). Regarding the role the community has been playing in the life of Armenians in various parts of the world, sociologist Stephane Dufoix continues by emphasizing that Armenians have preserved a sense of community even without a nation-state, unlike most of the other classical diasporas (Dufoix, 2008: 51).

The role of the national religion, as it is recognized as such, has been instrumental in this regard. For instance, political scientist John Armstrong, in his *Nations Before Nationalism*, emphasized that especially among Armenians and Jews "the highly evolved network of religious officials and institutions was able to ensure the subjective unity and survival of the community and its historical and religious traditions" (Armstrong, in Smith, 1991: 38). Such a network has become not only a provider of religious service but also served as a social network with the homeland included in it. Under such a condition or evolution of the network, the diaspora and the homeland naturally (should) seek engagement rather than separation.

Nation Beyond the Nation-State: Homeland and Diaspora Return

With more people traveling and settling in new lands (hostlands), the study of diasporas is enriched, it becomes more complex, and, at the same time, more demanded. It would be simplistic to view 'diaspora' and 'identity' only from the perspective of the contemporary migration. Diasporic identities reflect migration that has been taking place for decades and even centuries. Moreover, identity, even if it is hidden or silent for a long time, can revive among the descendants of migrants even many years after they, their parents or grandparents settled in a new land. The 'law of the third generation' (Kenny, 2013: 109), revival of identity among grandchildren of the first generation of migrants, emphasizes the significance of a more in-depth understanding of diasporic identity and its transformation over time.

The primary criteria that differentiate diaspora from 'non-diasporan ethnies' are probably 'diaspora mobilization' and 'return.' According to Roger Brubaker, the difference is in the 'homeland orientation' (Brubaker, 2005: 5). James Clifford, on the other hand, stresses that "the transnational connections linking diasporas need not be articulated primarily through a real or symbolic homeland" and that "decentered, lateral connections may be as important as those formed around a teleology of origin/return" (Clifford, 1994: 306).

Regarding the difference between ethnic and diasporic communities, Razmig Panossian, a scholar of the Armenian diaspora, argues that diasporans make a well-thought choice to preserve their identity and not to assimilate into the host country (Panossian, 1998: 151). Diasporas, each different from another in terms of geographic distribution, demographic or social structure, assume interaction with the homeland. Diasporans, unlike non-diasporic 'ethnies,' participate in the creation of a transnational space, which engages the homeland as well and implies "transnational commitment to each other" (Ben-Rafael, 2013: 845). The creation of such transnational spaces, as argued here, takes place through the process of permanent return.

Diasporans are always in return, as mentioned above, and the concept of 'diaspora' itself assumes permanent return (Vardanyan, 2016: 76), be it of real, virtual, imaginary or metaphorical nature. Real return is physical, with diasporans returning to the homeland, which can be permanent, one-time, or repeated (temporary), either short- or long-term. Permanent physical return is what can be referred to as 'diaspora repatriation.' The latter is traditionally considered the ultimate purpose of any diaspora. It is another question whether the return is permanent physical (repatriation), especially when there are favourable opportunities for it, with no barriers existing on the way.

Virtual return can take place through the use of communication technologies. Imaginary return can be expressed, for instance, as attending a church liturgy service with fellow diasporans or playing on a sports team with other members of their own community. Such participation implies going back to the roots, to the homeland, to its culture. A diasporan, for example, by dining with another diasporan, discussing news from the homeland, or participating in a community network, through these acts, in a way, returns to the homeland.

Return is also participation in the homeland's affairs, its economic or social life. Diasporans are in an ongoing relationship with the homeland, caused by social-cultural, economic, or political motives. Diasporans as historical formations, as social anthropologist Pnina Werbner emphasizes, are in process and represent a "multiplicity of discourses" (Werbner, in Knott and McLoughlin, 2010: 74).

Debatably, as proposed, not only 'diaspora' assumes return, but its existence itself is 'return' (Vardanyan, 2016: 76). Return to the homeland should not be seen as a derivative or a condition of diaspora's existence. Instead, as argued, 'diaspora return' forms the diaspora, and any policy of the homeland toward its diaspora is about 'return.'

The whole concept of 'return' is romanticism-based (Skrbis, 1999: 43). Stephane Dufoix emphasizes that any diasporic nation was once "together before being dispersed" (Dufoix, 2008: 35), and for many diasporans 'return' is not real, but is "a way of keeping alive and reinventing" the historical homeland, "whose territory is the memory of dispersion itself" (Dufoix, 2008: 15). The social, economic, or political engagement of diasporans, as well as the geographic distribution of diasporic communities in the world, assume interaction with the homeland, i.e., representing 'return' in a certain way. The idea of 'return' is featured in almost every case of a diaspora, as Kevin Kenny emphasizes (Kenny, 2013: 61). For William Safran, 'return' is a key factor for the definition of 'diaspora' (Safran, in Baubock and Faist 2010: 12).

'Return' should not necessarily be understood as only that of those diasporans who have left their homeland and migrated to a new land, but also those who have no personal first-hand experience of being in the homeland. 'Return,' as a concept, represents a process of going to the roots through routes. This makes 'return' different from simply 'immigration', and, as Kenny stresses, they should not be mixed up (Kenny, 2013: 72). Understanding the routes, as a complex endeavor, assumes identification and knowing how communities, their heritage, and interaction within the host country have been formed.

Katherine McKittrick, a specialist in gender studies, emphasizes that the diaspora addresses the question of nation, home, and location. To her, "lack of a stable nation space and geopolitical independence, and transnational dispersals can shape the possible desire to establish and secure a location that can replace former geographic losses" (McKittrick, 2009: 156). Diasporas are "imagined communities" (Sokefeld and Schwalgin, 2000: 3), and the connection between the diaspora and the homeland is a connection over spaces. This connection, arguably, takes place through the perception of an imagined identity, to borrow and re-phrase Benedict Anderson's renowned phrase. With such a perception formed, diasporans return to the homeland; they also return from the homeland to the diaspora (their community) and perceive it as their particular space in the broader global diasporic space.

Diaspora and Homeland: Inclusion of the Transnational Formation

'Diaspora' has been a subject of intensive study over the past several decades. Development of technology and increasing mobility of people have transformed diasporas from being a collection of separate communities, which have preserved their national identity in their hostland in a passive way, to an extraterritorial body that includes active participants in the homeland. On the other hand, more nation-states are turning toward pursuing an inclusionary approach with regard to their diasporas, "in a variety of domains, such as citizenship, economic development or diplomatic service" (Ragazzi, 2014: 74). Such an inclusionary position aims to strengthen the national identity, economic opportunities for the homeland, and is perceived as a rational choice. Inclusion assumes more active participation of the diaspora in the political and economic life of the homeland.

Strengthening the power of a nation and promoting its national identity can be among other strong rationales for inclusion. Diaspora organizations, individuals, and communities, as Kathleen Newland from Migration Policy Institute emphasizes, "are increasingly vocal and influential" in both their country of origin and settlement (Newland, 2010: 3). Governments of homeland nations are applying an inclusionary approach by reaching out in "new ways" to their people overseas in search of support, be it economic or political (Kenny, 2013: 9). They also use diasporas "to pursue agendas of nation-state-building or controlling populations abroad" (Baubock and Faist, 2010: 11). Diasporas are a powerful tool for political and cultural mobilization, and they are expected to play an even bigger role as diasporans "continue to forge links among themselves and with their homelands" (Kenny, 2013: 109).

As glue for this two-way relationship, inclusion is by no means (and should not be seen as) an act of absorbing one side by another. Instead, it assumes understanding each other first. As in any relationship, trust and direct knowledge should be vital in the homeland-diaspora relationship. Diasporans are nationals of other (host) nation-states with traditions and culture of those hostland countries carried over the years. Khachig Tölölyan argues that diasporic communities carry "a paradoxical combination of both ethnic and diasporic cultural identities and political practices" (Tölölyan, 2000: 109). The development of diaspora communities makes them powerful participant in host nations, with their established institutions, economic, political, social, and religious participation. They are also bound by responsibilities as nationals of their host states. Even though the 'diaspora world' is often perceived as one space, in its global sense, the 'dual orientation of diasporas' (Werbner, in Knott and McLoughlin, 2010: 74) makes 'diaspora' a very complex phenomenon, understanding of which is a continuous process and is never complete.

To understand the inclusion of a diaspora it is essential to identify different factors that influence a homeland's policies to engage its diaspora. Inclusion is often seen strategically important, and more nation-states try to engage people with the same cultural, ethnic, and religious heritage abroad. Inclusion can be justified for a broad range of political, economic, social, cultural, environmental, and demographic reasons. For instance, a diaspora and its homeland, being close to one another, first of all, empower the entire nation to be stronger with regard to negotiating power and lobbying. Jewish or Armenian lobbies are such well-known examples. For instance, the Armenian diaspora "is widely considered one of the most effective ethnic lobbies in Washington, D.C." (Newland, 2010: 11). Political engagement of the diaspora enables both sides of the nation to be united when it comes to promoting their pan-national goals, or to block undesirable outcomes or solutions to issues of importance for either side of the nation. Under the local threat, it is likely that diasporans become more oriented toward moving to the homeland. The immigration of Armenians from Syria since the Syrian civil war began in 2011 can be considered as a justification of such a change.

From pursuing purely economic objectives, such as implementation of joint projects or attracting foreign investments, to meeting strategically important demographic objectives such as increasing the population number, engaging the diaspora can strengthen the homeland nation-state's political power and has a potential for improving its competitiveness abroad. Other possible reasons for the inclusion of diaspora in homeland affairs can be the restoration of wealth (property) as a result of forced expropriation, inflow of finances (with tourists, medical tourists, athletes, through remittances), promotion of the homeland and its geographic regions, reinforcement of the homeland's role as a transit location, as well as enriching the experience of dealing with people from different countries, including people of the same cultural, religious, or ethnic heritage.

The inclusion of diaspora into its homeland can also help the latter develop and promote its national reputation and brand overseas. At the same time, such cooperation between the diaspora and its homeland, debatably, not only strengthens the unity of the nation in the international arena but can also create problems between the two parties. History knows cases of independent existence of both sides or even an exclusionary position toward the diaspora. The exclusion of the Armenian Revolutionary Federation – ARF, a major Armenian diasporic organization – from Armenia in the early 1990s affected the overall participation of diasporans in the homeland.[*] The primary justification used for such a position was the protection of local (homeland's) interests from interference by the diaspora, mainly political. Generally speaking, as political scientist Kristin Cavoukian argues, during Armenia's first President Levon Ter-Petrosyan's presidency, the Armenian state "did not include any diaspora-specific institutions in the new republic, and relations between Armenia and the diaspora were strained during his tenure, from 1991 to 1998," when diasporan criticism of Armenia's state policies was treated as a threat to the regime (Cavoukian, 2013: 716).

Interestingly, relations between the diaspora and the homeland, as mentioned earlier, have been transforming over time as a result of political changes, such as achieving political independence and the establishment of a sovereign nation-state in the homeland. Moreover, diasporas, being "marginal groups who do not give up easily on matters that are related to homelands" (Baser and Swain, 2010: 40), are "wellspring of nationalism" and often support the establishment of a sovereign nation-state in the homeland (Kenny, 2013: 52). Diasporas as agents supporting "sovereignty goals in the homeland, whether on radical or moderate terms" (Koinova, 2009: 9), support nationalistic movements and, as Pnina Werbner quotes Benedict Anderson, are engaged in "long distance nationalism but with no accountability" (Werbner, in Knott and McLoughlin, 2010: 74).

Inclusion does not happen by itself and requires consistent and focused efforts. Ranging from granting citizenship and planning and implementing settlement programs, which build long-term attachment with the homeland, to attracting business projects, including transnational

---

[*] The activities of ARF-Dashnaktsutyun were "temporarily suspended" in Armenia by the Armenian authorities on December 28, 1994, as part of the "anti-ARF interdictions by the Armenian authorities" (ARF, *Background*).

megaprojects, business trips, participation in art and industrial exhibitions, conferences and forums, student exchanges, camps, and formal study, all such measures can aim at placing the homeland in the geographic center of diasporans. Supported by media coverage of events, whether they are organized through diaspora institutions or representatives of the homeland state, fundraising initiatives, remittances, and benevolent contributions or cultural events, and even exported products from the homeland, all these provide connection over spaces.

The inclusion of diaspora does not happen by itself and requires consistent and focused efforts. Despite actual and potential benefits, the inclusionary endeavor may not be effective, arguably because of a lack of continuity or if, for instance, the place-centric perception of the homeland is not seen as the target of the policy. Problems can arise when return is spontaneous and not planned, for instance, with an inflow of refugees into the homeland.

Other problems that might pop up with inclusionary measures, as argued, can be

- resistance at the local and hostland levels,
- financial limitations (lack of funding),
- lack of relevant regulations in the homeland,
- possible interference in hostland's affairs,
- existence of geographical or geopolitical barriers (remoteness, lack of common borders, historically-formed hostile relations between the two sides),
- language barriers between the diaspora and the homeland and differences in understanding each other and in perception of the historical homeland,
- lack of expertise and lack of experience of how to deal with each other, of mutual understanding of the diaspora and the homeland.

Generally speaking, the homeland as a space of return is what keeps diasporans united, as Panossian emphasizes when discussing the case of the Armenians. At the same time, Panossian's strong argument is that the way the diaspora is included, or how it is related to the homeland is what can keep diasporans separate (Panossian, 1998: 185). Often, diasporans know the homeland only as a concept, with no first-hand knowledge, and, so long as this is the case, the sense of home might not be applied to the homeland. The question is whether it can be developed. What is the role of the homeland (and its government) in it?

Policies of a nation-state regarding its diaspora aim at creating and maintaining "ideologies of singularity – of singular loyalties, of the singularity of the national space ownership and of clear-cut borders" (Georgiou, 2006: 9). The process of de-territorialization and re-territorialization diasporans undergo, as well as the multiple identities they carry, shape the context where these national ideologies are being challenged, and, in parallel with calls for loyalty by the homeland, the host nation-state expects a similar attitude toward it from diasporans (Georgiou, 2006: 9). Georgiou suggests that this re-territorialization is taking place in both the new country and the homeland (Georgiou, 2006: 11).

While living in an increasingly globalized world, countries turn to emphasize their identity, which they try to strengthen and promote beyond borders. Sociologist Avtar Brah points out that "the concept of border and diaspora together reference the theme of location" (Brah, 1996: 180). He sees 'diaspora space' as a category that brings 'dispersion' and 'staying put' together, and diasporans being dispersed over spaces but, by 'staying put,' maintain a sense of loyalty to the homeland (Brah, 1996: 181). Arjun Appadurai, a social and cultural anthropologist, even argues that loyalty to a non-territorial transnation is put first (Karla et al., 2005: 36). According to Samuel Huntington, many diasporans, in particular, those in Western countries, even remain loyal to their home-, rather than the hostland (Karla et al., 2005: 36). Sociologist Eliezer Ben-Rafael stresses his view that diasporic communities "belong to another world – through their close contact with their original homeland and fellow-diasporics living elsewhere" (Ben-Rafael, 2013: 854).

The relations between the homeland and its diaspora lie at multiple levels and have differing implications for both. As a framework for understanding the development of a diaspora and its role in transnational development, geographer Giles Mohan categorizes diaspora's development in three dimensions – "development in," "development through," and "development by." The three dimensions facilitation of the diaspora's development where it currently lives ('in'), transnational development processes between diaspora and the world, including homeland ('though'), and benefits that diaspora brings to the homeland ('by') (Page and Mercer, in Knott and McLoughlin, 2010: 105).

The inclusion of diaspora assumes mutual understanding by the diaspora and the homeland and, most importantly, of the need for that inclusion from the strategic and national development perspectives. Diasporas, being in permanent return, even of virtual or imaginary nature, can be "a force for stability' or one "that amplifies and even creates conflict" (Cohen, 2005: 179). Inclusion assumes understanding the diaspora and the homeland by each side and, most importantly, of the need for that inclusion from strategic and national development perspectives.

There is no final answer to understanding a diaspora, as it is not a homogeneous static space but is in dynamic progress. One answer opens a new question and, despite living in one 'diaspora space,' there are differences from country to country. Political scientist Gabriel Sheffer underlines the crucial importance for any diaspora to have and maintain its national identity, so that diaspora communities can develop and prosper (Sheffer, in Sarkisian et el, 2014: 117). The existence of a diaspora gives the homeland an opportunity to reach "new cultural spaces," taking it beyond the physical boundaries of both home- and hostland countries (Kenny, 2013: 12).

Can the homeland engage its diaspora? Or will problems that exist in relations between the two sides limit the ability of the homeland to engage its diaspora? What is the role of places in this task? David Morley, a specialist of communication studies, and Kevin Robins, a geographer, discuss the approach presented by sociologist Antony Giddens that "the effect of the great dynamic forces of modernity," in contrast to the premodern times, "disengage some basic forms of trust relation from the attributes of local contexts" and, therefore, that places are no longer seen as "clear supports of our identities" (Morley and Robins, 2002: 87). Simultaneously, Morley and Robins refer to sociologist Michael Rustin, who stresses the increasingly stronger need "for attachment to particular territorial locations as 'nodes of association and continuity, bounding cultures and communities,'" and they emphasize the "desire to be 'at home' in the new and disorientating global space" (Morley and Robins, 2002: 87). The emphasis on this desire to be at 'home,' driven by historical connection and cultural association, as it can be argued, is what diaspora return assumes. Diasporic identity goes through a transformation process over time and space and is influenced by the environment and time. Space perceived as place, as argued, is what makes diaspora return less idealistic and abstract but more concrete and physically attractive. Places, as stressed, are essential keys that motivate the diaspora, its return.

Engaging the Diaspora: Transformation Over Time

Diaspora needs to be included in the homeland. If left to itself, as argued, it tends to become self-isolated and even exclusionary in its nature, but it will continue developing its own elites and resisting change or transformation. Diaspora can be a powerful actor for the homeland state since it "can mobilize resources outside of the national territory, perform bridging functions or play peace-building roles in the service of the state" (Ho and McConnell, 2017: 16). The inclusion of the diaspora into the homeland is an active process, which, debatably, depends on the rationality-based goodwill of both sides, as well as the good treatment of one another. Diaspora geography is about connections between people and their "'territorial identity,' often over transnational space and via transnational networks," argues geographer Alison Blunt (Blunt, 2007: 689). Reaching the diaspora is a process that involves connections between private individuals, various types of organizations, including religious, as well as the state (homeland nation-state). In cases of reaching ordinary diasporans and their communities, private connections have been useful in reaching the diaspora's elite, as geographer Elaine Ho emphasizes, and "the state has been a prime actor" in this regard (Ho, 2011: 760).

Diaspora should not be viewed as "lost actors, but as terrific a national asset" as, for instance, taking only the total unilateral remittances contributed by diasporans worldwide makes 560 billion US dollars (Atkins, *TedTalk*, 2014). The unilateral remittances contributed by diasporans worldwide total 560 billion US dollars. Diaspora-state relationship and communications are being transformed in the current rapid globalization stage when geographical borders and location are becoming a minor obstacle in transnational communication (Skrbic, 1999: 2).[*] The transnational nature of a diaspora, as Georgiou argues, emphasizes the possibility for development of meaningful relations and social formations across borders, which embraces the connection between "co-existence of the local, the national and the global" (Georgiou, 2006: 10).

---

[*]   In fact, the COVID-19-related measures imposed worldwide since early-2020 have made state borders a significant obstacle for travel.

When analyzing the diaspora-homeland relationship, it becomes important to understand what 'diaspora community' means. It will be a simplistic approach to define a minimum community size. This, however, might lead to very small communities being ignored or, at least, not receive enough attention from the homeland, and, as a result, not being a target for inclusion in the homeland. In any case, "people can't be dispersed without first being together" (Dufoix, 2008: 35). This argument emphasizes that states and their diasporas have mutual connection, and it is only geographic distances that separate them, and that homeland and diaspora are linked over space. According to historian Judith Brown, a successful diaspora first becomes established in host lands, after which its diasporans become related to the 'public space' of their new countries. Only then they revive their connections with their homeland (Brown, in Gottschlich, Roots and Routes, 2012: 5).

The diaspora-state relationship assumes that both sides pursue a specific approach toward each other. Since diasporas, by default, as it is argued here, are in 'permanent return,' it is also suggested that diasporas, when connected to the homeland, cannot pursue an exclusionary approach toward it (possibly with exception of ideology-based exiled diasporans, such as the Cuban diaspora in the U.S.). It is likely, for instance, that in some cases, first-generation diasporans can speak negatively about the homeland. However, this still does not mean that they do not carry a sense of return toward the homeland. This way, possibly, such diasporans try to justify their exodus. Otherwise, it is assumed that diasporans always welcome their homelands' inclusionary approach toward them. The situation can be different from the homeland's perspective. Their policy approach can be inclusionary or exclusionary, as mentioned previously, and accepted or rejected by their diasporas. In either case, there can be reasons, mainly political and economic, which lead to such an approach.

Geographer Francesco Ragazzi specifies five ideal-types of state policies regarding diasporas: "the expatriate, the closed, the indifferent, the global-nation and the managed labor state" (Ragazzi, 2014: 75). Following Ragazzi's analysis, it can be argued that the Armenian state belongs to 'the global-nation state' ideal-type, which, as Ragazzi generalizes, provides its population abroad (the global *Armenianness*, in our case) "the broader number of rights," cultural and language programs, and is "interested in extracting economic and political resources from the population abroad"

(Ragazzi, 2014: 80). In exchange, the Armenian state agrees to include foreign Armenians as its citizens.

The inclusion of a diaspora into its homeland state is a two-fold process. On the one hand, it is about integration in the host country. Here, as a reciprocal process, the latter's acceptance of that inclusion is essential. On the other hand, it is an inclusionary approach from the home(land) country, primarily, its state. Diasporas exist beyond borders, and, as Avtar Brah stresses, the diasporic space not only crosses nation-state borders but also "in so doing evokes transgressive potential" (Brah, in Kalra, Kaur, Hutnyk, 2005: 36). Diasporans, especially immigrants (first-generation diasporans) can successfully integrate with the host country; many even weaken their own ties with the homeland. Over time, some even assimilate and "abandon all ties with their countries of origin" (Newland, 2010: 2). Geographer David Ley's argument that "migrants with the most extensive transnational economic ties are those who are most assimilated" (Ley, 2009: 392) can stress the significance of the economic aspect as an effective motivating tool for the inclusion of diaspora by the homeland and for transforming non-diasporan 'ethnies' into 'diasporans.' As specified earlier, not every 'ethnie' is a diasporan. Diasporans, being in permanent return, maintain links not only with the homeland but also their communities. The modern stage of technological development, in particular, communication technologies, allow the establishment of direct and efficient links with the homeland.

Arjun Appadurai and Anthony Smith emphasize that transnational relations can prevent assimilation and that "identities are deterritorialized" (Erhkamp, 2005: 346). As geographer Patricia Erhkamp suggests, due to transnational connections, it becomes even possible to 'place' identity in the new country, meaning that culture, traditions, and language, can all become placed within a new space, where being concentrated, they transform into a micro-representation of a home-nation (Erhkamp, 2005: 346).

Diasporans, despite being 'others' in both home- and host countries, are present in both spaces. Myria Georgiou argues that a diaspora is positioned in a "particular local and national context" and communication between the spaces, between the homeland and the diaspora "does not erase difference in context" (Georgiou, 2006: 162). Diaspora, being transnational and extraterritorial, can expect protection from its home nation-state; it has a potential, and often contributes toward economic, political, and educational development, to influence the homeland, including its government with regard to strategic, geopolitical, and economics goals; from the other side, a home government attempts to use its diaspora for its political and economic goals (Esman, 2009: 122-130). Diasporans may also support or oppose processes and practices taking place in their homeland (Brah, 1996: 243). With its ability to influence international affairs and politics, as well as to enjoy "some degree of autonomy," a diaspora possesses power to limit actions of nation-states, including the homeland, to have an impact on events, both "in an autonomous capacity" and "as an instrument," as Dimitry Constas and Athanssios Platias, specialists of international relations, emphasize (Constas and Platias, 1993: 10-12).

In their work on the Greek diaspora, Constas and Platias provide a comparative perspective with two other 'classical' diasporas – Armenian and Jewish. They argue that the influence a diaspora has on its host-country depends on the degree of diaspora community organization and tolerance toward its activism by the host state (Constas and Platias, 1993: 12). As argued, a similar argument can also be brought regarding the homeland's influence on its diaspora. However, the homeland state, in its inclusionary policy, is more interested in diasporic community mobilization, particularly when it comes to promoting its (homeland's) interests and identity in the host country's space and even beyond it. Thus, the approach and interests toward diasporas by home and host nation-states can be different. Milton Esman, a specialist of international studies, suggests that diasporans "maintain a transnational existence" and "remain socially and culturally in the homeland" (Esman, 2009: 121). This process transforms the space, which can be "real and/or virtual and imaginary" (Georgiou, 2006: 5), and, as philosopher and sociologist Henry Lefebvre argues, the process "links the mental and the cultural, the social and the historical" through three stages: discovery of unknown spaces, production of spaces, and creation of landscape (Lefebvre, in Georgiou, 2006: 5).

Diaspora, being an extraterritorial phenomenon, assumes that "geographical boundedness and dualities are being constantly challenged," and, at the same time, diaspora's belonging is non-exclusive in terms of its ability to "shape a sense of commonality and (imagined) community in their engagement with transnational communication" (Georgiou, 2006:

149). This idea can assume communication with the home nation-state as well. It should be noted that although diasporans are linked with the homeland, their relationship is "in the context of a hybrid – decentralized, multimodal, conditional – imagined community," and they, by representing different identities of both home and host lands, are positioned in local, national, and transnational spaces (Georgiou, 2006: 155). Georgiou continues that transnationalism of the diaspora is "less about place and more about space," "less about the boundary and more about imagination" (Georgiou, 2006: 135). The extraterritorial diaspora space knows no borders. Thus, the role of boundaries, specifically during the modern era of communication technologies, is beyond argument. However, it can be argued that places continue playing an important role in including diasporans in the homeland since, to a significant degree, those are places that create an emotional attachment to the homeland. Doreen Massey views the diasporic world within the context of "global sense of place," which goes into "interconnectedness rather than separatism, routes rather than roots" (Massey, in Hubbard and Kitchin, 2011: 216). In the process of creation and maintenance of that interconnectedness, the role diaspora institutions play, becomes critical.

Following her argument, Georgiou mentions that diaspora networks are not "linear one-way flows" but "follow the routes and the rules of human mobility, deterritorialization and relocation" (Georgiou, 2006: 147). Being relocated, however, diasporans, from place to place, have differing motivations to support their homelands. Thus, to Kathleen Newland, diasporas that have a strong sense of existential threat or injustice are more supportive (Newland, 2010: 216). Esman's description of the diaspora's involvement in its homeland's affairs presents the mutually beneficial nature of the relationship. With regard to trading diasporas (with many relevant examples, such as the Lebanese, the Armenians before the Genocide, or the Chinese), they form "a nation of socially interdependent but spatially dispersed communities," as Robin Cohen specifies (Dufoix, 2008: 20) and, in general, diasporans reside and act in host countries but maintain "strong sentimental and materials links with their countries of origin" (Dufoix, 2008: 21).

The special focus of this book is on the role diaspora institutions play in the process of inclusion of diasporas into their homelands, as viewed by diasporans. Institutions are instrumental in diaspora-state relationships, and as Dufoix argues it is through the intermediation of these institutions that diaspora communities in host countries undergo "the process of (re)constituting fellow feeling" and "the local then becomes the place where community identities are forged on the model that prevail in the home country" (Dufoix, 2008: 71). Even back in 1972, political scientists Robert Keohane and Joseph Nye emphasized "the growing importance of networks and non-state actors" in international affairs (Dufoix, 2008: 31).

This new paradigm of diaspora-homeland connection is "reshaping geography" by making "the construction of nonphysical territories possible" (Dufoix, 2008: 104). Moreover, the rapid development of communication technologies strengthens the role the Internet plays in strengthening national identity (Ortmann, 2009: 39) and in communicating geopolitical imaginations (Beck, 2006: 521). The Internet serves as a tool the state uses for communication and "developing contact policies" with its diaspora (Dufoix, 2008: 101) and for supporting the pan-nation and not simply transnational identity (Dufoix, 2008: 102), as it allows people to "be united in their dispersion" (Dufoix, 2008: 105).

Utilization of this technological opportunity might even help diaspora institutions, particularly religious ones, to preserve their national identity. The Internet has become an important and powerful tool "for both formal and informal connections among diaspora networks, individuals, and policymakers" (Newland, 2010: 11). This opens new horizons in terms of opportunities to reach other diasporans and beyond in their cities, countries, and farther, in the homeland and the rest of the world.

Engaging the Diaspora: The Role of Religious Institutions

Diaspora institutions can be represented by a broad range of religious and educational organizations (many of which are linked to religious ones), charities, political parties/branches, and lobbying groups and associations, trade organizations and chambers. All these institutions attempt to establish a good rapport with both home and host states, as their effective functioning, among other factors, depends on useful links and networks with both sides. Among them, the role of religious institutions is considered here as of particular importance. With regard to this, sociologists Helen Ebaugh and Janet Chafetz emphasize that transnational religious networks connecting immigrants play a central role in the 21st-century transnational world (Ebaugh and Chafetz, 2002: 190).

Nation-states understand that their country serves as the 'emotional home' for its diaspora (as Judith Brown notes) and that "religious networks can be a source of both linkage and division" (Brown, in Gottschlich, Roots and Routes, 2012: 6). Brown stresses the essential role of religious institutions (in her example – temples) and religious traditions in forming "a strong bond within a diaspora" (Roots and Routes, 2012: 6). For instance, in Armenia, which was a part of the Soviet Union and not considered the historical homeland by many Armenians in the diaspora, it was the Armenian (Apostolic) Church and the Armenian language that "played a crucial role in maintaining national unity" and connecting communities (Dufoix, 2008: 52).

Transnational religious organizations, sociologist Peggy Levitt classifies, fall under one of three forms: 'extended,' such as the Catholic Church, 'negotiated,' like Protestant Churches, and 're-created,' "when believers migrate to a country where no structure exists and they must build from scratch" (Levitt, in Dufoux, 2008: 77). In the case of three 'classical' diasporas – Jews, Armenians, and Greeks – the opportunity to practice religion, as it can be argued, has been of crucial importance for keeping the nation centered on it. Interestingly, even many centuries back, as Stephane Dufoix states, after Constantinople was seized by the Ottomans in 1453, these three communities were "allowed to establish an autonomous religious community" (Dufoix, 2008: 39). To Dufoix, it is through the mediation of institutions that diasporic "community identities are forged on the model of those that prevail in the home country" (Dufoix, 2008: 71).

Belonging to a diaspora organization or being active in one has two sides: rational and emotional. Many diasporans belong to religious organizations purely based on emotional (including nostalgic) or spiritual needs. The case of Croatians and Slovenians in Australia is such an example, which shows that even the second generation of diasporans identify themselves with the (Catholic) church, although they do not necessarily see advantages in "being a part of this organization" (Skrbic, 1999: 77). While, in the case of trade or political organizations, the rational motives are easily observable, belonging to a religious organization is not only an issue of emotional and spiritual attachment, but can also be a rational choice. The role of a widespread religious institution such as the Armenian Apostolic Church is later discussed in greater detail. Networks of institutions that link the diaspora and its homeland become powerful tools to strengthen and promote national identity, as well as to influence the power of the home nation-state to reach its diaspora and the rest of the world through the diaspora.

Engaging the Diaspora: A Homeland's Rational Choice

The inclusion of a diaspora in its homeland, arguably, is an outcome of an emotional attachment and rationality – two conditions, which are quite distinct from each other. Geographer Elizabeth Mavroudi stresses that a strong sense of diasporic identity is not a necessary determinant for diaspora mobilization (Mavroudi, 2017: 12). The study Mavroudi has conducted on the mobilization of Greek and Palestinian diasporas demonstrates a weaker-than-generally-expected mobilization based on the emotional factor. In particular, Mavroudi argues that "those in diaspora often appear to feel disillusioned by their attempts to help the homeland at a time of crisis" (Mavroudi, 2017: 12). In the case of the Greek diaspora, the origin of which is trade (as specified by Robin Cohen), the economic factor in diaspora formation can, to a certain extent, justify rationality in the approach to diaspora-homeland relations. In the case of the Palestinian diaspora, the situation is quite different. The diaspora, as its origin, has a major political event, the *Nakba* or catastrophe, as a consequence of the establishment of the State of Israel in 1948 (Mavroudi, 2017: 4). As such, the origin of the diaspora can assume more emotional (patriotic) and less rational motives behind the mobilization of the diaspora. However, even in the case of the Palestinians, there is another potentially strong political factor, which the Palestinian nation and its homeland can (and often does) rely on – the 'Arab World.' In the case of another classical diaspora – the Armenians, a significant part of the diaspora has an exile origin based on a political condition – the Armenian Genocide. As argued, the emotional factor can be expected as the main driving force for mobilizing the Armenian nation worldwide, including within the homeland (the Republic of Armenia). This is a major topic for further study. However, at this stage, it cannot be concluded that, in the case of all diasporas, the emotional belonging is not directly linked to diaspora mobilization, as Mavroudi argues with regard to both Greek and Palestinian diasporans. During the history of independent Armenia (from 1991 onward), after the War in Artsakh (formerly known as Nagorno-Karabakh), which ended in a ceasefire with neighboring Azerbaijan (mentioned previously), a sudden need for political mobilization in the diaspora appeared during the unexpected Four-Day War in the first days of April in 2016 and the Second Artsakh War (the 44-day War) of September-November of 2020. A study of the Armenian diaspora's behavior in such critical times will be needed before any conclusion on possible factors of its mobilization can be presented regarding the Armenian diaspora's mobilization capacity. Mavroudi brings an argument, which is one of the core points identified through an empirical study in this work, "that homeland governments cannot necessarily rely on the support or help of diasporas," but they, as well as diaspora elites, "need to do more to win over trust of those in diaspora" (Mavroudi, 2017: 12).

The policies nation-states pursue toward diasporas are indeed within the context of their geopolitical interests. The nation-state, being a derivative of an already-formed society and community, is an "artificial form that protects the interests of those who belong to it" (Dufoix, 2008: 70). While nation-states remain key players in world politics, the whole conceptual framework of cross-cultural and political communication complicates matters. Regarding the process of changes, Khachig Tölölyan stresses that while nation-states remain leading political organizations, "nonstate forces threaten the stability of borders" (Dufoix, 2008: 32). Globalization processes influence space and time. 'Global narrowing of space and time,' which is inherent to these processes, "does not, paradoxically, refer to the loss of identities or cultures," suggests ethnographer Warren Kidd (Kidd, 2002: 195).

The nation-state, while being a dominant player in the international political arena, recognizes that, on the one hand, it is to its own benefit to engage its diaspora in local affairs to serve political, economic, and even social-demographic interests. At the same time, being under the sovereign jurisdiction of foreign nation-states, interference of diasporans and their organizations/institutions in the homeland's affairs can lead to a weakening of the home nation-state and its power over its internal and foreign affairs. Globally spread diasporic communities transform the concept of 'national identity.' Simultaneously, Avtar Brah emphasizes that in the contemporary world, nation-states find it difficult to refuse their diasporization (Brah, 1996: 243). Brah argues that the "contemporary form of transnational migrancy of capital, commodities, peoples, and cultures is the very condition of both the persistence and erosion of the nation state" (Brah, 1996: 243). Besides, diaspora-state networks are gradually creating a new phenomenon of 'brain gain,' as opposed to 'brain drain' (Dufoix, 2008: 104), which transforms the quality of the relationship diasporans have with the home nation-state.

In her analysis of contemporary diasporas (based on the Greek diaspora), Myria Georgiou emphasizes that continuity and sense of belonging that a diaspora is carrying have been formed "in the tense heterogeneous space of imagined community" (Georgiou, 2006: 49). Georgiou also argues that the transformation shifts "the centrality of the nation-state and the homeland" (Georgiou, 2006: 49).

An in-depth analysis is needed to identify whether a newly established home nation-state is willing to sacrifice its power by sharing it with its diaspora or instead to preserve and strengthen it independently. If the diaspora had been carrying the identity and culture, as well as promoting transnational geopolitical interests for centuries, then, after a sovereign nation-state is established, would the diaspora-homeland relationship change? Another point of interest is whether national identity is limited to national borders, something that acts as "symbols of sovereignty" and holds "emotive significance" (Kuzio, 2007: 38-39).

According to geographer Lily Kong, "physical presence in a territory is not a necessary condition for a feeling of nationhood" (Kong, 1999: 584), and residence in a country's "territory is unnecessary for the development of national identity; indeed, residence beyond the politically defined territory appears to enhance the sense of attachment" (Kong, 1999: 577). Diasporans can be engaged in national-level projects, which geographer Tim Bunnell suggests "may extend beyond the bounds of the national territory to include nationals overseas," (Bunnell, 2002: 4). Diasporans can be engaged in the creation and maintenance of rituals or traditions, which are "as important as, if not more so than those of the state in constructing community (both real and imagined) and maintaining identity" (Kong, 1999: 584). If actions of the home state can be considered or perceived to be binding or pressuring, then a diaspora's activities are more voluntary in nature and, typically, reflect the social needs of diasporic communities.

The homeland, to be identified as home, assumes "attachment and associations, rather than residence in or possession of the land that matters for ethnic identification"; it is "where we belong" and is "also often a sacred land" (Smith, 1991: 23). In his analysis of the Armenian diaspora, Khachig Tölölyan separates it from all other diasporas with regard to its attitude toward adaptation. There are some communities, for instance, in India (Kolkata), Ethiopia and other countries, which have become residual, as Tölölyan defines it. Meanwhile, unlike other 'emerging diasporas,' Armenians "respond to changing local conditions through emigration rather than by adapting and developing new institutions, cultural and social practices, or identities" (Tölölyan, 2000: 112). Such a process, as might be argued, is not only applicable to the Armenians outside of Armenia, but also to the Armenians who live in Armenia, who have emigrated since independence, with an increase in numbers during economic and political turmoil and hardship, or because of a lack of positive expectations.

Changes in the total population number in Armenia can lead to an assumption that the Armenians either impose and follow their own order or simply emigrate. This makes the Armenian diaspora's engagement complicated since a well-established diaspora would not be willing to give in, while the nation-state, following its most recent experience of its own traditions and order, developed during and after the Soviet era, tends to defend its system, its space. This is like a different sub-identity within the broader Armenian identity, which has a potentially resistant nature to any transformation of its space. This and other aspects of the Armenian diaspora's nature are discussed later in this book.

Understanding National Identity

The concept of "nation" involves a broad spectrum of constituent elements which are "valid only for a certain historical period" (Uzelac, 2002: 43). The case of Israel demonstrated, for instance, that mobilization could be driven by ideology – Zionism, since the late 19th century – which took place when no common language, common territory, or economy existed. Geographer Derek Gregory points at what Theodor Herzl, the founder of Zionism, emphasized, "that it was only through the birth of their own nation-state that Jews would emerge into the world of modernity" (Gregory, 2004: 79). Thus, driven by the ideas of a group of people, the imaginary existence of the nation (as a state) preceded its real existence. This point coincides with the definition of the nation given by sociologist and anthropologist Liah Greenfield, who points out that the national consciousness of the intelligentsia is crucial in forming the nation (Greenfield, in Uzelac, 2002: 36). Such an approach may signify the notion that national consciousness and self-perception of distinctiveness will remain key mobilizing factors of national identity.

According to sociologist Edward Tiryakian and political scientist Neil Nevitte, a nation is "a historically evolving reality" (in Panossian, 2002: 123). As an 'imagined community' (if we apply Benedict Anderson's concept), a nation "is more specifically a remembered community, a community with an imagined history, and is defined by its historical memory of itself" (Huntington, 2004: 117). At the same time, despite numerous attempts aimed at defining 'nation,' viewpoints vary, and "the distinction between nation-as-state and nation-as-people is vague" (Szondi, 2008: 6).

Concepts of 'nation' and 'national identity' are interlinked. The need to differentiate the 'self' from the 'other' does not appear spontaneously. According to political scientist Samuel Huntington, "people develop their sense of national identity as they fight to differentiate themselves from other people with different language, religion, history, or location" (Huntington, 2004: 29). Permanent differentiation between 'self' and 'other' forms the need for a distinct identity. Being in permanent change, on the other hand, identity "can be understood in the relationship between the past and the present" (Mohamadi, 2011: 412), as "it looks both to the past and to the future" by "allowing dispersion to be thought of either as a state of incompleteness or a state completeness," when the "issue of origin arises in both cases" (Dufoix, 2008: 34).

Identity is always in "permanent identity negotiation" (Ranjan, in Roots and Routes, 2013: 6). Cultural theorist and sociologist Stewart Hall argues that 'identity' is not "an already accomplished fact," but, rather, a 'production,' "which is never complete, always in process" (Hall, 2003: 222). Identities can be multiple, based on gender and age, space and territory, social class and ideology, etc. Identity represents, as historian Dipesh Chakrabarty emphasizes, "some kind of narrative consensus in which everybody or every group knows who or what they are" (Chakrabarty, 2002: 94-95), and it "can never be reduced to a single element" (Smith, 1991: 14). In her definition, sociologist Gordana Uzelac emphasized the role of political factors in forming a culture, as the latter becomes "a social agency politically organized as a community which claims its rights on the basis of a culture defined as its own" (Uzelac, 2002: 49). Uzelac accentuates that nations are rooted in national ideology (Uzelac, 2002: 43), and through the development over centuries they have arrived at the current stage when "subnational cultural and regional identities are taking precedence over broader national identities" (Huntington, 2004: 13). Historian and political scientist Hugh Seton-Watson argues that the significance of "national consciousness" in forming a nation cannot be underestimated, as it is "first developed within a narrow circle of the population, like the intelligentsia, political elite or aristocracy" (Seton-Watson, in Uzelac, 2002: 36).

National existence, Uzelac summarizes, requires a number of factors to be present. A common language is seen as the primary factor by B. Anderson, J. G. Herder, K. Kautsky, and K. Deutsch, and "control of a specific territory is stressed by A. Hastings, A. Giddens, M. Billig and J. Breuilly as a crucial constituent element" (Uzelac, 2002: 35). Apart from these, myths of common descent (W. Connor) and common economy are considered critical by Anthony Smith (Smith, 1992: 60).[*] Smith also emphasizes that a nation is "first and foremost a community of common descent" (Smith, 1991: 11).

Nowadays, identities are seen broader than what national borders determine. They can "span over multiple scales, and their boundaries are social rather than geographical," should neither be perceived too narrowly within a certain territory, nor be deterritorialized, but rather be seen as "the persistence of thick cultural identities imbricated with territory in multiple relations" (Antonsich, 2009: 801).

Identities are not constant and fixed. As imagined selves, identities are in permanent change (Huntington, 2004: 22-23); its formation is a continuous process (Huntington, 2004: 109). The perception of identity at a time may be totally different at another time, even politically incorrect, as stressed by cultural geographer Victor Savage (Savage, 2012: 1). Political geographer Doreen Massey argues that identity is relational in 'spatio-temporal' way, and in addition to being "the narratives of the past" and "inherited resources," the process of identity construction is ongoing now (Massey, 2012: 192).

---

[*] Joseph Stalin considered a common economy as a crucial factor too (Uzelac, 2002: 35).

The identity of a nation, according to political scientists Richard Mansbach and Richard Rhodes, is "a social construct, created or modified daily through internal cognitive processes and social praxis" (Mansbach and Rhodes, 2007: 434). It can be wrong to state that the formation of identity started at some fixed point in time. As identity assumes a "meaningful sense of belonging" as a necessary emotional motive (Panossian, 2002: 124), then in the case of many nations, the historical memory and links to their ancient past serve as roots of their identity. In this long-term process, religion, literature, language or dialect, poetry, and rituals, among other factors, nourish ancient identities and support the continuousness of identity (Mansbach and Rhodes, 2007: 436).

In her analysis, sociologist Montserrat Guibernau proposes that national identity is composed of five key elements:

(i) psychological: consciousness of forming a community;

(ii) cultural: sharing a common culture;

(iii) territorial: attachment to a clearly demarcated territory;

(iv) historical: possessing a common past; and

(v) political: claiming the right to rule itself (Guibernau, 2004: 135).

At the national level, identity is seen as an outcome of politicization of cultural identity, the same way as nations serve as carriers of that identity as a result of the politicization of culture through nationalism (Uzelac, 2002: 50). Identity is intertwined with culture, which opens "the relationship of the individual to the wider group" and cultures (Kidd, 2002: 3). Being time-bound, particular and expressive, identities "are tied to specific people, places and periods" and "are bound up with definite historical identities" (Smith, 1992: 66-67). The argument historian Martin van Creveld brings is that there is a need for a "push" from a nation toward a national state by strengthening the appeal of national identity (Mansbach and Rhodes, 2007: 434) and further stresses the importance of national identity for both the nation (including its diaspora) and the nation-state, categories, which, as geographers Peter Taylor and Colin Flint point out, provide individuals "with their fundamental space-time identities" (Taylor and Flint, 2000: 234).

Identity as a category has different interpretations and meanings. Until some three hundred years ago, as "the vast majority of analysts" state, the ideas of 'nation,' 'national identities,' 'national states,' and 'national ideologies' did not exist; they are "recent and novel" (Smith, 2002: 6).

When referring to the modernists, Anthony Smith continues that nations and national states are viewed as 'inventions' "of the ideology of nationalism, which is itself wholly modern," and that for modernists, the causal chain "runs from modernity to nationalism to nations" (Smith, 2002: 6). This explanation can be essential for understanding the evolution of nations, in this particular case, the Armenians and their national identity in its contemporary form. A specialist of constitutional identity, Gary Jacobsohn mentions, "a person may be said to have an identity even in the absence of widespread agreement on what exactly it is" (Jacobsohn, 2006: 370). Ethnic and cultural identities, including language and religious identities, are mainly viewed from the perspectives of anthropology and cultural geography; class identities are mainly seen from the viewpoint of sociology and political economy; and national identities from the viewpoint of political geography and geopolitics.

Anthony Cohen, a social anthropologist, argues that "identification with a community is largely a symbolic process" and identity is not limited to geographical boundaries of countries but is based "on the establishment of shared sets of meaning, the use of which enables people to act and interact with others, and with whom they can identify (Cohen, in Kidd, 2002: 27). As a relative phenomenon, identity is always in comparison and in "contrast with others who are deemed to be different" (Kidd, 2002: 131). When contrasting between 'self' and 'other,' philosopher and cultural theorist Kwame A. Appiah argues that "identities are multiple and overlapping and context-sensitive, and some are relatively trivial and transient" (Appiah, 2005: 100).

Identity assumes differentiation and, therefore, comparison (Huntington, 2004: 26). Being rooted in emotions, "in particular, those of fear, hope, and humiliation," Dominique Moisi, a French political scientist, says that "identity is strongly linked with confidence, or the lack thereof" (Moisi, 2009: 12). Many nations have experienced certain periods in their history, including tragic times and events, which have significantly influenced, even shaped their identity. This experience is particularly important when a nation has passed through a continuous historical decline in terms of its political standing, be it regional or broader. Such decline becomes the most important cause of the dominance of humiliation (Moisi, 2009: 60). Humiliation can be an outcome of a loss of a country's territory (for example, the loss of what Japan calls 'the

Northern Territories' to Russia). A cause for humiliation can be originated by a "difficult search for identity," such as in the case of Muslims in Europe (Moisi, 2009: 79), or by a threat that the nation and its identity will be destroyed (e.g., the Holocaust or the Armenian Genocide – the *Medz Yeghern*). For Armenians, the losses in the *Second Artsakh War*,[*] is another example of such humiliation, outcomes of which can remain for a relatively long period of time.

To sum up, the concepts of 'nation' and 'national identity' with regard to nations, which are spread beyond territorial limits of their nation-states, accentuate the extraterritorial nature of the concepts. There is no unified approach toward the concept of 'national identity' and how it has been shaped, at least in the modern times. For instance, with regard to a 'classical' diasporic nation – the Jews, whose scattered communities "retained their unique identity" (Kotkin, 1993: 31), a strong Marxist stance has been prevalent in the foundation of national ideology – Zionism (Rodinson, 1973: 83), even though the religious identity is the core of Jewish national identity. With regard to Armenians, studied as an empirical case here, their religious identity is often viewed as identical to their national identity. National identity, thus, combines ethnic and religious identities in this particular case, and, in order to maintain consistency in terminology, 'identity' here in this work means 'national identity' in its broader meaning, not limited only to nationals (citizens) of the nation-state.

---

[*] The *Second Artsakh War,* as briefly mentioned above, was unleashed by Azerbaijan against Artsakh on September 27, 2020. The War (its military part) ended with a three-party declaration mediated by President Putin of Russia, with Prime Minister Pashinyan of Armenia and President Aliyev of Azerbaijan as two other signatories. As a result of the War, more than 3,500 Armenians (mostly military personnel) were killed (search efforts continued even after 2020), and Artsakh lost about one third of the territory of the former Soviet Nagorno-Karabakh Autonomous Oblast proper (NKAO) and the seven districts around it (CarnegieEurope.eu and News.am), which were acquired by the Republic of Artsakh (or Nagorno-Karabakh) as a result of the counter-offensive in the *First Karabakh War*.

PART 2

Chapter 4

A CLASSICAL DIASPORA: THE ARMENIANS

The Armenians: Diaspora and National Identity, Dimensions and Roots

"The sun never sets on the Armenian diaspora" (Tölölyan, 2000: 107). Used as a joke in Armenia, when an Armenian is leaving for overseas, he or she is not asked if there are Armenians in the country of destination but if there are many of them there. For a diasporic global nation, the concept of '*Armenianness*' is not limited to the borders of the Republic of Armenia. Diaspora, being extraterritorial, as it can be strongly argued, becomes a bridge connecting the homeland state (of Armenia) to the rest of the world, at least the part of it where the diaspora is found. Living overseas, diasporan (not simply 'ethnie') Armenians connect the two spaces, of the homeland and the host country. Let's go through an overview of how 'diaspora' as a concept is applied to Armenians, as of a classical diasporic nation.

Diasporans, thus, are 'intellectual amphibians,' because of the "hovering position between cultures" they stand on (Ranjan, in Roots and Routes, 2013: 6). Samuel Huntington argues that diasporas are "cultural communities cutting across the boundaries of two or more states, one of which is viewed as the homeland country of that community" (Huntington, 2004: 262). Diasporas, their ethnic identity, and culture have a power to have an impact on others (Gilroy, in Kidd, 2002: 194). However, without underestimating the importance of such cultural influence, a diaspora should not be viewed, as historian Kim D. Butler emphasizes, as an ethnicity, but as a "framework for the study of a specific process of community formation" (Butler, in Rios and Adiv, 2010: 3). A diaspora can play an important geopolitical role, according to Fiona Adamson, a specialist of international studies (Adamson, 2008: 2) and, therefore, it needs to be well examined to understand transnations and their identity.

'Diaspora' as a phenomenon has come into existence and has broadened the concept of a 'nation.' The term 'diaspora,' despite being old (derived from Greek), was rarely in use until the nineteenth century. It was since the early 1930s (Dufoix, 2008: 14, 17), when the concept was suggested (by Simon Dubnov), then the term entered into use. However, its use was still limited to Jewish or other religious histories, up to the 1960s (Dufoix, 2008: 17, 19). Since then, several other diasporas, specifically the Armenians, have been considered 'classical.'[*] Even as the term 'diaspora' came into modern use, it wasn't until the mid-1980s (more specifically, in 1986) when the study of diaspora "shifted to a general theoretical approach based on a comparative perspective, comparing Jews, Armenians, Turks, Palestinians, Chinese, Indians, and so on" (Dufoix, 2008: 20).

During the first decades after 'diaspora' entered its modern era as an area of study, there were mainly political scientists and sociologists who used the concept. In France, the concept was also an important object for study among geographers. Thus, in 1957, Maximilien Sorre used the term 'diaspora' to mean "the space that national minorities occupy in foreign countries" (Dufoix, 2008: 26). Pierre George (in 1984) went further and suggested a more specific application of the term, with emphasis on "successive exodus" and "ethno-cultural segregation and conservation of cultural practices" (Dufoix, 2008: 26). In 1989, Yves Lacoste suggested limiting the application of the term 'diaspora' to only people whose majority lives abroad, therefore, leaving only five diasporas for consideration: the Jewish, Armenian, Lebanese, Palestinian, and Irish cases (Dufoix, 2008: 22). The process of determining how far the concept of 'diaspora' can be extended has remained ongoing. Richard Marienstras, a French specialist of literature, suggests a condition in 1985 that makes the application of the term toward other diasporas possible" by introducing "the central role of time in determining "true diasporas" (Dufoix, 2008: 26). More than a decade later (1999), sociologist Dominique Shnapper suggested to broaden the concept by making it based on two conditions: neutrality of the concept and inclusion of the dispersed populations "that maintain ties among themselves, and not only to the Jews, Armenians, Greeks, or Chinese" (Dufoix, 2008: 30). The significance of these criteria has been brought into the context of territoriality. Permanence, as a crucial condition for a diaspora's existence, Dufoix argues, "is possible only when

---

[*] Apart from the Jews and Armenians diasporas, the Greek and, to some extent, Chinese and African diasporas are also considered 'classical' (Brubaker, 2005: 2).

it involves a territory that has no borders and is not limited to a specific piece of ground" (Dufoix, 2008: 27).[*]

To be classified as diasporas, transnational communities, arguably, should be dispersed and have their collective memory of their homeland (Safran, Cohen, Butler), alienation from host lands (Safran), collective trauma and sense of community (Cohen), minimum two destinations and minimum two generations after dispersal (Butler) (Rios and Adiv, 2010: 3). Preservation of national culture is seen an essential condition for classification of transnationals as diasporans (Dufoix, 2008: 17). That being said, French geographer Michel Bruneau named diasporans "world people," who "have occupied and politically or culturally dominated vast spaces," which is tripartite with a state established in modern times (last two centuries), "a broader cultural realm, and finally a 'world diaspora' – classification, which counts the Chinese, Indians, Greeks, and Armenians" (Dufoix, 2008: 38).

Robin Cohen, a scholar in migration and diaspora studies, classifies diaspora based on its origin - victim, labor, trade, imperial, and cultural (Cohen, in Rios and Adiv, 2010: 3). He uses examples of Jews, Armenians, Africans, Irish, and Palestinians as victim diasporas, Indians, Chinese, Sikhs, and Italians as labor diasporas, Lebanese as a trade diaspora, British, Spanish, and Dutch as imperial diasporas, and the Caribbean as a cultural diaspora (Alonso and Oiarzabal, 2010: 5-6). Indeed, within the diaspora, there are differences as well, based on "complexities of class, race, gender, generation and other social divisions" (Rios and Adiv, 2010: 11). However, Fiona Adamson argues that such classifications are oversimplified "because they suggest that diasporas exist as homogenous groups" (Adamson, 2016: 292). Even in case of the Armenians, who have been classified as victim diaspora people by Robin Cohen, there have been significant diasporic communities originated before the dispersion caused by tragedies such as the Armenian Genocide. For instance, the communities in East and South Asia, with the most notable one in Kolkata, India, are some of the Armenian 'trade network' examples, as Sebouh Aslanian names such (Aslanian, 2017).

Understanding diasporas requires accepting the heterogeneous nature of diaspora communities, despite having a common cultural and even

---

[*] Dufoix brings an example of the Torah as the abstract territory for the Jews (Dufoix, 2008: 27).

language umbrella. An ethnic diaspora is essential to form a transnation, and a diaspora has the potential to "succeed in maintaining links and in developing a 'nation abroad'" (Kong, 1999: 586). However, not all transnational migrations result in forming diasporas. Khachig Tölölyan, in his studies of the Armenian diaspora, insists that efforts aimed at the creation of discourses and cultural works that "fuel the diasporic consciousness and identity" are what is essential to make the diaspora "worthy of that name" (Tölölyan, in Yeoh and Willis, 2004: 183). Tölölyan and sociologist Dominique Schnapper stress upon the expansion and more diverse meaning of diaspora, based on 'classical' diaspora experiences in order "to accommodate it to new contemporary transnational realities" (Schnapper, in Alonso and Oiarzabal, 2010: 5). However, critics of dilution of the concept, such as political scientist William Safran insist that "diaspora status can be applied only to Jews and Armenians" (Safran, in Alonso and Oiarzabal, 2010: 6).

Diasporas assume interaction with both host and home states. Linking both societies, diasporas draw "attention away from the single nation-state and towards a potential multiplicity of nation-states or regions within states" (Kalra, Kaur, and Hutnyk, 2005: 17). The identity of a diaspora **thus** carries common features of both states. In that case, which nation do diasporans belong to – the homeland or the hostland, or both?

Diaspora, by definition, assumes being separated from its homeland, to which it seeks to join or return. Nations (nation-states), being "inherently exclusionary" and considering "the majority of the world's people to be outsiders," as social psychologist Michael Billig describes them (Billig, in Antonsich, Mavroudi, Mihelj, 2017: 159), at the same time, tend not to apply such approaches toward their own diasporans. In practice, as argued, this exception is mainly rooted in the emotional-historical perception of the diaspora. Michael Billig stresses that nation-states, with their exclusionary nature, are such because of their "fundamentally exclusive ideology of nationalism *tout court*" (Antonsich, Mavroudi, Mihelj, 2017: 159-160).

Anthony Smith proposes that in the current stage of global geopolitical development, "national identification has become the cultural and political norm, transcending other loyalties in scope and power" (Smith, 1992: 58). The phenomenon of loyalty is crucial as far as the diaspora-homeland relationship is concerned. Smith suggests the following minimum factors necessary for the formation of a nation: a collective proper name, myths and memories of communal history, a common public culture, common laws and customs, and a historical territory or homeland (Smith, 2002: 16-17). In the case of the Armenians, a proper name, historical myths and memories, and common culture are present; however, homeland is perceived differently – the whole territory of the Armenian Highlands is perceived as the historical homeland and territory of the modern Armenian nation-state (the Republic of Armenia) as only a part of it. The Armenian Highlands, as stressed, is the historical-geographic reason for the existence of Armenians in at least the territory where modern Armenia and Artsakh are located. Not to take for granted, as Sökefeld and Schwalgin stress, the Armenian identity is perceived in a way that "it has to be maintained through constant activities and sacrifices if it is not to be lost" (Sökefeld and Schwalgin, 2000: 4). Being a key element of Armenian diaspora identity, the concept of sacrifice assumes "efforts to preserve the Armenian language, the transmission of Armenian names, the foundation of a purely Armenian family as well as commitment to the local community and the community's institutions" (Sökefeld and Schwalgin, 2000: 5, 9).

Together with its global diaspora, the Armenian nation-state represents a portion of the Armenian (trans)nation. Khachig Tölölyan argues that the diasporic home is not to be confused with, or be located in, the ancestral homeland (Tölölyan, 2011: 11-12). Being an Armenian goes beyond the nation-state and includes the diaspora as well[*] and, as argued by Joseph Masih and Robert Krikorian in their study of post-Soviet Armenia, "the diaspora has played a critical role in the formation of Armenian national consciousness throughout the last several centuries" (Masih and Krikorian, 1999: xxii).

In Armenian, the word *spyurq* or *spiurk*, means (as a collective noun) 'spread-out people' or 'dispersed people,' which is the term used to refer to the 'diaspora.' At the same time, diaspora communities are often referred to as *gaghut* or *kaghout*, which translates to "living in diaspora," unlike "the situation of (forced) dispersion," as in the case of the term *spiurk* (Sökefeld and Schwalgin, 2000: 4). This, arguably, can be an important difference in

---

[*] The Armenian Highlands is now spread over Turkey, Iran, Azerbaijan, Georgia, and Armenia. In 1990, when discussing the name of the post-Soviet Armenia, there was even an idea proposed by one of the members of the Armenian parliament to call the new state the Republic of Eastern Armenia.

terms of how diasporans perceive themselves. With *gaghut* they can be more self-isolated within their community and community affairs, while considering themselves part of the *spiurk* makes them feel part of the globally-dispersed nation, as emphasized, a key for effective engagement within the diaspora communities and the homeland.

Razmig Panossian suggests that there are three core narratives of Armenian identity or '*Armenianness*': i) belonging to the first Christian Nation; ii) Armenia's pre-Christian history, and iii) the Armenian Genocide (Panossian, 2002: 125-126). Khachig Tölölyan argues that the nature of the Armenians is like one nation, irrespective of their location, in their homeland (Armenia) or outside of it. To him, "like the Jews, Armenians worldwide consider themselves essentially one people, albeit living in numerous different countries" (Kotkin, 1992: 29). An indirect evidence of such a perception is that 'a national' among many in Armenia is largely perceived as ethnic Armenian.[*] Tölölyan continues that diasporas like these are "fundamentally different from other emigrant peoples" in the sense of either keeping alive a historical memory of their homeland or dreaming of a return to it or interacting with it in some way (Kotkin, 1992: 29). In general, diaspora and its culture "are not simply traveling and migrating with ease," but those are particular events, which have initiated flight, and "this movement is difficult psychically because it is wrapped up in loss and different types of return" (McKittrick, 2009: 158). The Armenian Genocide became such an event for Armenians. As Panossian underlines, it seems ironic that "the destruction of Armenians in their homeland is the point of reference for the survival of the nation" (Panossian, 2002: 139). French-Armenian historian Anahide Ter-Minassian called the Genocide a 'foundational event', which has created 'the Great Diaspora' and separated Armenians from their homeland (Ter-Minassian, in Dufoix, 2008; 52). The diaspora has been instrumental in its

[*] In Armenia, the term 'nationality' denoted 'race' throughout the decades under Soviet rule. As a result, for example, an Armenian living in Russia, when asked about nationality, might reply 'Armenian, with a Russian passport.' Even now, in Armenia, the concept of 'nationality' is commonly perceived as 'race.' When passports of newly-independent Armenia were introduced in the mid-1990s, many strongly opposed the idea of having 'the Republic of Armenia' mentioned as 'nationality,' instead of 'Armenian' meaning 'ethnic Armenian.'

strive for recognition of the Genocide, for it is driven by the tragedy and the very origin of the post-Genocide diaspora (Martirosyan, 2014: 59). Moreover, another tragic event, such as the earthquake of 1988, "has further buttressed the Armenian identity" (Kotkin, 1992: 239).

Anthony Smith recognizes the unique case of the Armenian national identity and points out that "among the Armenians the development of organized religion, liturgy and religious law produced a growing sense of what we can term incipient 'national identity,' even if it did not last in the subsequent diaspora epoch" (Smith, 2002: 26). Contrary to the argument that "'national identity' does not go as far as to prescribe that the nation is inexorably bound-up with the state, and that it can only survive through the existence of a state apparatus" (Fowler, 2002: 6), in case of Armenians, national identity has been shaped and strengthened by its diaspora decades before the modern Armenian nation-state was established in 1991.

After achieving sovereignty, debatably, a nationalistic stance that has existed in the diaspora faced a demand for change, since the nation-state had become a separate participant in transnational affairs. Moreover, throughout the past nearly three decades, Armenia has been particularly trying to position itself as the core of *Armenianness* by organizing various political, cultural, economic, and sports events.* As generalized, the establishment of the nation-state is a process that takes place based on "a psychological bond that joins a people and differentiates it" (Mansbach and Rhodes, 2007: 435). In the case of the homogenous Armenian state, as argued, ethno-nationalism has remained dominant – a phenomenon, which, as Jan Beck, a scholar of national, in particular, of Basque identity, formulates (when discussing the Basques) as an "alternative vision of a

---

* The 1ˢᵗ Armenia-Diaspora Conference and the Pan-Armenian Games were initiated and organized (both in Armenia) in 1999. The 5th Conference was held in Yerevan in September 2014 (Ministry of Diaspora of Armenia, Conferences). The Conference used to be conducted once every three years, and the 6th one (in which the author of this book participated) was organized in September 2017. The Pan-Armenian Games were held once every two years, starting in 1999, and later changed to once every four years, with the most recent games organized in August 2019 (PanArmenianGames.am, *History of the Games*).

nation-state" where "both territoriality and national belonging is combined" (Beck, 2006: 508).

Unlike heterogeneous societies, where the "sense of belonging and feeling of togetherness ('oneness') will not develop naturally" and interference of the state is needed (Ortmann, 2009: 31), in Armenia, driven by nationalism for a long period in history, the nation has achieved its nation-state as (by applying Fowler's idea) "nationalism demands the nation-state, and the creation of the nation-state strengthens nationalism" (Fowler, 2002: 1). Anthony Smith advocates that "the 'ethnic' nationalist components tended to predominate over the more territorial and civic-political components of the concept of the nation" (Smith, 2002: 28). This thought can be applied to Armenia too, following Anthony Smith's argument that "the emphasis fell less upon territorial political community and the ideals of mass citizenship, and more on the selection of the contents of the myths, memories and traditions of earlier 'ethnies', and on communal attachments to the homeland and rituals of membership" (Smith, 2002: 28).

Sociologist Anny Bakalian stresses that nowadays, "the emerging diaspora identity is much more of a 'symbolic' notion of Armeniannes" (Bakalian, in Panossian, 2002: 138). Despite these dynamics, the modern Armenian state is determined to become the representative of all Armenians and, therefore, of global Armenian identity. Has the establishment of the Armenian state strengthened Armenian identity and improved communication of diaspora communities with the state? How strong is the racial element of Armenian nationalism and national identity, in particular, concerning communities in the selected two cities of this study? What are the main recognizable attributes of the Armenian (trans)national identity?

To the question: 'Who are Armenians?' probably the most commonly given answer is "the first Christian nation in the world." Despite having many pre-Christian national myths, celebrations and symbols incorporated into its modern identity, the Armenian Apostolic Church, arguably, represents the core of Armenian national identity and the strongest factor that determines it. As the late Garegin I (Karekin I), the Catholicos of All Armenians once stressed, "the (Armenian) Church and the nation are not divided" (Panossian, 2002: 144). It has served the nation as a carrier of its history, a supporter of its culture, language (and scripts), science, and the organization that brings Armenians and their dispersed worldwide communities closer to each other.[*] The Armenian ethnic identity, thus, becomes inseparable from the religious identity of the people, and the role of transnational religious institutions becomes instrumental for the unification of the diaspora. This argument can be buttressed by a Romanian anthropologist Silviu Rogobete's general statement that, despite overt and subtle attacks against it, religion "was, and still seems to remain, one of the strongest markers of human identity" (Rogobete, 2009: 563).

Throughout the last two decades, there have been various initiatives and projects aimed at linking the Armenian diaspora with the nation-state. However, despite the strong sense of national identity, the cooperation link between the Armenian nation-state and the diaspora is not strong enough and, as Keith Dinnie, a marketing professor, points out, the Armenian state has "failed to benefit from its diaspora" (Dinnie, 2008: 228-229). The Ministry of Diaspora and, later, since 2019, the Office of the High Commissioner for Diaspora Affairs created to substitute the functions of the Ministry,[†] aim at facilitating communication between the state and diaspora communities. The status of ministry in the government enabled policy planning and implementation, which, however, as many argue, could have been more effective in terms of diaspora engagement and integration. Established in 2008[‡] and functioning until the change of power in Armenia in May-December 2018, the Ministry became affected by the government restructuring, a political decision made to reduce the number of ministries in the government, as a result of which the Ministry of Diaspora has been transformed to the Office of the High Commissioner for Diaspora Affairs, which reports directly to the Prime Minister. By agreeing that the Ministry could have been more effective in pursuing its mission, in January 2019, an open letter sent by me to Armenia's Prime Minister Nikol Pashinyan argued for keeping the status of a ministry for the body dealing with the diaspora, i.e., allowing it to plan and pursue the

---

[*] It performs a similar role to the Vatican for all Catholics, with a major difference that the Armenian Church is a national church.

[†] The Ministry was transformed into the Office of the High Commissioner for Diaspora Affairs, whose head was appointed (14.06.2019) to report directly to the Prime Ministry of the Republic of Armenia. (Government of Armenia, www.gov.am)

[‡] Source: Ministry of Diaspora of Armenia, *About Us.*

policy toward the diaspora.[*] The open letter highlights the most essential four policy areas of the Ministry. Previously, throughout the decade of the Ministry's existence, its structure was based on a geographic principle, i.e., each department was specialized in a particular region. Four functional areas could have raised the effectiveness of the Ministry's (and the whole government's) diaspora engagement and integration policy implementation. The areas are:[†]

(1) Promotion of Armenian national identity within the diaspora and strengthening ties with Armenia;

(2) Prevention of anti-Armenian campaigns and propaganda, including actions aiming to inflate the meaning of the concept of 'genocide';

(3) Making the diaspora better known in Armenia (as argued, this has been completely overlooked as a critical aspect of Armenia-diaspora cooperation);

(4) Strengthening the Armenian national identity among non-diasporan Armenian 'ethnies' aiming to transform them into diasporans.

At present, the Armenian nation-state has been trying to pursue an inclusive approach toward the diaspora.[‡] This is seen as a way to improve communication of diasporans with the homeland nation-state and, thus, to strengthen their affiliation with it. The Armenian state's inclusive approach toward the diaspora, despite the potential problem of 'dual loyalty,' provides the diaspora with an opportunity to continue being the other part of the whole nation. The reasoning behind this measured approach is that the diaspora, an extraterritorial phenomenon when it comes to its connection to the homeland, is a complex of smaller communities, all of which are territorially defined and bound by local traditions, customs, and laws.

---

[*] *Open Letter to Prime Minister Pashinyan* (Vardanyan, Aravot.am news. 2019).

[†] Vardanyan, Aravot.am: 2019. https://www.aravot.am/2019/01/15/1009679/.

[‡] One of the measures implemented is the simplified procedure of naturalization and settlement in Armenia. The requirements of minimum residency, as well as knowledge of the Armenian language and Constitution of the Republic, are waived for applicants of Armenian ethnicity. Thus, as guaranteed by the Constitution, any person of Armenian descent can acquire Armenian citizenship and keep their existing one for permanent residency in Armenia (Refworld, *Law of Armenia on the Citizenship of Armenia*).

Inclusiveness of the diaspora faces limitations, even if the Armenians abroad are citizens of Armenia. For instance, Armenian citizens who do not reside in Armenia have been technically deprived of an opportunity to vote in political elections. Moreover, unlike before, the most recent constitutional amendments of December 2015 changed the inclusionary nature of the policy toward more exclusion by limiting the diaspora's participation in the political life of the state. To be elected or appointed to a political office, there is a minimum residency requirement of 731 days in a four-year period preceding the elections to parliament.[*] In daily life and activity, with multiple or 'flexible citizenship' opportunities, "affluent migrants seek different locations for economic gain and political security" (Ong, 1999: 25). Armenian nationals can choose to maintain their citizenship in most of the diaspora space.

The inclusion of diasporas in national affairs becomes instrumental for the solution of pan-national problems. Despite differences in terms of internal policy (similarities exist with Zionism and the State of Israel), the Armenian diaspora, divided in its approaches and tactics, is unified "in its insistence" that Turkey acknowledges and apologizes for the genocide of 1915-16 (Esman, 2009: 112). The diaspora has been an important and influential player in preserving the nation's ethnic, cultural, and religious identity. At the same time, the diaspora is also seen by the home nation-state as a strong supporter of its geopolitical interests abroad, as it attempts to influence host governments or international organizations to promote its interests (Esman, 2009: 124).

It can be argued that the Armenian diaspora has been successful in preserving the Armenian national identity through decades of isolation from the homeland during the Soviet years. Even though independence and return to the motherland were seen (then) as the ultimate goal of the diaspora, political changes following the independence of Armenia came as a surprise (Libaridian, 1999: 137). The diaspora was not prepared for open relations with the homeland. At this stage, when political sovereignty has

---

[*] The constitutional amendments changed the state system from semi-presidential to parliamentary, and this residency requirement has been established by the new Electoral Code (Radio Liberty, *Armenian RM*)

Epic Armenian folk hero, Sasountsi Davit
(David of Sasoun)

been achieved and leadership over the nation is contested, diaspora communities have begun facing challenges relating to effective communication with the homeland.

Distribution of the Armenian Diaspora

The objective of this book is not to conduct a statistical analysis of the Armenian diaspora across the world, but to provide general insights into the dispersion of the diaspora and its largest communities as a diverse, extraterritorial, transnational body.

The Armenian diaspora is diverse and does not exist in an abstract homogenous space. As briefly mentioned above, prior to the Genocide, the diaspora was formed mainly of "merchants, labourers, fortune seekers, intellectuals and political exiles," while, after WWI it was mainly formed of "refugees, starving survivors and a deeply scarred people" (Panossian, 2002: 137). Possibly because of its sharply distinct identity and such factors as culture, religion, ethnicity, and even climatic conditions, as well as the lack of aid for refugees, South (and South-East) Asia did not become a destination for Genocide survivors. However, Australia, which is located farther east, can boast an estimated 50 thousand Armenians today.[*] Armenian communities in Asia, which have originated from the inflow of migrants from the Persian Empire, arguably, had a weaker Genocide-related sense of loss, as their ancestors migrated from areas not affected by the Genocide. Thus, to a certain extent, it can be argued that for the Armenians in Asia, the sense of 'lost motherland' is weaker compared to most of the others in the diaspora.

The global Armenian diaspora across the world is a predominantly urban phenomenon. Armenians, who lived outside their traditional homeland "tended to live in the big cities" (Herzig and Kurkchiyan, 2005: 68). Here, it should be mentioned that the diaspora community in Javakhetsi region in Georgia, which is not only urban, does not fully match all the criteria to be considered 'pure' diaspora. In this particular case, after state frontiers were drawn by the central authorities in the early years of Soviet rule, not the people crossed the border but the border crossed the people.

The Armenian nation is dispersed worldwide, with its diasporic nation-state – the Republic of Armenia – and the global diaspora located on all the continents. As mentioned above, Armenians make a particular case, since they constitute about 2-2.5 times more in numbers outside Armenia compared to the number of Armenians in Armenia.[†] Based on the estimated number of Armenians in the world, the following table reflects on most of the largest communities in the world.

Some countries, such as Russia, the U.S., and France, have hundreds of thousands or even millions of Armenians living there. The vast majority of Armenians live either to the north or south of the tropics.

Some countries, such as Russia, the U.S., and France, have hundreds of thousands or even millions of Armenians living there. The vast majority of Armenians live either to the north or south of the tropics. Even in the case of countries whose territories extend into the tropical zone, such as Brazil and Australia, the largest Armenian communities can be found in cities located beyond the tropics. It is roughly estimated, only 1 out of 1,000 Armenians, who live outside Armenia, live in the tropics.[‡] Apparently, it is

---

[*] This figure is based on estimates provided by ANC Australia in *Armenian-Australian Community.*

[†] The number is based on estimates provided in Martirosyan, 2014: 57

[‡] The estimated number is based on OST Armenia, *The Armenian Diaspora.*

TABLE 1

City	Country	Population of city ('000 people)	Estimated No. of Armenians ('000 people)	Proportion of Armenians of in city (%)	Percent of Armenians in world(%) [a]
Yerevan	Armenia	1,065[b]	1,045[c]	98.1	10.4
Moscow	Russia	12,190[d]	800[e]	6.6	8.0
Krasnodar (region)	Russia	5,097[f]	700[g]	13.7	7.0
Los Angeles (metro)	U.S.	12,829[h]	450[i]	3.5	4.5
Tehran	Iran	8,300[j]	110[k]	1.3	1.1
Paris (Greater)	France	10,000+[l]	100[m]	1.0	1.0
Marseille	France	1,600[n]	100[o]	6.3	1.0
Buenos Aires (metro)	Argentina	13,528[p]	80[q]	0.6	0.8
Aleppo (2004)	Syria	2,132[r]	80[s]	3.7	0.8
Beirut	Lebanon	1,916[t]	70[u]	3.7	0.7
New York	U.S.	8,550[v]	70[w]	0.8	0.7
Tbilisi	Georgia	1,049[x]	53[y]	5.1	0.5
Boston	U.S.	4,590[z]	50	1.1	0.5
Kiev	Ukraine	2,798[aa]	50[ab]	1.8	0.5
Sydney	Australia	5,570[ac]	42[ad]	0.8	0.4
Sao Paolo	Brazil	11,900[ae]	30[af]	0.3	0.3
Montevideo	Uruguay	1,271[ag]	15	1.2	0.2
Melbourne	Australia	4,500	13	0.3	0.1
Isfahan	Iran	1,547[ah]	11[ai]	0.7	0.1
Cairo (metro)	Egypt	20,500[aj]	6[ak]	0.03	0.1

a. The global Armenian population, as estimated, is considered 10 mln people, as mentioned earlier in the work. However, this number may include the number of crypto- or hidden Armenians in Turkey, who have converted to Islam and do not openly show their ethnic identity because of possible persecutions or a perception of such, throughout the post-Genocide history.
b. National Statistical Service of the Republic of Armenia (http://www.armstat.am/en/?nid=420)
c. Based on the overall ethnic proportion data of Armenia (Nee, 2014: Ch. 3)
d. World Population Review, *Moscow Population 2017*, http://worldpopulationreview.com/world-cities/moscow-population/
e. Unofficial estimates of the Ministry of Diaspora of Armenia, provided in a personal communication.
f. Encyclopaedia Britannica, https://www.britannica.com/place/Krasnodar-kray-Russia
g. Panarmenian.net, 08 June 2012, http://www.panarmenian.net/arm/news/110953/
h. Encyclopaedia Britannica, https://www.britannica.com/place/Los-Angeles-California
i. According to Archbishop Hovnan Derderian of the Armenian Church of North America, as of 2007 (unofficial estimate, http://www.prolades.com/glama/la5co07/armenian_community.htm)

j. World Population Review, *Tehran Population 2017*, http://worldpopulationreview.com/world-cities/tehran-population/

k. According to the Ministry of Diaspora of Armenia unofficial estimates

l. Encyclopaedia Britannica, https://www.britannica.com/place/Paris/People

m. An unofficial estimate of the Ministry of Diaspora of Armenia

n. World Population Review, *Marseille Population 2017*, http://worldpopulationreview.com/world-cities/marseille-population/

o. According to the Ministry of Diaspora of Armenia unofficial estimates

p. Encyclopaedia Britannica, https://www.britannica.com/place/Buenos-Aires

q. The number of Armenians in Buenos Aires and Montevideo is based on Ghanalanyan, T., 2011, http://noravank.am/eng/articles/detail.php?ELEMENT_ID=5722

r. World Population Review, Syria Population 2017, http://worldpopulationreview.com/countries/syria-population/

s. World Population Review, *Population of Cities in Lebanon*, http://worldpopulationreview.com/countries/lebanon-population/cities/

t. The Armenian population in Lebanon is largely concentrated in Beirut metro area. The total number of Armenians in the country is 4% of the total population (The CIA Factbook Lebanon) (https://www.cia.gov/library/publications/the-world-factbook/geos/le.html)

u. Warren, A., 2013, http://www.eastbook.eu/en/2013/08/12/desperately-seeking-refuge-the-syrian-armenian-humanitarian-crisis/

v. World Population Review, *New York City Population 2017,* http://worldpopulationreview.com/us-cities/new-york-city-population/

w. An unofficial estimate of the Ministry of Diaspora of Armenia

x. World Population Review, *Georgia Population 2017*, http://worldpopulationreview.com/countries/ukraine-population/

y. National Statistics Office of Georgia, *General Population Census 2014, Total population by regions and ethnicity*, 2013, www.census.ge

z. Douglas, C., Boston Business Journal, 24 March 2010, http://www.bizjournals.com/boston/stories/2010/03/22/daily22.html

aa. World Population Review, *Ukraine Population 2017*, http://worldpopulationreview.com/countries/ukraine-population/

ab. Estimated as an average number, based on *Largest Armenian diaspora communities explained*, http://everything.explained.today/Largest_Armenian_diaspora_communities/

ac. Population number for Sydney and Melbourne, as shown above in the work, have been taked from Population Australia (http://www.population.net.au/)

ad. The number of Armenians in Sydney and Melbourne has been taken from the Ministry of Diaspora (Passport of the Armenian Community in Australia, 2017: 5)

ae. World Population Review, *Sao Paolo Population 2017*, http://worldpopulationreview.com/world-cities/sao-paulo-population/

af. According to the Ministry of Diaspora of Armenia unofficial estimates

ag. World Population Review, *Uruguay Population 2017*, http://worldpopulationreview.com/countries/uruguay-population/

ah. World Population Review, *Population of Cities in Iran*, http://worldpopulationreview.com/countries/iran-population/cities/

ai. The number is the average on an estimate of 10-12 thousand people, according to D. Petrosyan (The Armenian Community in Iran, 1998, http://www.ca-c.org/journal/15-1998/st_10_petrosjan.shtml)

aj. World Population Review, *Cairo Population 2017*, http://worldpopulationreview.com/world-cities/cairo-population/

ak. Zohry, Ayman, *Armenians in Egypt*, XXV IUSSP International Population Conference, International Union for the Scientific Study of Population, American University in Cairo, 2005 not the distance from Armenia that matters, as there are sizable communities in South America such as Buenos Aires, Montevideo and Sao Paolo, as well as in Australia, such as Sydney and Melbourne, all of which are geographically far from Armenia. Such distribution of Armenians worldwide, arguably, may be caused partly by their willingness to live in areas with distinct seasonal differences, somehow close to climatic conditions in the historical homeland.

Worldwide, the number of Armenians living outside Armenia is about seven or even eight million, according to some estimates, and they can be found in about 85 countries on all the continents (RepatArmenia). The largest communities can be found in Russia (2.25 million), the United States (1.5 million), France (450,000), as well as other relatively large communities in Georgia, Argentina, Lebanon, Iran, Poland, Ukraine, Germany, Australia, Brazil, and Canada. (Martirosyan, 2014: 57). The exact numbers of Armenians in various cities and countries vary and are largely based on estimates. There is also a number of smaller communities, with hundreds of Armenians living there, including some, which have been historically notable, such as the communities in Asian cities of Kolkata, Singapore, or Yangon. Even though small communities seem to possess a weaker overall potential, some can be disproportionately active and well connected with the homeland (such as the community in Singapore over the past decade).

Geopolitical developments over the past century have led to the existence of the unique two-sided Armenian diaspora – 'internal' or *'nerkin spyurk,'* which traditionally includes Armenians in the post-Soviet area/ countries and 'external,' which covers the rest of the diaspora (Cavoukian, 2013: 712). Diaspora communities are complex and involve communication among their members, and also by members and the outside world, including the homeland. This process, to a significant extent, happens through diaspora institutions. When talking particularly about formal relations, it can be argued that nearly all communication has been through diaspora institutions. Nevertheless, there is a noticeable transformation taking place nowadays, largely influenced by advanced communication technologies, most significant of all, the Internet.

Larger communities have traditionally been the focus of the relationship, especially from the homeland's perspective. Some of the main factors which have determined this stance are probably limits to financial means and human resources. Because of the importance of these two factors, smaller communities have tended to be marginalized, to a certain extent. By stating this, it does not necessarily mean that the smaller communities are weaker since, as also discussed later, the organization within communities is not less important than their size, as some of the interviewees in this study have also emphasized.

Table 1 (see above) presents the largest cities (in terms of their Armenian population) in their respective countries, which are geographically spread out. On top of the list is the largest Armenian-populated city - Yerevan, which is presented to compare the large (diasporic) cities with it. The mentioned 20 cities only are home to about 40% of all Armenians worldwide. It should be noted that one of the communities, in Aleppo, has been significantly damaged over the recent years because of the civil war in Syria. However, one can assume that most of the Armenians from Aleppo moved to other cities with relatively large Armenian communities, and, therefore, the total number of Armenians in the specified 20 cities remains more or less the same.[*] Worldwide, the largest Armenian diaspora communities (about 10,000 and more Armenians in each) can be found in the following urban areas:[†]

Europe: Amsterdam, Brussels, London, Valencia, Barcelona, Athens

* France - Paris, Lyon, Marseille

* Eastern Europe - Minsk, Kiev, Kharkov

* Black Sea region: Tbilisi, Sukhumi, Akhalkalaki, Akhaltsikhe, Ninotsminda, Istanbul, Sofia

Russia: Moscow and St. Petersburg;

* Krasnodar (and region), Stavropol and region), and Rostov (and region) in southern Russia

* Volgograd, Saratov, Samara, all three on Volga river, in central Russia

* Vladikavkaz (North Ossetia) and Maykop (Adygea) in northern Caucasus

Middle East: Tehran, Beirut, Aleppo, Isfahan

Central Asia: Almaty, Ashgabat, Tashkent

South America: Sao Paolo, Buenos Aires, Montevideo

United States: Los Angeles, Fresno, Boston, New York

---

* It is estimated that only 20,000 Armenians from Aleppo have settled in Armenia, mainly in Yerevan (Foreign Policy, *The Syrian Refugees*).

† These lists are made on the basis of conservative population estimates.

Canada: Toronto, Montreal

Australia: Sydney, Melbourne

Probably with the exception of Russia and the United States, in all other countries, the Armenians are concentrated in mainly one to three cities or metropolitan areas. This condition enables the communities in these countries to be engaged in their core of political, economic, and social-cultural life. The same goes for Australia with its two largest cities being the primary spaces for Armenian communities in the country. As already stated above, the two Australian communities include about 40,000-50,000 Armenians, and about 35,000-40,000 of them, as estimated, live in Sydney and about 10,000 in Melbourne.

The Armenians in Australia: An Insight into the Community

Following a discussion of concepts forming the framework of 'diaspora' ('nation' and 'national identity,' 'space' and 'place'), we can look at the narrative story of diasporan Armenians, which, to a certain extent, reflects the current state of diasporic life in our selected two cities (Sydney and Melbourne), and their challenges and expectations for the future. In particular, our study, as specified previously, aims at advancing our knowledge about the Armenian diaspora, particularly diasporic identity, through an understanding of, possibly, the central aspect of 'diaspora' – the phenomenon of 'diaspora return,' that connects home- and hostland spaces.

The Armenian community in Australia is among the largest in the whole Armenian diaspora space. In the world, some communities are fragmented, such as the Armenian communities in Russia, as social anthropologist Marina Oussatcheva describes (Oussatcheva, 2001: 20). The community in Australia is concentrated mainly in two cities, as mentioned earlier. The study of these two particular diaspora communities (diasporas' perspectives of national identity and sense of belonging) can shed light not only on an overall understanding of the diaspora but also help to understand challenges faced by remote diasporan communities.

The Armenians, with their strong sense of communal identity, seek to settle in spaces where they can find other Armenians. Such an attitude, probably, has been one of the motivating factors for those who followed the first wave of migration to Sydney and Melbourne. The Armenian diaspora is an urban diaspora, as already mentioned, and the Armenians in

Australia are only found in large cities. With a tiny exception of a couple of hundred people in other cities in the country, the community is mainly present in two – Sydney and Melbourne.

Many Armenians moved to Australia because of political, economic, and security concerns related to the Lebanese civil war, the Iranian revolution, the Israeli-Palestinian conflict, and the aftermath of Indian independence in 1947. Most of these Armenians settled in Sydney, the center of the diocese of the Armenian Apostolic Church in Australia, and Melbourne (Angold, 2014: 455). The Armenian communities in Australia are among the most remote ones, certainly, by taking into consideration the distance from the homeland (Armenia). The perception of space differs from one location to another. The expression "in remote Armenia" used by Archbishop Najarian during a liturgy service (mentioned earlier in the book), was unexpected and thought-provoking to me as an Armenian from Armenia. Before, I used to perceive Australia as a remote space. This short phrase led me to think about how Australian Armenians see Armenia and how geographical and financial barriers limit their physical connection to it.

Armenia is perceived far away for Australians, and so is Australia for Armenians in Armenia. Arguably, distance and costs are the main reasons why Armenia has no resident diplomatic representation in Australia. Since Armenia's independence in 1991, the highest-level visit there was paid by the head of the Armenian Parliament (in 2000), as well as visits by the Minister of Diaspora, and Minister of Foreign Affairs in 2005, 2011, 2012, and 2015 (Ministry of Diaspora of Armenia, 2017: 1). Over 25 years of bilateral diplomatic relations, official visits from Armenia to Australia have not been frequent.

Immigration of Armenians to Australia in relatively large numbers started in the second half of the 20th century, and by the end of the 1950s, there were already about 1,000 Armenians in the country and about 13,000 in the 1970s (Ministry of Diaspora of Armenia, 2017: 1). The Australian Armenian communities are diverse in terms of diasporic origin or roots. With regard to the responses provided by interviewees, large numbers of Armenians in Australia originate from Iran, Iraq, Syria, Lebanon, Cyprus, Egypt, Sudan, Ethiopia, Greece, Romania, Bulgaria, and India (descendants of Iranian or then-Persian Armenians), as well as Turkey (in particular, Istanbul). There are also those from the former Soviet Union and, later, after the 1990s – from the Republic of Armenia. According to the interviewees' responses, the main immigration wave of Armenians to Australia took place throughout the 1960s to the 1980s, as a result of the establishment of nationalist regimes in several countries in the Middle East (in particular, Syria and Egypt), as well as the civil war in Lebanon between 1975 and 1990. As of 2001, officially, about 14,667 Australians of Armenian origin lived in Australia. The number is presented on a glass banner installed by the city authorities in downtown Riverside, Melbourne. The numbers do not include Armenians born in Australia. However, as estimated by the Armenian National Committee of Australia (ANCA, 2016), and mentioned earlier, there are about 50,000 Armenians in Australia. The Profile of the Armenian Community in Australia, prepared by the Ministry of Diaspora, specifies 42,000 and 13,000 Armenians in Sydney and Melbourne respectively (Ministry of Diaspora of Armenia, 2017: 5).[*] Other than in the main two communities of Sydney and Melbourne, smaller ones can be found in Perth, Gold Coast, Brisbane, Adelaide, with some 50-150 Armenians living in each of the cities. Overall, the Armenians migrated to Australia "from forty-three countries, held twenty-five nationalities, a reminder of the vast spread of the Armenian diaspora" (Babkenian and Stanley, 216: 268).

The Sydney community is the largest not only in Australia but also in the vast Asia-Australia region. Sydney has cultural centers, day schools, Saturday schools, a weekly newspaper, as well as churches. Meanwhile, the community in Melbourne has cultural centers, a church, and a Saturday language school (ANCA, 2016). At the same time, it should be mentioned that in a large community like Sydney, there can be an estimated 6,000-7,000 people of school age, while only about 250 students study in the only secondary day school and about 40 in a primary school.[†] Thus, the number of Armenian school-age children studying in both day schools is only about 5% of its total potential number.

The Armenian Apostolic Church, the Armenian Catholic Church, and the Armenian Evangelical Church are all present in both Sydney and

---

[*] The numbers are slightly different from those mentioned by other sources; however, they are still comparable. For instance, the Armenian National Committee of Australia estimates that there are 40,000 Armenians in Sydney and 10,000 in Melbourne. (ANC Australia, 2016).

[†] The numbers have been related in personal conversations with former and current heads of the schools.

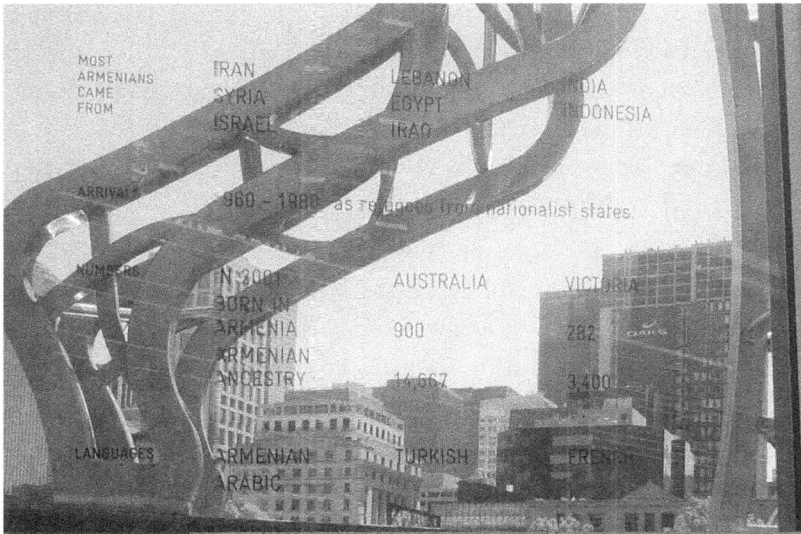

Commemorative glass banner in Melbourne celebrating
Armenian presence in Australia (2001)

Melbourne, four periodicals being issued in both cities, two days schools (as mentioned earlier) and six one-day weekend schools operating in both cities (Ministry of Diaspora of Armenia, 2017: 5). Sydney and Melbourne's communities are home to various Armenian political and charity organizations: *ARF – Dashnaktsutyun*, with its cultural, sports and educational institutions, *Ramgavar Azadagan (Liberal) Party*, *Social-Democratic Hnchakian Party*, a number of social and cultural organizations, the *Armenian General Benevolent Union (AGBU)*, clubs, as well as various events organized in the cities (e.g., dance performances, parties, fundraising activities). The community has a broad range of institutions with a potential to provide a rich and varied political, economic, social and cultural life for their diasporic communities and members. A special role is carried by religious institutions, most notably, by the Armenian Apostolic Church. More on the role of the Apostolic Church is discussed separately later.

The Australian Armenians: The Roots and the Routes

The policy of the homeland toward its diaspora assumes adequate knowledge of its different diasporan communities. It is a fallacy to think of the diaspora as one homogenous body and consider an approach toward one community as equally valid toward another one. Knowledge assumes understanding the political, economic and social-cultural environment, as well as the main challenges diasporans experience regarding the space surrounding them and their community. On the other hand, from the diaspora's side, it is also essential to know the homeland well. Both sides have certain expectations of each other, and the issue of trust, arguably, becomes critical in their relationship.

When trying to understand the diaspora and formulating an inclusionary policy, with the ultimate goal of facilitating diaspora return in whatever form, identification of the roots of diasporans becomes essential. Where do diasporans come from? What is common in their origin?

Diaspora communities have a different historical development than their homeland. The interviewed community members represent their roots quite well. The glass banner mentioned earlier shows that most Armenians in Australia have arrived from Iran, Lebanon, Syria, Egypt, Iraq, Israel,[*] as well as India and Indonesia. This range of countries, to a large extent, matches the countries of origin the interviewee in this study specified. Three to four generations of Armenians, within a century, changed at least three countries of abode – the Ottoman Empire (later - Turkey), another country in the Middle East, where they escaped to during or after the Genocide, and finally, Australia, which has become their permanent geographic space. Other than English, the main languages spoken by Armenians in Australia are Armenian, Arabic, Turkish, French, and, to some extent, Russian, spoken by some Armenians, who have migrated from Armenia and other parts of the former USSR.

The geographic origin of the interviewees in this study is diverse. They were born in Cyprus, Armenia (then a part of the Soviet Union), Egypt, Syria, Jordan, Turkey, and Australia. Moreover, those born in Australia also had their roots different from each other. Parents of these diasporans also originated from areas of modern Lebanon, Egypt, Syria, Iraq, and various parts of Turkey.

Understanding diasporic roots helps diasporans in their self-perception of their own identity. A better understanding of diaspora communities, as argued, also enables the homeland to formulate and implement a more effective approach and policy toward communities in various parts of the world. Understanding roots, however, is not enough. Knowing the 'roots'

---

[*] Including areas of de facto (modern-day) control, in particular, East Jerusalem.

without understanding the 'routes' is like knowing how a fruit looks like without knowing how it tastes. Those are the routes that provide essential information on how diasporans have ended up in their current hostland destination. Lack of knowledge of the 'routes' makes the understanding of homeland-diaspora relations superficial. A strong support of this argument is one shared by Archbishop Haigazoun Najarian in Sydney, who has stressed the importance of identifying and understanding how communities appear and how they perish.

The routes of the interviewed diasporans are complex. There are some born in Australia years after their parents migrated there. There are also people with complicated journey maps which covered half-a-dozen countries before they arrived in Australia. For instance, one of the interviewees, Mr. Michael Bazikian, a retired man in his late 80s, was born in Cyprus to Genocide survivors. Seeing the great hardship and recession in Cyprus, he moved to England. However, in 1964, after living there for years, he moved to Australia, mainly because of the poor weather in the UK, as he explained. On the other hand, Bedros, a retired businessman, is a relatively new member of the Sydney community and is not a citizen of Australia. He is originally from Kessab.[*]

The parents of Vahe, an administrator in a diaspora organization, in his late 20s, had arrived in Australia from Lebanon (the father) and Egypt (the mother), before the civil war took place in Lebanon. Another interviewee, Helen, is of Armenian and Assyrian descent. Her parents arrived in Australia in the late-60s, from Iraq, following her grandparents who had migrated to Australia earlier. Australia was considered a good choice, among other countries under consideration.

Anahit was born in Armenia and migrated to Australia when she was in early primary school age. In another case, both parents of Vrej, an IT-

---

[*] Kessab is a small Armenian-populated village in Syria, with a population of around 2,000 people, only a kilometer away from the Turkish border (World Heritage Encyclopedia, *Kessab*). People in Kessab, which is located about 25km from Mousa Dag (where Armenians defended themselves successfully in 1915), are known for their strong identity preservation stance throughout history and maintained their identity over centuries. Mousa Dag was the location of a cluster of Armenian villages whose inhabitants fought back during the Armenian Genocide of 1915 and were rescued by French warships. They were evacuated to Egypt. Franz Werfel's novel, *Forty Days of Mousa Dagh,* is based on this epic resistance of Armenian villagers.

industry manager, migrated to Australia from Egypt after a nationalistic political regime came to power there. Egypt is the origin of another participant in this study. As in the previous case, here, too, the ancestors originated from what is historically-culturally known as 'Western Armenia' – the areas in eastern Turkey today. A high school teacher in her 30s, Lily's parents migrated to Australia from Alexandria and Cairo in Egypt. Her grandfather, as she told, did not want to raise his children in a non-Christian religious environment and brought them to Australia. They first settled in Queensland, where they had a friend, and then moved to Melbourne.

The modern Middle East has been home to hundreds of thousands of Armenians mainly because of its proximity to their original areas of inhabitance, the Ottoman Empire, from where they were deported or fled during the Genocide, before 1923. For instance, Antonio, one of the interviewees, in his late 50s, explained as follows. Born in Syria, when he was seven, his parents moved to Lebanon to avoid military service in Syria. After the civil war broke out in Lebanon in the mid-1970s, the family was forced to leave the country. His father had a friend in Australia. While still in Lebanon, he met a young Armenian woman visiting Lebanon, married her, and migrated to Australia with her. Other family members joined them later. Antonio stated that he had been trying to raise his children in an Armenian cultural environment, even though he himself is of mixed background, with an Italian paternal great-grandparent. Despite this fact, he mentioned that all the men in the family had married Armenian women, and, apart from the inherited Italian surname, everything else remained Armenian. The sense of diaspora return that Antonio has passed to his children has motivated them to visit Armenia. "I find myself strange in Australia," he says. "Even though it is secure and safe, I do not belong here. One day I am going to live in Armenia. Physically I am here, mentally in Armenia," he stresses. His perception of the homeland as an imagined space is strong even though he has no direct connection to modern Armenia.

Two other participants in the study had direct ancestors in Syria. One of them is Levon, a young company manager, whose family was initially from Aintap in modern Turkey. They were deported to the Der-Zor desert in Syria,[*] survived, and later ended up in Australia in the 1970-1980s. In this particular case, too, the Civil War in Lebanon was the reason for their migration to Australia.

Cilicia, the area of the last Armenian kingdom,[†] is the origin of many Australian Armenians. In the case of Garo, an engineer in his mid-30s – his maternal side is from Kharpert, and the paternal one from Sepasdia (or Sivas). They were able to survive the Genocide, and in the 1950-60s, their parents moved to Istanbul, so that the children could have an Armenian education and go to the Armenian Church. However, as Garo explained, "being an Armenian in Turkey is very difficult; you are always under persecution; if you have a faith other than Islam and a national identity other than Turkish, you are always a second-class person." To escape that persecution and be accepted, the family moved out and headed to Australia, as "it was easy to move to Australia at that time." Another interviewee, Aram, a middle-age lawyer, pointed out that his maternal ancestors were from Marash, also in modern-day Turkey, while his paternal ancestors came from an area near Adana in Cilicia. Aram grew up in Jordan, where his father's family moved after the Genocide. Before migrating to Australia, they lived in Muscat (Oman), for a while, and eventually arrived in Australia in the 1980s.

Armen, an education administrator, related a detailed story of his family's origin. With ancestors from Cilicia, where his father was born (on the Syria-Turkey border, near Kessab) and his mother from Lebanon, Armen was also born in Lebanon. He describes how, as a child, he was confused: "I asked my aunt about it, whether some of my ancestors were Turkish, as my relatives could not speak Armenian and were speaking Turkish." Many families continued speaking Turkish as their home language even after leaving their original land in the Ottoman Empire and, later, Turkey.

---

[*] According to the Armenian National Institute, "Der Zor was designated by the Young Turks as the destination point and final killing center of Armenian deportees. Those who survived the death marches were brought to the desert of Der Zor and murdered in this area. The desert contains a large number of mass graves" (ANI, *Monument at Der Zor*).

[†] The Armenian principality and kingdom of Cilicia (1199 until 1375) on the Mediterranean Sea is now part of Turkey (as mentioned earlier in this book).

As in the case of many other diasporans, Lebanon was their secondary environment. In Lebanon, about which Armen was speaking appreciatively, the government named some districts, where Armenians lived, after historical regions of their ancestors, such as Nor Cilicia, Nor Hajen, etc.* Due to such a positive attitude, the Armenians living there did not feel foreign in their environment and felt as if they were on their historical land. This was an attempt to name the new space by such geographic names in order to endear Armenians to favor their new host land and to develop it. Generally speaking, as geographer Yvonne Whelan argues, "naming and claiming spaces of the cultural landscape takes on particular significance" for diaspora communities (Whelan, 2011: 11).

Again, similar to the case of other Armenians who migrated to Australia from Lebanon, Armen also emigrated from Lebanon because of the civil war there. "We came as refugees, in 1984. We left Lebanon in 1983, then lived in Cyprus, until immigration documents were prepared, before we could come to Australia," Armen explained.

A unique interpretation was given by a hidden or crypto-Armenian. Mateos was born and grew up in Turkey, and only in 2010 moved to Australia as a student. The difficulties of being an Armenian in Turkey, as he specified, were the reasons for his decision to move out of Turkey and to settle in Australia. Mateos' ancestors had been living in Sepasdia (Sivas) from the 15-16th century, until the Genocide. When the Genocide took place, there were Armenians in a number of big cities in the region such as Sivas and Moush. The authorities deported the Armenians to Der Zor desert in Syria, many died on the way, and some were killed by the Turkish army, as mentioned. Mateos' great-grandfather was only aged 11-12 years then and was taken as an orphan. The interviewee makes his point clear:

> They did not save him in fact. When the Genocide took place, the government held their wealth until they would come to pick it up. As Syria was a part of the Ottoman Empire, they were deported as if they moved the people from one part of the Empire to another one. After staying for a while, it was assumed that they could come back and take their properties back. If you take an orphan, you take him or her with the wealth. The Genocide was an economically motivated act, also politically, but mainly economically. The government said it would keep the wealth of the deported people

---

* 'Nor' means 'new' in Armenian.

Opera House, Yerevan

Matenadaran (manuscript depository), Yerevan

under protection. In those cities, in the Ottoman Empire, the authorities were working with big families in the land. Some big guys were looking after 5-6 cities. They were looking after the Armenian property as well and were giving tax to the government as well. The government was thinking that it could change the identity of the Armenians to Muslim and they would either forget or not demand their property. The big families took the orphans with their money. They were way too young to demand anything.

Vartan, an executive of a diaspora organization, shared his view about personal diaspora roots and routes, about his geographically rich migration history. He identifies Cilicia as his historical homeland and possesses a mix of values from the broad range of countries he has lived in. Vartan's ancestral lands "have been lost forever," he said sadly. Australia, he is hoping, provides a safe environment for his children, "so that they do not need to go through the nightmare again, to suffer for who they are." History, to him, "is a fact, memory is a perpetual phenomenon, sometimes it can be imaginary." Throughout the decades before Armenia achieved its political independence, the Armenians "were imagining their homeland" and "many never had a chance to see it." Vartan continues that after growing up in Europe, and then living in the Middle East again, he became frustrated with the conditions there. He reached a point when he felt that he could not continue that way any longer and chose Australia as a country of final destination, "one of my first choices and I am glad I chose it." Other than opposite climatic conditions (winter-summer), Australia's location was taken into consideration. When talking about Australia, Vartan mentioned the geographic distance and its remoteness from Armenia. This point is quite interesting. It was the distance from Armenia that was considered and not that of the country he moved from.

With a strong communal identity, Vartan, as many other diasporans do, tends to orient himself toward the historical or cultural homeland as his geographic center – the core space of his national identity. In the early years, after migration to Australia, as Vartan explained, he used to go to Armenia every year but had not been there for 30 years until 2014. "I enjoyed it, but I was disappointed, as what I used to see and do there when living five years in Etchmiadzin were not there at all.[*] Apart from the center of Yerevan, which is very European and modernized, everything else was my Armenia, what I recognized." He continues talking about the differences in the country by adding that "sometimes tourists coming from

The Republic Square with the Government House and the exit to
Tigran Medz Avenue to its right, Yerevan, Armenia, July 2017

Armenia are very happy and telling what Armenia is. I keep asking them whether they talk about Armenia or only Yerevan. Many correct themselves and say that they mean Yerevan." Such misperception of the Armenia space is common since tourists mainly spend their time in the center of Yerevan, and most of them only travel to other regions and return to Yerevan often within the same day. Thus, Yerevan is what they perceive as the space of their stay in Armenia, whereas the rest, including most of out-of-center in Yerevan, is seen as a periphery.

The modern-day Republic of Armenia, despite its relatively small territory, is geographically located on the border of Eastern Europe, Northern Middle East, and Western Asia. Thus, being on the crossroad of these civilizations, throughout its history, it has become a space where the European, Middle Eastern, and, to some extent, Asian cultures and traditions meet and mix. Located on the maps of all these three parts of the world, in little Armenia, there are areas where specific attributes and features, such as social life, are closer to Europe or the Middle East or Asia.

---

*   He was a student at the Gevorkian Theological Seminary. The seminary is an institution located in the Holy See of Saint Etchmiadzin in Armenia (The Armenian Church, *Gevorkian Seminary*).

This is particularly true regarding the center of Yerevan, as the above-mentioned interviewee also referred to. The city's small downtown of only about two kilometers in diameter, as many would argue, is a collective representation of the three parts of the world. Even when narrowed down to a geographically tiny place, the city's heart – the Republic Square – with several streets leading off in different directions, one could, as a joke, point where the borders between Europe, the Middle East and Asia are located. In particular, the exit to Tigran Medz Avenue from the Republic Square (beside the Government House) can be perceived as one such border.

An understanding of roots and routes of diasporans enriches the whole framework of our diaspora-homeland study since the purpose of such an endeavor is to know how to approach a particular community as a group or even as a consolidation of individual diasporans. On the one hand, in the contemporary globalizing world, it is becoming more difficult not to assimilate in a new social-cultural environment, and, on the other hand, communication technologies make it possible to reach every diasporan, irrespective of distances, and to engage them in the homeland. Globalization processes, arguably, stimulate countries to be more particular about their uniqueness and even their origin, which they see as a way to position themselves in the world, following both emotional and rational motives. Globalized extraterritorial spaces create a necessity to track the origins, the roots, as well as the homeland as the link to these roots, even if it is only that of ancestors and not a direct space of origin. It becomes essential to develop a sense of self-identification and belonging, even if questions about belonging and identity are rarely asked and answered. The development of a sense of belonging among diasporans, as proposed, becomes the cornerstone for the engagement of diasporans and their inclusion in the homeland. Let's see how the interviewed Armenians in the selected cities of the global diaspora perceive their own space of belonging and identity, and whether they have experienced any transformation of identity over time.

Chapter 5

DIASPORIC IDENTITY AND BELONGING

Space of Belonging and Identity

Diasporans live in a two-faceted space. Geographers James Sideway and Carl Grundy-Warr argue that territories of states are "spatial containers in which people are socialized through various social practices and discourses" (Grundy-Warr, in Daniels, Bradshaw, Shaw, and Sideway, 2008: 400). Diasporans are bound by laws and customs of their hostlands. They work and study in that environment and may live their whole life there. At the same time, a part of their existence is over spaces in the homeland. This is a paradox; however, diasporans can 'live' in the homeland even by never being there. Such a sense of belonging is due to their attachment to or the perception of the homeland, even in cases where the boundaries of the homeland do not exactly match those of the historical homeland as perceived by diasporans.

Sideway and Grundy-Warr bring an interesting connection between territoriality and identity. They identify three components: material, which is land, functional, which is control over space, and symbolic, which "is associated with people's social identity" (Grundy-Warr, in Daniels, Bradshaw, Shaw, and Sideway, 2008: 400). Thus, as they quote geographer Jan Penrose, people's identification with territories takes place in such a way that both "material requirements of life and the emotional requirement of belonging" can be satisfied (Grundy-Warr, in Daniels, Bradshaw, Shaw, and Sideway, 2008: 400).

The concepts of 'place' and 'space,' as the core of political geography, form the geographic framework for the study of diasporas and the homeland-diaspora relations. Over time, people have developed their "practical knowledge of the spatial," as geographer Helen Couclelis summarizes (Couclelis, in Longley et al., 2005: 31). Space, at the same time, as a "socially-produced phenomenon" (Soja, 1989: 80), cannot be absolute, as it is closely linked with social activity and is "relativized and historicized," philosopher and sociologist Henry Lefebvre argues (Lefebvre, in Hubbard and Kitchin, 2011: 5-6).

Space is not always visible (Couclelis, in Longley et al., 2005: 37), and, as geographer Doreen Massey stresses, the 'spatial' can only be conceptualized together with the 'social' (Massey, in Hubbard and Kitchin, 2011: 302). Geographers D. Lowenthal, A. Buttimer, D. Ley, E. Relph, and Yi-Fu Tuan specify that living in space is living "in a world of meaning," and not in a framework of various connected relationships (Hubbard and Kitchin, 2011: 6). In categorizing propositions of space, Massey separates space as "the product of interrelations," which is "always under construction," and maintains that spatiality is co-constitutive with identities and relations between them (Massey, 2012: 9-10).

Geographer Yi-Fu Tuan proposes that there are three levels of knowing space and place: intimate (direct), knowledgeable, and conceptual (indirect) (Tuan, 2011: 6). To him, "geographers study places," which is a "concretion of value" (Tuan, 2011: 3, 12). How can the homeland, being a conceptual space for diasporans, who have not lived there, transform into one with concretion of value? For those diasporans, who have no first-hand personal experience in the homeland, the latter, tends to be perceived as a mythical space, rooted by ancestry.

With these three levels of space, geographer Nigel Thrift goes farther and categorizes four kinds of space: space as 'empirical constructions,' 'unblocking space,' 'image space,' and 'place space,' each "undergoing continual construction" (Thrift, 2003: 96-104). Thrift pays particular attention to the last one and summarizes his thought on 'place' by indicating its embodied nature (Thrift, 2003: 103). With regard to the social aspect, Thrift emphasizes the ability of a place to produce effects (Thrift, 2003: 104).

When space and place are compared, the former is perceived as more abstract than the latter (Tuan, 2012: 183) since place is space with an ascribed meaning (Massey, 2012: 183). More specifically, regarding the diasporic world and its sense of place, Doreen Massey argues that it is important to understand that culture and identity are always related to geography (Hubbard and Kitchin, 2011: 216).

The concept of 'diaspora' is all about space, about its dispersion over space; and the concept of 'space' is directly related to 'identity,' which, by its nature, changes from space to space. James Clifford and Avtar Brah propose that the concept of diaspora is not limited to a historical experience; instead, it "functions as at once a theoretical concept, [and] a complicated imagined space of relations" (Campt, 2009: 171).

The imagined home(land) space can be key to understanding the concepts of national identity and, thus, of diaspora itself, as the homeland's representative abroad. Following the logic presented by sociologist Myria Georgiou, 'homeland' provides the emotional parameters of 'identity' as a category (Georgiou, 2006: 13).

Diasporas do not exist in isolation. While they exist in their space, the relationship between a homeland and its diaspora is a relationship between two spaces. As a transnational formation, a diaspora is not just a space that is connected to a homeland space. Rather, diasporic transnationals connect spaces by serving as a link between them. With two faces, one turned toward the hostland and its society and the other permanently facing the homeland, a diaspora develops its identity that reflects these two faces or sides. Since diasporas are in permanent return, as argued in this work, they are also in search of their own homeland. Diasporans participate in their hostland's social and even political life and, at the same time, as Bahar Baser and Ashok Swain, researchers of peace and conflict, emphasise, they "keep their emotional attachment to the holy homeland" (Baser and Swain, 2010: 40-41). It can even be argued that any diaspora (diasporic communities), being well-established in its hostland, tries its best not to destroy its own two-sided identity, which would be an inevitable outcome after diasporans make their 'ultimate goal' come true – the final physical permanent return (repatriation). Such resistance can be expressed at various levels – by the whole diaspora, a particular community, or even individual diasporans.

A diaspora's power to mobilize is probably the most important tool it can use to help and, at the same time, to influence the homeland's affairs. According to sociologist Nauja Kleist, a diaspora's force as an "identity marker in political mobilization" is that "it can signal universalism," by addressing pan-national issues, sometimes "by ignoring or blurring different positions." At the same time, "it can be used in more exclusionary ways to address particular groups and positions," be they of economic or political nature (Kleist, 2008: 1139).

In general, the concept of 'diaspora' assumes migration and relocation. National identity, it can be argued, is reflected by geographic and psychological conditions and environment. In particular, to a certain extent, it is affected by the perception and influence of 'space' and 'place.' A diaspora's engagement in the homeland cultural world, as proposed, assumes processes directed toward the transformation of the perception of space and places by diasporans. The sense of home for diasporans has two sides. Edward Said points out that most people know one culture, one home; however, "exiles are aware of at least two" (Said, 1995: 84). Many diasporans, even after they return physically, find themselves in-between two cultures but in none of them as at home (Kenny, 2013: 89), and they might also face integration problems (Sarkisian et al., 2014: 141).

When studying diasporas, it is essential to understand the particular location of communities, as well as their origins, since their environment can have a significant impact on their character. However, the 'routes' of a community formation can also shape such communities. For instance, the influence of the environment on diasporans and their national identity can differ to a significant extent, between a person whose ancestors originated from one location, then lived in another country, after which they migrated to a new destination, and a person whose parents or grandparents moved from the first country directly to the current (last) one.

The concepts of 'identity' and 'place' are in a "natural relationship" (Kenny, 2013: 108), in which, arguably, place becomes a determining factor. The role of places as "centers of felt value" (Tuan, 2011: 4) cannot be overestimated. Home is perceived through places; for effective connection through spaces in the homeland-diaspora relationship and strengthening the national identity of diasporans, the sense of home becomes central.

The identity of diasporans, Razmig Panossian argues, is created and is not just an extension of the homeland (Panossian, 1998: 151). Diasporic space can still exist in relative isolation from the homeland, in the continuous state of permanent return, even in its imaginary form, as diasporans can follow their traditional (homeland-origin) life practices, traditions, and norms. There are examples of such communities in the world, such as the Russian community in Bolivia (Fedorov: 2016).

The contemporary technological era makes the diasporic connection between diasporic spaces smooth and creates conditions for them to unite. According to Kevin Kenny, technology has become the most significant factor in strengthening "diasporic connectivity" (Kenny, 2013: 98). As some argue, strengthening the connections between the homeland and the diaspora has the potential to change the whole diaspora space into one transnational space.

The abstract sense of space keeps diasporans conceptually attached to or only knowledgeable about the homeland. Homeland itself can be perceived in an abstract way and, certainly, not as a concretion of values, as Yi-Fu Tuan would describe it (as mentioned previously). Homeland-diaspora relations can potentially create the problem of contested leadership by both sides of the nation. Arguably, for diasporans, who have developed only a conceptual sense or abstract knowledge of the homeland, the contested leadership between the homeland and the diaspora can prevent the diasporans from being effectively included in the nation, and it becomes a significant political barrier in homeland-diaspora relations and the development of one transnational space.

When trying to engage its diaspora, the (homeland) state tries to spill across its borders in search of its own people, as geographers Alexandra Delano and Alan Gamlen emphasize (Delano and Gamlen, 2014: 45). It can also be argued that diasporans, being in permanent return, are also in search of their own homeland, based on the foundational assumption that, by definition, diasporans are in permanent return.

Through modern technology, the whole diaspora space has become reachable by the homeland. National art, religion, myths and traditions, lifestyle, and social norms, even though often adapted to the local environment, throughout time, have enabled communities in the diaspora to create their physical environment within the framework of their diasporic identity. Religious institutions, political associations, cultural clubs and societies, even the home environment – all can contribute to the empirically constructed diasporic space (if Nigel Thrift's categorization of space is applied).

When dealing with the diaspora, many in the homeland, even policymakers, tend to make the mistake of perceiving the diaspora as a single homogenous space. The importance of distinguishing between two views on cultural identity (what diasporans also carry) is clearly explained by Stewart Hall. Apart from the view that shared culture is "common historical experiences and shared cultural codes which provide us, as 'one people,'" there is also the view, which recognizes the "deep and significant difference" which makes cultural identity "a matter of 'becoming' as well as

Khor Virap with Mt. Ararat (Masis) in background

of 'being'" (Hall, 2003: 225). This second view, arguably, emphasizes the necessity of understanding diasporic 'routes,' and not only 'roots.'

In the course of 'unblocking space,' the interaction between the homeland and the diaspora allows a potential for the formation of one transnational space. This process can also be applied to connections between diasporic communities, as well as connections within communities. In fact, diasporas, as James Clifford writes, "connect multiple communities of a dispersed population" (Clifford, 1994: 304). The 'Armenian World' and the 'Jewish World' are such examples.

The role of 'image space' cannot be overestimated. People think in symbolic terms. The homeland is a symbol for homelanders, as well as diasporans. Symbols help to strengthen diasporic attachments to the homeland. Diasporans, especially those who have never been to the homeland, perceive the latter mainly through symbols and images. Symbolism, it could be argued, is one of the strongest driving forces behind the diaspora's existence. They help to create an idealistic perception of the homeland and its history. Symbols can represent various religious, cultural and political sites, as well as images. For instance, an image with a view of Mount Ararat from the Church of St. Gevorg in Khor Virap in Armenia is a symbolized image of the homeland by Armenians in various corners of the world. This particular example represents one of the main (if not the main) symbols of Armenian identity – Biblical Mount Ararat,[*] and at the same time, the nation's religious affiliation, represented through a church, symbolizing the origin of Christianity in Armenia. Images can also represent the diaspora space. They can be unique identifications of particular spaces of where diaspora communities exist. Images are important elements of space because it is often through images that we understand the spaces surrounding us, now and in the future (Thrift, 2003: 100).

Thrift pays particular attention to space as place and summarizes the geographical thought on 'place' by indicating its embodied nature and, at the same time, by raising a question of what embodiment means (Thrift, 2003: 103). Then, compared to individuals, who interact socially, he emphasizes the ability of a place to produce effects and admits that places "can change the composition of an encounter by changing the affective connections that are made" (Thrift, 2003: 104).

Space as place assumes specific locations; it is "place involved with embodiment" (Thrift, 2003: 103). Places have differences, and these

---

[*] According to the Bible, Mount Ararat is the resting place of Noah's Ark after the Great Flood. For this reason, Ararat and Armenia are often referred to as "the cradle of humanity" (*National Geographic*, October 1915: 330). Mount Ararat has been considered the main symbol of the Armenian people throughout history. The Armenians usually call it Masis. The mountain, which is a dormant volcano, has two peaks – Greater Ararat, or Masis, 5,165 meters above sea level, and Lesser Ararat, or Sis, 3,896 meters above sea level (Encyclopaedia Britannica, *Mount Ararat*). Mount Ararat is sacred to Armenians, "who believe themselves to be the first race of humans to appear in the world after the Deluge" (Encyclopaedia Britannica, *Mount Ararat*). Nowadays (since 1920), the mountain is located in Eastern Turkey, few kilometers from the Armenian border. It can be viewed from both Turkish territory and Armenia. The view from Armenia's side is usually considered a more complex and a better vantage point, with the symbolic church at Khor Virap in the foreground. This church was built on the site where, according to tradition, St. Gregory the Illuminator, the founder of the Armenians Apostolic Church, was imprisoned for his Christian belief. After serving 13 years of imprisonment, St Gregory persuaded king Trdat III to convert the nation to the Christian faith. On that very place, the above-mentioned church was constructed and completed in the 17th Century. The name Khor Virap literally means 'deep dungeon' (Armenian Travel Bureau, *Khor Virap Monastery*). Khor Virap is a popular destination for pilgrims and tourists, many of whom visit it to view Mount Ararat.

differences come out before they enter into contact with each other, explains Doreen Massey (Massey, 2012: 69). Space as place has an emotional aspect, it is "more 'real' than space," as it links the way places are perceived "through memories of places" (Thrift, 2003: 102). Thrift analyses the recent trend on how geographers see the limit of being in new kinds of space or experimenting with them (Thrift, 2003: 100). Can this work for diasporans in their permanent return? For diasporans, who live in permanent return, their willingness to reach new spaces, arguably, is blocked by that need for return. Even if physical return never happens, the imaginary nature of return maintains the connections between two spaces alive. Return, Kevin Kenny stresses, can "be even more powerful in allegoric form" (Kenny, 2013: 84), or metaphorical return. The 'real' nature of the homeland space is thus, its nature as place, or at least a need for transforming the space into place. "Places stay put" (Tuan, 2011: 29). By accepting this feature of places, it is proposed that attachment to particular places and making diasporans place-centric in the homeland creates the strongest potential for transforming the abstractly perceived homeland space into a specific place of return. For people, feeling "a need to anchor their personality in objects and places" (Yuan, 2011: 32) is probably the best justification for the above-stated argument.

In modern society, geographer Michael Curry emphasizes, "to say that something is where it belongs is to say that it ought to be there" (Earle et al., 1996: 20). Each of the interviewees was asked the same set of 28 questions, and, as it became evident, the shortest question – "Where do you belong?" – was the most difficult to answer. Indeed, with no visits paid to the homeland, it is not easy to have a physical attachment to it. However, the sense of belonging to a non-territorial and more abstract identity, such as belonging to the 'Armenian World,' or *Armenianness*, has been stressed by many interviewees of different backgrounds.

Two interviewees were struck by the question and said that they had never thought about their space of belonging, after saying that they could not answer the question clearly. Five respondents specified that their space of belonging was non-territorial *Armenianness*, the community, the 'Armenian World.' Thus, it can be argued that the perception of national identity in such cases is inseparable from the sense of belonging. Belonging to space is a complex phenomenon, and, apart from geographically specific physical space, it can also mean belonging to abstract non-territorial space.

Belonging is associated with the development of the sense of home, which can be essential for understanding the emotional aspect of the perception of national identity and connection to the homeland. As proposed throughout this work, apart from the economically-motivated side of diaspora's inclusion in the homeland, the inclusionary process can be effective if it is developed based on the place-centric emotional approach toward the homeland. Here we need to differentiate between physical belonging and a virtual or imaginary one.

An exciting observation makes it clear that the sense of belonging to global *Armenianness* and the 'Armenian World' is equally strong among interviewees of different ages. Thus, a third of the interviewees emphasized that Australia was only a physical space they had been living in and did not represent their space of belonging. Among them is Michael Bazikian, a retired man in his late 80s, Bedros, a retired businessman in his 60s, Maria, a school teacher, and Mateos, a crypto-Armenian from Turkey. Armen, an education administrator in his 40s, even specified that with a non-territorial sense of belonging, they had created their space.

In the case of diasporans, who possess a strong sense of extraterritorial belonging, their sense of belonging to their physical space of living tends to be weaker compared to the extraterritorial transnational space. Mr. Bazikian, who has lived five decades in Australia, makes it clear that geographically, it does not matter where he belongs, as his cultural space of belonging is clearly Armenia. He admits, "culturally I belong to Armenia because I enjoy the culture, but Australia is my country, and I will do everything possible to see Australia prosper." According to Bedros, his presence in Australia does not have any impact on his sense of belonging. It is only the connection to Armenia, the Armenian community, and *Armenianness* that shape that sense.

Vahe shared his feeling of traveling to Armenia: "When I travel to Armenia and get out of the plane, I think I am at home." If such an attitude and perception can be easily understood in the case of Anahit, a housewife, who was born in Armenia and migrated to Australia with her family when she was only seven, then for someone born in a different land, the home-like perception of the homeland (even in case of those, who have never been there before) underlines the strong connection to the cultural heritage. Anahit proudly stresses, "not only me, but also my whole family would say that our space of belonging is Armenia." Being emotionally attached to the homeland as a whole and their hometown, in particular, central to the identity of which is 'memorialization' (Mohan, 2008: 473), the interviewees' attachment to specific places becomes essential. During the conversation, Anahit went as far back into her childhood memories as her bedroom in her house in Armenia when she was a child.

Vrej has never lived in Armenia and only visited it twice on short trips. However, with such a brief experience of being in Armenia, he talks about an emotional attachment to it and his strong sense of belonging there. An interesting observation brought by Vrej was his strong feelings experienced during the second visit. When talking about visiting Armenia, Vrej used a phrase which showed, probably subconsciously, his perception of Armenia. He said, "when I went back…," and not "when I visited it for the second time," a phrase that indirectly reflects his willingness to return.

Helen, who is half-Armenian by blood, has lived in several countries and regions; nevertheless, she has never been to Armenia. She found it hard to provide a straightforward answer to the question of belonging. Similarly, Garo said that he felt more belonging in the Armenia space.

As proposed, virtual and imaginary return, fostered by the idealistic perception of the homeland, is possibly a factor that contributes to the emotional perception of the homeland, even without a particular place of attachment. The argument here is that such understanding can make the perception more specific and real and, thus, further strengthen the links to the homeland. Perception of return by diasporans, who have never been to the homeland and perceive it only idealistically, arguably, takes place mainly through the homeland space as image.

Vartan's language has been more of an uncertain, even pessimistic, nature. Despite being a diasporan engaged in diaspora-homeland relations on a daily basis, he has been struggling to understand where he belongs:

> Unfortunately, my culture being Armenian does not let me have an exact feeling of belonging. It is more of an older generation issue. My belonging is to Armenia but by 80%. Geographically, I am totally lost. I do not have the sense of belonging. I was born in one country, studied in a different country, grew up in a different country, lost my parents very early, have lived all by myself in a different environment. Australia, taking into consideration that I am maturing in this country, makes me feel more and more that this

is my home, this is my place, not as belonging but as space I am living, where I will be ending my days. Deep I would prefer to have my tomb in Armenia or somewhere where historical Armenia was.

There were interviewees who developed a clearly perceived sense of belonging to the hostland, to Australia. If in the case of belonging to extraterritorial *Armenianness*, these were people of different occupations and of age; but those who responded, 'I belong to Australia,' were all younger, their age ranging from their late 20s to early 40s, all of whom were working professionals – a high school teacher, a lawyer, and a private company manager. Two of them had never been to Armenia. The social space or environment was also specified as a space of belonging. Levon, for instance, identified his belonging to the family and continued:

> From the pure physicality, culturally, it is the family in its broader sense. Geography, it is where I can provide my family to the best. At this moment, it is Australia. In the future, I do not know now yet.

The sense of belonging, either to a geographically-bounded territory or an abstract non-territorial space, such as '*Armenianness*' or the 'Armenian World,' as it is strongly argued, is related to what diasporans perceive as their homeland.

Historical Homeland: Perception of Reality or a Dream?

Armenians, with regard to the perception of their historical homeland, considerably differ from many other diasporic nations. Not only the homeland space is perceived differently, but also the homeland's transformation over time has changed that perception, with 1991 being the cornerstone when Armenia acquired its political sovereignty – becoming a nation-state after about six centuries of being deprived of statehood.*

In the diaspora, before 1991, Armenia was a myth, a dream. For the generation in its mid-40s and above, a part of their life coincided with Armenia as part of the Soviet Union. However, the generation that is

---

* As mentioned above, since the 14th century, there was a very brief period of two years (1918-1920) when Armenia was a politically independent nation-state (the Republic of Armenia, or the 'First Republic'), until it was absorbed by Soviet Russia, and later, by the Soviet Union, within the Transcaucasian Republic and, since 1936, as the Armenian Soviet Socialist Republic, also known as the 'Second Republic.'

currently in its 20s and 30s has grown up knowing that there is a Republic of Armenia. Nonetheless, for many older diasporans, the homeland was eastern and central Turkey, often referred to as 'Western Armenia,' where Armenians lived for thousands of years.

During most of the 20th century, "Armenia was sort of far away, but we knew it existed," said Armen and continued:

> Since independence, it changed. When I visited Armenia in 1986 for the first time, my sense of belonging from then has strengthened, a personal attachment too. I felt it as my land. It was also part of my history. For instance, *Sasountsi Davit*[*] was not from there, but seeing the statue in Yerevan somehow made me feel it was present there. To me, Armenia means a sense of belonging, a place connected by language and religion.

Now, the Republic is the only Armenia. Two-thirds of the interviewees pointed out that their historical homeland was left in modern Turkey. Among the Armenians, that space is often referred to as 'Western Armenia.' Nowadays, there is probably no one with a first-hand experience of living there before the Genocide, and, therefore, nobody can remember the lost homeland. This means that the dream of physical return contradicts its rational perception and reality since diasporans understand that such an emotion-based dream cannot be fulfilled. In their perception of 'Western Armenia' as the homeland, many diasporans commit a fallacy by perceiving that territory as the same space that used to be there before. It has changed to a significant extent, demographically. With about 15 million ethnic Kurds inhabiting Turkey,[†] mainly in its eastern provinces, the space of 'Western Armenia' has become different from what it used to be a century ago. A new space has been created on that territory, and 'Western Armenia' has turned into a merely imagined space for many diasporan Armenians.

This reference to 'Western Armenia' by many diasporans as the homeland is a crucial point because, for a significant part in the diaspora, the modern Republic of Armenia is not associated with their historical homeland, but is mainly perceived as the cultural representative of their

---

* Sasountsi Davit or David of Sasoun is a mythical Armenian national hero. The statue mentioned here is one of the most recognized landmarks in Armenia's capital city of Yerevan.
† Source: The CIA World Factbook, *Turkey*

heritage. Armenia is a concept, as some interviewees say. It is broader than the Republic; it is a complex of "our land, our culture, our religion, but is not just a geographical land."

The Republic of Armenia, as mentioned above, is a monoethnic nation-state. In the early 1970s, Walker Connor estimated that the true definition of a 'nation-state' could be applied to only about 10% of states, "in the sense that the state's boundaries coincide with the nation's and that the total population of the state share a single ethnic culture" (Connor, in Smith, 1991: 15). Armenia, thus, after 1991 can be classified as such. "In reality, the perception of Armenia is broader," explains Bedros. Such an opinion was also expressed by Aram and Vahe. Belonging to modern Armenia, even without any ancestral links to it, has also been expressed by Antonio. The reason is emotional. He says, "I have found spiritual healing in Armenia; have visited it three times. I always felt the need and found it there, an emotional affiliation." Does this mean it is possible to transform a space into one that can be perceived as a homeland? To what extent do emotions matter? In the understanding of homeland-diaspora relations, this can be essential, as the whole inclusionary policy of the homeland toward its diaspora can be built on the identification and strengthening of the emotional factors in the perception of the homeland.

By possessing communal identity, Armenian diasporans tend to emphasize *Armenianness* despite being born and raised in another land. As Ulf Bjorklund argues, "Armenians have more or less well-founded, well-articulated ideas about what Armenians are like in other parts of the diaspora, and now in Armenia proper – what it means and what it takes to be an Armenian elsewhere" (Bjorklund, 2003: 350). This point presents Armenia in the eyes of diasporans in a particular way. Thus, Vrej, for instance, whose parents were descendants of Genocide survivors, arrived in Australia from Egypt, and specified that modern Armenia could be a representative of his culture and identity. "It is where the people of my identity live. I can say that current Armenia can also be identified as homeland." Vrej also mentioned that before 1991, it was quite difficult to explain to friends and classmates what Armenia was when it was part of the USSR. Besides, being a son of Egyptian-born Armenians, he found it hard to explain his origin and identity, when he was introducing himself as an Armenian but not Egyptian. When it comes to the modern Republic, "it is where the people of my identity live. I can say that current Armenia can also be identified as homeland," says Vrej.

For most of the diasporans, modern Armenia is not the direct historical homeland and is only a small geographic part of what used to be Armenia for centuries, located on the Armenian Highlands. It extended from eastern Turkey to Azerbaijan (which until the 20th century used to be the name of only an Iranian, then-Persian, province) (Brockhaus and Efron, 1899: 55-56). There was also the Armenian principality and kingdom of Cilicia on the Mediterranean Sea. These factors can be taken into consideration in the formulation and implementation of the inclusionary policy of Armenia toward the diaspora. Armenia, even though it is not the direct historical homeland for many diasporans, remains the core, the center of their belonging. Michael Bazikian, who has lived in several countries before moving to Australia five decades ago, stated: "My cultural center is in Armenia," and this is said by a person who visited Armenia the first time at the age of 80. Besides the modern Republic, the abstract de-territorialized space of *Armenianness* is the space of belonging for many other interviewees too.

The cultural sense of belonging to Armenia in its broader meaning has remained strong over the decades. Indeed, a significant number of 'ethnies' are neither diasporans, nor culturally linked to *Armenianness* or the 'Armenian World.' For younger participants in the diaspora, Armenia has always been there as an independent state. For the older generation, who have been teenagers or older when Armenia became independent in 1991, a drastic transformation process took place along with independence. Armenia has become more open toward the diaspora, and, arguably, it has acquired a new meaning.

An interesting reflection given by Vahe from Sydney identifies the perception of Armenia "in-between historical Armenia and the modern one." To him, Armenia is an "unhealed wound," "a landmass taken away during and after the Genocide," "a monumental loss in the national identity." However, when someone now asks where Armenia is, "you can point on the map at Armenia now."

"Strength to make a new life," "ability to recreate," "the sadness of the Genocide memory" have been among many other phrases and thoughts the interviewed diasporans mentioned. A common line has been a strong emotional and patriotic feeling toward Armenia expressed even by those diasporans who have never been to Armenia. At the time the interviews were conducted, only about 55% of the interviewees had been to Armenia, and only one was born there (emigrated at the age of seven, as mentioned above). Anahit, who has lived in Australia for about two decades after moving there, says proudly, "when people talk about Armenia, I feel that I have to defend it." To her, it does not matter what the media says. "My concern is that I wish there is always a better Armenia."

For many diasporans, Armenia is a representational homeland space. Garo from Melbourne shares his feelings that even though the Republic of Armenia does not represent his historical homeland, he recognizes it as such. Vrej, who has been to Armenia only twice, reflects on his two trips differently. He speaks about "the sense of feeling Armenian changes with the trips, especially with the first."[*] It is interesting to mention the perception of Armenia by Bedros, who has visited Armenia many times. "For me, the concept of Armenia is two-fold," Bedros claims and clarifies that, when it comes to the geographical area, Armenia is the Republic of Armenia. The reason behind this is that the Republic possesses "all the features and elements of Armenia I have in my mind. You can find all these there that you cannot find elsewhere in the diaspora, like the development and preservation of culture, of language, of religion." Thus, the significance of having a sovereign nation-state is emphasized. Bedros says that the diaspora is perceived as a strong contributor to the preservation of identity; it should support Armenia and not give up "for any political or bourgeois reasons." However, the Republic has a higher-level participation and should be seen as the leader of the 'Armenian World.' "It bears a big historic role for leading the 'Armenian World.' It can preserve the elements that constitute the identity," Bedros added. "I live the whole thing," he summarized when speaking about Armenia as of a concept.

Those diasporans, who have never been to the homeland, may have different expectations of it prior to their visit. Other than the idealistic perception of the homeland space, which is often perceived as an 'image space,' there is no emotional attachment or memory related to it, particularly, to a specific place there. On the other hand, being the only representative of the broader historical homeland (ancient Armenia as an area in the Armenian Highlands), many in the diaspora have certain

---

[*] After spending three weeks in Armenia during his first trip, in 2011, he went there again for 10 days in 2013.

expectations toward the Republic, before their first visit there. Idealistic perceptions might serve as a barrier for first-time visitors. As stressed by a diasporan in Kolkata, who has studied in the Armenian College there and considers Armenia his home, even though he has never been there, the idealistic perception of Armenia might change after the first visit.

Armenia, in a broader sense, is perceived as the homeland, "but the Republic is a different story," specifies Lily. "It is my country, a country that is very rich in culture, religion, history that I do not understand a word of when I communicate with anyone,[*] beautiful music, traditions, that's what I think of."

For Mateos, Armenia is perceived "as a country where Armenians live." Then he touches on a point, which is very common for the people who have experienced genocide and deportation – humiliation, an "uncured confidence," as Dominique Moisi names the lack of hope of a nation (Moisi, 2009: 5). Mateos speaks about a potential threat and of Armenia as a space to feel secure: "If there is something happening to me, I know I can go there and live there." At the same time, he admits that Istanbul and Sivas[†] in Turkey are where he belongs and feels at home. Mateos is not alone in his perception of Armenia as a safe space, a land, which is a safe haven for Armenians (in case anything happens in the hostlands Armenians live in). Many Armenians, who leave Armenia for good, try to keep one residential unit, an apartment, "just in case," as many say, to be sure that they will have a safe place to live if they are "forced to return."

For Mateos, as he clarifies, Armenia is not where he belongs. He elaborates:

> The homeland is not where you go and live. It is a space you feel you belong, where, for example, your ancestors' graves are. I have no relative in Armenia. It is neither nothing nor also not too important for me as well, like any other country. In case of Armenia, I cannot say it is exactly like any other country for me. I will feel sad if something happens to it. But it is not like Turkey for me.

---

[*] Such problems are mainly due to the use of some Russian words and phrases in the informal language in Armenia, an influence of Russian culture and language over the past decades.

[†] Also known as Sepasdia [Sebastia].

As an Armenian, who has lived most of his life in Turkey and where his main social environment has developed, Mateos admits the difficulty of living in Turkish social surroundings for an Armenian and, at the same time, he feels firmly attached to it. Thus, the Turkey space for him (and possibly, for many other crypto-Armenians) is perceived contradictorily. Our purpose here, however, is not to analyze the perception of Armenia among crypto-Armenians, which is a topic of a separate study.

Armenians, as it is argued throughout this book, have a strong communal identity. As opposed to territorial identity, the sense of belonging to the imagined community of *Armenianness* (the 'Armenian World') can be understood, as Antonio, who is part Italian, explains:

> The country has a strong influence on me; I have not felt it with any other place. Italy is a touristic place for me, nothing more. All my female ancestors were Armenians. Only my surname and name remained Italian by a tradition. In Armenia, I felt a sort of rebirth, when I encountered that everything in the environment was Armenian.

Such a nationalistic stance is not peculiar to only those diasporans who have been to Armenia. Aram, a mid-career lawyer, who has never visited Armenia, speaks in a very nationalistic and possessive manner about it. Aram's very idealistic perception of Armenia is strong, and he justifies it, "maybe because I have never been there. If I visit it, I might change my perception; I do not know." This can lead to the point that without an intimate knowledge, such a perception shapes an indirect knowledge of the homeland space, as it keeps that knowledge only at a conceptual level, if we use Yi-Fu Tuan's classification (Yi-Fu Tuan, 2011: 6). Garo, who had also never been to Armenia at the time of the interview, stated that Armenia was associated with his ancestry, history, and culture. A similar interpretation was reflected by an official of a diaspora institution in Sydney – "Armenia is our values, heritage, culture, and is my past and future. There is no doubt it will always be my essence of who I am culturally."

Two of the interviewees in Melbourne spoke about Armenia as a country that "means to me who I am, where my ancestors came from, it represents how hard they fought for who we were, so we have Armenia in the first place, we have an identity" (Maria, a teacher in Melbourne) and as a country associated with culture, the origin of his religion (Levon, a company manager also from Melbourne). Levon, a person, who has never been to Armenia, sees Armenia as a country his children can go to, as his home, a spiritual space, where he "can help it develop."

Perception of National Identity

National identity, arguably, is the perception of the 'self' in the world of hundreds of nation-states and thousands of ethnic peoples and tribes. Political scientists Richard Mansbach and Edward Rhodes identify the following five markers of national identity: blood, language, religion, culture, and citizenship (Mansbach and Rhodes, 2007: 443). Indeed, there are features of national identity that are carried by people from their birth. Blood is such. People can choose their religion, nationality (citizenship), to some extent, even culture and language. Blood is something people are born with, and it determines how they look and sometimes how they are perceived and even stereotyped.

When trying to understand and approach (engage) any diaspora, it is essential to distinguish between diasporans and 'ethnies.' Many carriers of the same blood, even living out of their homeland, are not diasporans, which assumes that they are not in permanent return, whatever form it may take. It is a fallacy often committed by homeland nation-states when all 'ethnies' are perceived as diasporans. Such misperception can mislead the homeland itself in pursuing its policy toward the diaspora and, therefore, make their inclusionary efforts less effective. This problem exists in case of the Armenians. Armenia, as the homeland, often perceives all ethnic Armenians in the world as diasporans. As proposed, it should be the ultimate aim of the homeland to engage all the diasporans in the homeland effectively and to motivate the 'ethnies' to transform into diasporans. That transformation assumes a change in the perception of their own national identity.

In their self-identification, a reflection of being Australian and Armenian is common. Nearly all the interviewees responded that they are proud of being Australian. A strong Armenian cultural heritage, as a pillar of Armenian identity, was emphasized by four interviewees. Eight interviewees, including seven citizens of Australia, stressed that for them belonging to the Armenian nation prevails over their citizenship identity. The processes of globalization have led to an argument that nationness, or national citizenship, as sociologists Yasemin Soysal and David Jacobson have argued, becomes less important and irrelevant with globalization

(Sousal and Jacobson, in Hansen, 2008: 3). However, by contradicting such an argument, based on responses given by the interviewed diasporans and observations in this study, one can propose that the weakening of nationness can be more relevant to peoples with a distinct territorial identity. In cases of communal identity (the Armenians, in our case), when citizenship is not specified as a pillar of identity, the extraterritorial communal identity makes the above- mentioned argument (discourse about it) less relevant. Anyway, this is an area with much room for further study, in particular, regarding the link between the engagement of extraterritorial diasporans in the homeland as its citizens and the possible strengthening of their national identity.

When reflecting on their own national identity, the following have been the interviewees' responses: "fully Armenian, born in Australia," "being an Australian of Armenian heritage," "living with a two-fold identity," "being part of two cultures, of two societies, of two very distinct and different cultural dimensions," "belonging to the Armenian nation," "an Armenian living in Australia," "even if born in Australia, feeling Armenian, as was raised within the culture," "national identity is the feeling of belonging and in our case belonging to the Armenian nation," "an Armenian living in Australia, an Australian Armenian," "feeling Armenian 100%," "pure Armenian," "as a citizenship, it is hard to say, I feel I am a citizen of this country (Australia), but not part of the national identity of the locals," "I consider myself as Armenian, even though I have Australian and Lebanese citizenship."

Thus, the majority of the interviewees view national identity as part of two cultures, of two societies, "of two very distinct and different cultural dimensions," as Vartan concludes. He points at a problem that "the new generation has no idea where their ancestors come from, and that is a huge loss in national identity." As a historical homeland space, 'Western Armenia' used to be a pillar for decades. As seen by Vartan, partly, this ignorance was rooted in the decision made by many Armenians (first-generation migrants), who, after surviving the Genocide, chose to close the page and to start a new life in a new country.

Culture, religion, language, as markers of identity, can be inherited and surround a person from birth. However, they can also be acquired, even if a person has never been exposed to the environment of their original heritage. Citizenship, being a legal term, is usually conferred by birth or by acquisition. In either case, it is the person who eventually chooses to maintain one's identity or to develop (in case of citizenship, to acquire) one. As briefly mentioned above, there is only one determinant of national identity that cannot change – blood.

Blood as a Marker of Armenian Identity

In the case of Armenians, anthropologist Url Bjorklund argues, "the very fact of belonging to a diaspora of dispersed Armenians" has an important influence on "their lives, individually and collectively" (Bjorklund, 2003: 351). All the interviewees confirmed that they perceived themselves Armenian as their identity and affirmed their feeling of belonging to *Armenianness*, some even by using stronger expressions such as "of course, I feel" or "yes and am proud of it." At the same time, among the interviewed diasporans, only some specified blood as the most important marker of identity. Helen, for instance, being half-Armenian (half-Assyrian), admits that other pillars are also very important. She emphasizes that born in Australia, she feels being a proud Australian. However, "it is not who I am. I am Armenian," she adds, "by blood, I am 50%, but the culture, values prevail... the most important for my identity is blood, what my father is."

For Anahit from Melbourne, national identity is a combination of blood and the way a person is brought up. "From my childhood, I felt and thought that we were different, and even if some cultures were close, we were unique." The role of history in this context is emphasized. "The Genocide brings us together," and "the fact that we have suffered so much and are still standing."

A different view on the role of blood is brought by Mateos, the interviewed crypto-Armenian. By keeping his Armenian identity hidden in his Turkish environment, including in Melbourne, where he lives now, Mateos has been trying to return to his roots and has shown his willingness to connect to the community. He accepts the important role of other markers, such as culture, but considers blood as the main pillar of national identity. He does not speak Armenian and has been brought up in a foreign environment, from the national and religious viewpoint (in Turkey), and possesses Turkish citizenship. He discloses that as it is not easy to be in an Armenian environment in Turkey, "so I define myself as Turkish" says Mateos. "I consider myself Armenian, by blood, but I always speak Turkish, so I show my identity as Turkish." Mateos represents a

132

special case of a split perception of his own identity, and he cannot disclose his identity in his social environment the way he perceives it.

Blood is seen as a "national transition of identity from persons, the parents, who held that identity." To Bedros, with his rich experience of living in the diaspora and visiting Armenia frequently, blood is a factor that cannot change since the person is born with it. Only second, to him, is the environment and education. These three are considered crucial, with parental care of Armenian schools, of the community, of the Church viewed as very important in "nurturing and keeping and transferring of that feeling of identity to the next generation."

Culture and Language in Armenian Identity

As in the case of any Armenian, the diasporans interviewed for this study have their roots originating in either Western or Eastern Armenia, with the latter, to a significant extent, matching the area of modern Armenia. However, their routes differ significantly. For instance, Vartan, who has gone through geographically diverse and long routes, considers himself part of Australia but sees his culture as Armenian. "Culture is the most important, but the citizenship is the last one," he adds. Culture "is the umbrella for all other attributes, and it is the embodiment of identity." Since coming to Australia, he clarifies, his "concentration has always been what is culture-related." Levon, a young business manager from Melbourne, also ranks culture the highest.

The perception of identity can have ups and downs. Similar to nations being imagined (Anderson, 2006: 7), national identity, too, as it can be argued, is a reflection of how one perceives themselves within imaginary borders of that identity. Blood and culture, including family culture, are seen as crucial for self-identification of *Armenianness*. Feeling different from other local cultures from childhood, as reflected, is what makes the family factor important.

When speaking about Armenian culture, nearly all the respondents specified religion, the Armenian Apostolic Church in particular, as an essential part of it. Generally speaking, the history of the nation, as mentioned above, is seen as a glue that keeps several identity pillars together. In particular, the fact that the nation has been standing after much suffering throughout its history is viewed as a particular justification of this position. Various factors can determine and develop the Australian

Armenian sense of community and national identity, as specified by Vahe, who has been "immersed in Armenian culture in Australia" through his life and work at a diaspora organization. Is citizenship of any importance?

Overall, among the five markers of national identity, citizenship was not specified as significant by any of the interviewees. This fact can be seen as a justification of an argument that Armenian identity is strongly communal, with weaker, if any, territorial identity affecting it. "I am not a citizen of Armenia but Australia, but I feel myself an Armenian," says Vahe. The first pillar for maintaining his identity, as he specifies, is language. The unique language[*] and being the first Christian nation in the world are seen as the two cornerstones of Armenian national identity. Vahe stressed that it was the language that allowed the Armenian people to maintain continuity for so long. To him, for the parents' generation, who arrived in Australia from the Middle East, preservation of identity in the Middle East was more important as there was a more distinct cultural environment (first of all, religious, as specified). Thus, the main pillar had shifted from religion to language. In the Middle East, Armenian language "stays as your first language, while in Australia it becomes your second language, as most of the activities are in English," emphasizes Vahe and justifies why family culture and traditions are seen as crucial.

It was a typical reflection among several interviewees that family traditions and education stood out among the factors that build and maintain Armenian identity. It was stressed that, with the loss of the language, the identity might also be lost. In Australia, among the Armenians, the Armenian language becomes less critical socially, compared to the community environment in the Middle East. Unless the family environment promotes learning Armenian, language is perceived by many interviewees as less important, several interviewees emphasize.

Vrej from Sydney spoke about the way Armenia's independence has strengthened his perception of his national identity. He explained that before Armenia became independent, he found it difficult to explain his national origin to others. As an Australian Armenian, born to parents from Egypt, when introduced to others, he would identify himself as an

---

* The Armenian language is a separate branch of the Indo-European language family (Encyclopaedia Britannica, *Armenian Language*).

Australian Armenian. A typical response would then be, why not an Egyptian but an Armenian? Vrej clarifies that after 1991 Armenians can easily be associated with Armenia, the nation-state.

When talking about the role of Armenian culture, a complex of factors has been considered. Not only the heritage and blood, language, culture, and religion are seen as important, but also one's own name, as specified by Vrej. With his unique-to-Australia name, he says that every time he tells it, he has to provide some background on the name, on *Armenianness*. Speaking about citizenship as a determinant of identity, Vrej considers it very minor and insignificant. "I am an Australian, but an Armenian," he stressed and added that he had chosen to live in Australia, but it was not his main identity. Instead, it is Armenian.

It was hard for Vrej to point at one single pillar that has shaped his identity. He responded that more than others, it is the language, the loss of which, he argues, will have an impact on identity. As an example, he spoke about one of his colleagues, with whom he had worked for a decade. The lady always introduced herself as a Palestinian. Recently, when she visited her parents in Perth, she found out that she was Armenian. Before that visit, she had never been told about her roots, lived in Jerusalem, and considered herself an Arab until she was told the truth recently. "A 50 year-old lady! She did not even want to know her origin for so many years and just took the news as a piece of information," said Vrej in an emotional manner.

Michael Bazikian, the oldest participant in this study, has been trying for a long time to answer the question of what the real Armenian character is. "It is to be friendly and hospitable to others, even to a complete stranger. The Armenians have become such throughout history," he says and adds, "the Armenian identity is, to some extent, being lost by time," as, according to him, the religion and faith are different now. "People go to church as tradition, and they have lost their national identity," he stresses pessimistically and points at a weaker community awareness, which has, in turn, weakened the sense of identity. Mr. Bazikian could not believe, his entire life, in the revival of the nation. His expectations were that:

Nothing would remain after the Genocide, but so much of culture is there in Armenia. In the early days, after the Genocide, there was no diaspora, but only refugees. Today, Armenia has a prosperous diaspora, and there is no excuse for not providing massive help to Armenia.

Concluding the point about an ongoing loss of identity in the diaspora, Michael Bazikian explains that, as a derivative, the "loss of trust is the outcome of the loss of identity." Turning indifferent to the community, be it in Armenia or the diaspora, to Mr. Bazikian, are signs of losing the national identity.

Culture, as the main pillar for Armenian identity, was specified by more than half of the interviewees. In a broader sense, family traditions were mentioned as part of the culture. The justification behind the role of the family is "not because we speak Armenian, but because we are keeping the family traditions, which is the most important pillar that has been passed from generation to generation," says Michael Bazikian. A similar reflection was shared by a younger interviewee, who grew up while the homeland was already a sovereign political entity, unlike in cases of older diasporans, for whom the homeland was only a myth, an idealistic perception.

Culture is seen as a tool that keeps the community together, "for us to continue being Armenian," says Maria, a school teacher. An interesting observation is that Antonio, a Roman Catholic, ranks culture higher than religion: "I am a patriotic Armenian, have gone to Karabakh as well," he stressed.

To understand one's own Armenian identity and culture, Levon emphasizes the need to develop "some knowledge about Armenia, not necessarily to be proud of where you are from, but knowing where you are from is important." A similar reflection on identity is shared by Aram, a lawyer from Sydney, who has never been to Armenia. By putting culture on top as a pillar, he ranks citizenship higher than other identity pillars, but still lower than culture. "My family's background is Armenian, but I also have an affinity for being an Australian. Citizenship is number two, will not put much stock in blood, as many ethnic Armenians do not even think of themselves as Armenian." Regarding the place of language in the rank of the identity pillars, to Aram, language is important, but he knows "Armenians who do not speak the language but feel as Armenians."

Culture is the top attribute, says Vartan. He has spent decades within different religious, linguistic, and cultural environment. After his early life in the Middle East (Syria and then Lebanon), he lived in Italy (Venice), in the congregation of the Mekhitarist Fathers,[*] and was then, as he proudly said, "fortunate enough" to study in Armenia, at the Mother See of Holy Etchmiadzin,[†] for five years, which according to him, helped him "to discover lots of values" that built his nationality through culture and heritage. Afterward, Vartan lived in Italy again, where he served the community, then in Egypt, where he worked as a teacher at an Armenian secondary school (and concurrently served as a deacon in the Church there). Afterward, Vartan left for Sudan in the mid-1980s. That was the last step before moving to Australia in the early-1990s, which coincided with the time Armenia became a nation-state.

Vartan admits that the environment can strengthen or weaken the perception of national identity. Being involved in diaspora affairs on a daily basis, he is sure that "culture and language are the most important" elements in Armenian identity, explaining that, "while living in Lebanon, it was the language that connected everything. Of course, without the language, you will lose your identity." At the same time, Vartan accepts the strong role of religion – the Armenian Apostolic Church in Armenian identity – "as it is largely perceived that being an Armenian is to be Christian anyway," Vartan notes confidently.

Religion as a Component of Armenian Culture

Christianity (the Armenian Apostolic Church) has been emphasized as the main pillar of Armenian identity by several interviewees, including Garo, who stresses that, apart from language, it is the religion that has helped "to survive as a nation, through starvation, through the Genocide. It was due

---

[*] "San Lazzaro in Venice was established as the island monastery of the Mekhitarist Congregation in 1717. The congregation is Catholic, founded by Mkhitar of Sepasdia (born in 1676 in Sivas, in central Turkey today), who joined the Armenian Church, but whose monastic and intellectual pursuits did not receive the full support of the hierarchy of the time" (100 Years, 100 Facts, *San Lazzaro in Venice*).

[†] In the Gevorkian Theological Seminary in Etchmiadzin.

to the Church."* Religion and culture are seen in strong connection. The liturgy or *Surb Badarag* (Holy Service) in the Church is in Armenian, and attending it automatically means to be in the Armenian language environment. "Ancestors have fought for the religion and not only it but also to speak Armenian," says Maria from Melbourne and further clarifies that to continue being Armenian, it is essential not to lose the language.

"What you choose is very powerful," stresses Levon, the only interviewee who has lived in both Sydney and Melbourne. He sees religion, followed by culture, as key determinants of national identity and ranks blood the last. "Blood is genetic; you do not choose it," Levon clarifies. Aram, the lawyer from Sydney, identifies himself as a non-religious person. He assumes that the role of religion cannot be fully identified; however, the importance of being the first Christian nation in the world is perceived by him as essential for the Armenian identity.

The Church is present in many cities, where the Armenian communities are found, including in the two selected cities in Australia. Churches in Sydney and Melbourne both provide a regular weekly liturgy service. The head of the Church in Australia – Archbishop Najarian resides in Sydney and performs liturgy services predominantly there, with regular visits to other (smaller) communities in the region (in Australia, as well as in New Zealand, Singapore, Myanmar, and India).†

The Armenian Apostolic Church has become so involved with Armenian culture that it is usually perceived as the national church for Armenians worldwide. The role of the Church has been particularly emphasized by Lily, a high school teacher, who, as she said during the interview, had become increasingly involved in diaspora events after her marriage. It is an essential primary determinant of national identity, to Lily, even though she sees culture and traditions as more critical. She connects Armenian culture, religion, and language as essential pillars and puts blood lower in ranking. The reason behind this is, she emphasizes, similar to what Aram says (as mentioned above); there are pure-blooded

---

* When referring to the Armenian Apostolic Church in this book, the reference to 'the Church' is used as a shortened form for the Armenian Apostolic Church.

† These countries are included in the Asia/Australia diocese of the Armenian Apostolic Church (The Armenian Church, *Asia/Australia*)

ethnic Armenians, "who never participate in any event, do not speak the language, and do not identify themselves as Armenians."

Living the National Identity

National identity can be carried passively, by knowing one's own heritage, roots, and even routes; however, with no active steps taken toward being engaged in the community and the homeland. On the other hand, participation in diaspora events and institutions, financial contributions to the community are only examples of active engagement in the diaspora. Sometimes, as one interviewee explains, sacrifices made for being Armenian lead to losing something economically, which would not be the case if a person was not that devoted to *Armenianness*.

The connection to the homeland, including visiting it, is arguably a way of maintaining and strengthening national identity. "My identity or my belonging also gives me the sense of direction, a duty to look for justice for those lands,* and why I am not living there anymore. It is my duty to pursue it as part of my identity," says Armen from Sydney. He sees Armenia as the last hope for the Armenian nation, as a result of the loss of the historical homeland, and this hope presents a "need to contribute to the Armenian nation," be it in the form of financial contribution to disadvantaged children in Armenia, participation in cultural events, conducting business there, being there on a cultural visit or through participation in the homeland in any other way. National identity is not perceived and carried in isolation. Diasporans, being always in return, preserve their national identity through return. Identity can strengthen and weaken over time and from space to space. It is interesting to follow how the interviewed diasporans reflect on the transformation of national identity, in general, and their own identity, in particular.

Transformation of National Identity

National identity, as it is claimed, is a dynamic phenomenon. So, what makes it change? Is it common to experience one's own identity transforming through time and space and to understand that transformation? An interesting observation has demonstrated that only two

---

* The term 'the lost land,' refers to the area in eastern Turkey, commonly known as 'Western Armenia'

of our interviewees have never experienced any change of their Armenian identity through time and space. It is interesting to note that the two interviewees were the only ones with mix-blood (partly Assyrian and partly Italian, respectively). As it was presented, they chose the Armenian root as a dominant one, through which they perceived their national identity.

One of these two respondents, Helen, stresses that she has always felt being Armenian. To her, such a feeling was even stronger when she lived out of Australia, "especially being associated with Armenians from Armenia." During her years abroad, Helen specifies, she felt proud of her heritage and roots. In a foreign land (out of Australia), where she lived, "the important contribution of Armenians," she says, strengthened her identity, and she was prouder of being Armenian. "The environment matters; I was introduced to the Armenian Church, and I got a stronger connection there." To her, national identity does not change but only becomes stronger, depending on the environment. Another mix-blood interviewee reveals that, from his childhood until the present (in his late 50s), his identity has remained the same. "I grew up in the Armenian culture and among the Armenians. My kids have been educated in the Armenian school and the culture." It would be wrong to conclude that a favorable identity-preservation environment leads to strengthening the identity or maintain it, constant and not prone to any transformation (weakening). However, the presence of an educational institution that supports one's identity cannot be overestimated, according to many interviewees. This condition has been not only a case of communities in the two cities covered in this study but also in other observed ones. Thus, the presence of the Armenian College in Kolkata was pointed by community members as the most important factor for preserving the language and identity, even though blood and religion were seen as the main determinants of Armenian identity. One of the Kolkatan Armenians told me during our conversation that after building a church, wherever Armenians settled in earlier years, their second duty was building an Armenian school, aiming to preserve the Armenian identity.

Vartan from Sydney, a diasporan with a rich (broad) geography of life experience and exposure to pan-national diaspora institutions (such as the Armenian Apostolic Church or the Armenian General Benevolent Union), admits that perhaps heritage and culture will be lost in the future. "We will be part of the geographical space of the host country, with, maybe the language saved to a lesser extent," he states.

Michael Bazikian believes that any transformation of identity depends on the circumstances of life. After eight decades of carrying the diasporic identity, at the age of 80, when traveling to Armenia for the first time, he experienced a revival of identity, as revealed. That change motivated him to revisit Armenia several times again, despite his age. He added that he was determined even to stay there for the rest of his life if he was sure of accessible, high-quality medical services and medicines to maintain his health.

Vahe, too, agrees that "there has been a shift of identity." There are both optimistic and pessimistic sides to the situation, as he sees it. The community started from scratch in Australia, and people were looking for a common thing, mostly a church. However, now, "the same struggle is no longer around for a younger generation, and the importance of preserving national identity has eroded." The sense of community, Vahe explains, has become weaker over the years. When the community is gathered for various days/events, it gathers in relatively large numbers; however, this happens only several times in a year. He sees that over time, for more people, it becomes an obligation, not a choice. "For myself, the preservation is of great importance; it is the question of not only preserving the identity for this generation but also for those who are yet to come," he adds. To Vahe, the issue of preserving Armenian identity is of even greater importance since the communities are geographically very far from Armenia.

It is argued that not only the environment but also age can affect identity and encourage its progress and transformation. Anahit, who moved from Armenia to Australia at the age of seven, is sure that transformation of identity is possible over time and space. She spoke about the changes she had experienced while growing up, from the time of migration to Australia, until the end of her teens. As specified, over those years, she almost forgot her roots and "wanted to be Australian." Only, at 19, when visiting Armenia, did she feel a sudden revival of her Armenian identity. As she explained, "I started speaking Armenian again, and my language has improved dramatically." That visit had motivated Anahit to visit Armenia every other year. With everything re-discovered during the first visit, "now I live and dream Armenia and would like my children to go to an Armenian school," she said, adding that, despite the accusations by friends of betraying the Australian identity, the recovered heritage and identity prevails. Generally speaking, moving to a new space can potentially lead to complete assimilation. The ideal perspective can be to adapt to the new space and to integrate with it, i.e., not to sacrifice one's own heritage but to complement the host culture and social environment with it. It is a process of re-inventing identity.

"Identity is how you perceive it," according to Vrej. He believes that a person can choose their own identity, and it can change, particularly through the transformation of their own perceptions, when a person starts questioning their identity and space of belonging. According to him, national identity wavers, but becomes more stabilized over time. "It is affected by your surroundings," argues Vrej and adds that even though a person carries a specific identity since birth, eventually, preservation is what one decides to do. Not having direct roots in Armenia, and educated in a local Australian school and a university, Vrej was nevertheless surrounded by Armenian culture in his family. He further specifies that an essential stage when one is not influenced by the many factors of their birth-identity and surrounding comes in adolescence.

The role of the environment has been underlined by all other interviewees as well. Bedros from Sydney, who had lived and visited many countries before ending up in Australia years ago, stresses that the philosophy of the globalization era has led to the weakening of identity over time. However, he is a firm believer that, in reality, globalization cannot change identity. It "can have ups and downs, but you still maintain your identity," says Bedros and supports his argument by an interesting example. He told a story about an ethnic Armenian, whom he knew personally, who never cared about his identity and once attended a football match when visiting Germany. The German team was playing against Armenians. Without knowing the Armenian language and even with doubts about any benefit of being Armenian, he attended the match, which uncovered his sense of national identity. "When I saw the Armenian team, my entire body was quivering; I was crying," he told Bedros, who uses this story to emphasize that ups and downs in national identity perception are possible but not the disappearance of that identity. As an effective way for identity preservation, according to Bedros, is synchronized work between the family, schools, the Church, and various Armenian institutions "in order not to leave the preservation task to destiny."

The conversations with diasporans reveal that the most drastic transformation of identity probably happens during the adolescence period in life. Even after years spent in a particular cultural-language environment, the social surrounding can have a substantial impact on the perception of identity. According to Lily, a school teacher, even after going to an Armenian school and having always spoken Armenian at home, by her 20s, the sense of feeling Armenian had declined and also affected her ability to converse in Armenian. Lily named her marriage to an Armenian-Australian, who had a stronger sense of (Armenian) national identity as the primary factor that contributed to the revival of her own Armenian identity.

It can be possible that identity transformation happens at any age. This study demonstrates that there is no relationship between the place of birth, be it in the homeland or out of it, and the perception of national identity. Aram, who had never been in Armenia, lived his first 12 years in the Middle East, in Jordan, where Armenians were not as many as in neighboring Syria and Lebanon. Aram remembers that up to the age of 12, he thought of himself as a Jordanian Armenian. Afterwards, for many years, his identity was hidden. He stated, "I was not committed to being an Armenian for a while, then became very nationalistic, was involved in events, and helped to organize various events," Aram summarized.

This phenomenon is interestingly explained by Armen, according to whom, it depends on how identity is embedded. "People think they belong to a certain identity based on what they feel." Armen brought examples from his life experience; when in Lebanon, he had a different perception of himself, while afterward, the Australian environment had changed it. Despite the fact that he has never lived in Armenia and has been living in Australia for a couple of decades, his emotional attachment, as he emphasizes, is in Armenia. As an example, he specified, "if I were to attend a football match between Armenia and Australia, I would probably support the Armenian team, because the other is more the adopted identity." Armen justifies his perception of his own identity by saying, "I can be a proud Lebanese and a proud Australian, but I have my Armenian identity."

Living in the homeland or visiting it, as discussed previously, can contribute to strengthening the identity. Visitors "can touch and feel the homeland; it can transform their views," says Garo and emphasizes the importance of being exposed to Armenian schools, knowing more about the roots. Nevertheless, the identity transformation process is not straightforward, and it occurs in stages. "At a younger age, you would think you were more aligned to your heritage and perceived it blindly, as I did," says Levon and added that over time he realized the importance of heritage and had become more mature in terms of understanding it, which happened by 21, as he clarified.

To become more mature over time and more willing to understand and reinvent one's own identity, an important consideration is presented by Maria from the Melbourne community. To her, the career of a teacher also contributed to the need to be more mature, and she related to her own identity. Identity transformation is seen as a changing phenomenon by nearly all the interviewed diasporans. Mateos (the crypto-Armenian interviewee), for instance, admits that various environments affect identity and its perception:

> Friends, the host country, the political issues are all impacting. I do not see myself as an Armenian in America, France, or elsewhere, even though we have the same blood. We are not all the same. Even in the same city, we are different, from family to family. Maybe because of the age differences, it has been changing and, I believe, it is going to change in the future as well, because I do not have the same view on ideas or issues exactly same way as I have had before.

Understanding national identity goes beyond the diasporans' perception of it. It is broader and integrates two dimensions: the territorial and extraterritorial areas of existence. It can be argued that national identity, being supported by its pillars, not only combines elements of each of them but is also inevitably connected to the perception of the space of belonging. If briefly summarized, it is proposed that national identity is a coexistence (integration) of language mentality (culture, religion, and language make its core) and belonging to the homeland space. Having this integrated duo broken, arguably, can lead to a crisis of national identity.

Diasporans live in hostlands, in their political, social, economic, and cultural environment. Living simultaneously in the extraterritorial diaspora space, they are engaged within their community space and, to a certain extent, in the homeland. Now let's attempt to identify the links, which shape that connection.

Chapter 6

DIASPORA-HOMELAND: CONNECTION THROUGH SPACES

Engagement Within the Community

Geographer Elizabeth Mavroudi argues that for diasporans, communities continue to be important as they are "stretched and manipulated across time and space; places can become political tools in the process, symbolic and material stages on which people can perform acts of belonging" (Mavroudi, 2010: 251). Here we focus on the connections diasporans maintain within their community and with the homeland (Armenia, in our case), with a particular focus on types and places of engagement, and the different ways and frequency of their connection with Armenia, including physical connection. We also discuss knowledge of the Armenian language as one of the means of connection with the homeland.

Certainly, the discussion here cannot cover all possible aspects of diasporic engagement in their communities. As a narrative study of diasporans' experience in two selected cities, this study attempts to broaden understanding of diasporic life, challenges and concerns, rather than provide a statistical review. As in the case of any diaspora community, the Armenians in the two cities have also found their ways of return in part through community gathering and events. As anthropologists Martin Sökefeld and Susanne Schwalgin argue, a diaspora community is made of individuals who "are willing to identify themselves at least partly with a common imagination of identity or difference from others" (Transcomm.ox.ac.uk, 2000: 3). Certainly, not many in a diaspora community are equally active in community affairs. In the Armenian communities studied here (as estimated by the interviewed diasporans) on average, there is a community event taking place about once every three months. Diversity of events provides a good platform for those who are willing to participate in the community. Sometimes, there are also joint events organized between the Sydney and Melbourne communities. As

Helen from Melbourne says, "there is always something happening, and it has become more visible due to the Internet."

There is a range of Armenian organizations in both cities. However, as many interviewees have mentioned, the overall amount of participation and attendance in the events is not enough. This fact can be partly related to the relatively large size of the community, where members assume there will always be someone who will be actively engaged. Even if so, it does not mean that in smaller communities the sense of responsibility is necessarily stronger. Reflections given by the participants in this study provide a comprehensive picture of the overall level of diasporic engagement in the selected communities. All the interviewees emphasized their belonging to the diaspora – a fact which assumes their participation in community life, to a certain extent. Besides, in general, diaspora return is not limited to community gatherings or participation in events.

The physical connection to Armenia has been identified as an essential measure for the preservation of Armenian identity. Diaspora return, as proposed, is a three-dimensional phenomenon: within the community, between communities, and with the homeland. Possible differences between cultural and even language environments in communities and the homeland arguably can strengthen the role of intra-community relations. It is possible to feel foreign in the homeland, if one has not lived there for a relatively long time, or if the languages (dialects) spoken are distinct, or if the cultural environment is different. For instance, regarding the Armenians and Armenia, the influence of the Russian language (words, phrases, expressions) in the conversational language are often seen as a barrier for communication between Armenians in Armenia and the diaspora. Such a distinct language-cultural environment in the homeland can create a phenomenon when it is more comfortable to limit diaspora return to the intra-community level or, at its broadest level, to inter-community relations rather than to extend it and reach the homeland. Limited communication can potentially limit the extent to which both parts of the nation know each other, which, in turn, can affect their expectations of each other. Unrealistic expectations, if not fulfilled, can potentially cause mistrust in relations between the homeland and its diaspora.

Diaspora is an extraterritorial space, while cities, where diasporans live, are territorially defined spaces. Indeed, there are particular places diasporans gather or even associate themselves. At the same time, being diasporan is often perceived as being a part of that extraterritorial space. "I am the diaspora," says Vartan and continues, "I do not see myself as something else." He points out that it is quite difficult to explain to others what diaspora means. If said, by definition, that diasporans are people who live outside their homeland, then the explanation is incomplete. To Vartan, being a diasporan is a feeling, "which has some advantages, as it gives you strength and energy to continue your struggle." The sense of belonging to the diaspora is considered important and is seen as an inherent part of oneself. "When I am not around, some part of the diaspora will be gone with me," summarizes Vartan.

Helen considers herself an active diasporan, whose activity is mainly limited to intra-community relations, and her connection is "not so much with Armenia but with the community in Melbourne." Armen and Maria see keeping the connection within the community and with the homeland important as do other interviewees. Antonio emphasizes the need to maintain strong connections through diaspora institutions. He works with *Hamazkayin*[*] in his weekend (Saturday) school,[†] where, as specified, about 40 students study at the moment. "Their parents are of mixed nationality, one is normally Armenian," says Antonio. "They are trying to maintain the heritage. Almost every day I am doing something with the Armenians, be it electrical work free of charge or helping the Galstaun School,"[‡] he adds. Aram, a professional lawyer, comments that he is involved in a few organizations as well; for instance, he participates in organizing cultural and commemorative events and is involved in the AGBU.[**] "I would like to be more involved though," says Aram regretfully.

---

[*] Hamazkayin is the name of the Armenian Educational and Cultural Society, a non-profit organization, a structure linked to ARF (Hamazkayin, http://www.hamazkayin.com/en/history/).

[†] One of the six one-day Armenian schools in Australia (Hayern Aysor, http://hayernaysor.am/en/archives/date/2017/01/12).

[‡] One of the two Armenian day schools in Sydney and the whole of Australia, as mentioned above.

[**] AGBU, or the Armenian General Benevolent Union, is a global pan-Armenian institution, founded in 1906 in Cairo (Egypt), which "provides educational and cultural opportunities to Armenian youth" (AGBU, https://agbu.org/about/our-history/)

Types and Places of Engagement

Engagement of the diaspora in the homeland, first of all, aims at satisfying the emotional needs of diasporans, as well as contributing to the development of the homeland. Diaspora engagement, as proposed by ethnographer Giulia Sinatti and anthropologist Cindy Horst, identifies diaspora "as actual communities rooted in a national home and sharing a group identity" (Sinatti and Horst, 2015: 134-152). Connection within the community can be an expression of diaspora engagement. At the same time, however, the community is not seen as the only way of preserving the national identity and its roots. Michael Bazikian, after his nearly nine decades of diasporic life, reflects, "Yes, I feel part of the diaspora," and refers to Aghasi Aivazyan by quoting one of his works "forget about from-sea-to-sea-Armenia, make the current one developed."[*] Mr. Bazikian specifies that he is always in diaspora return; however, he has not participated in the community for a long time. To him, being connected to the homeland is, first of all, helping it financially, something, as he points, has not been done effectively. Mr. Bazikian expressed his disappointment at this and gave up being an active community member, "as there was no action in terms of helping on the individual level."

According to Mateos, the diasporic connection is a complex inter-spatial relationship. If seen static and one-way, it may lead to unreasonable and even false expectations. An interesting perspective was suggested by Vahe, according to whom, "the time has come to begin to move away from the emphasis on Armenia-diaspora into a model of one." Specific questions he brings up are: "What can an Armenian do for Armenia, either in the Republic or in the diaspora?" As presented, the dimension of the connection is seen not only through the diaspora-homeland prism but also from the standpoint of the Armenians in the homeland. So, Vahe suggests a very homeland-centric approach. The view is that the diaspora "was imposed upon us; we are one people," and adds that the inclusion of the diaspora as an active participant assumes making those active diasporans citizens of (the Republic of) Armenia.

There are schools, scouting groups, cultural, educational, sporting, political, and religious events in the diaspora. This diversity provides multi-

---

[*] Aghasi Ayvazyan (1925-2007) was an Armenian writer and film director (ArmenianHouse.org electronic library (in Russian), http://armenianhouse.org/aivazyan/aivazyan-ru.html).

faceted opportunities for those who want to continue to protect their identity, as Vahe specifies, and supports this view by specifying that "the Armenians have a strong sense of community and protection." He spoke about the community environment in the Middle East, where Armenians are a minority and are motivated to look for each other in such a distinct cultural and religious space. He brought an example of his recent visit to Jerusalem, where he spent most of the time in the Armenian Quarter in the Old City, with complete strangers, whom "you thought you knew for years."

The connection with the homeland, being through spaces, does face barriers. They can be geographic, determined by distances between communities and the homeland, and also between different communities. Barriers can also be of a non-geographical nature, with the most significant being intra-cultural and psychological. Such barriers assume difficulties in terms of understanding the other side, mainly because of differences in language and cultural environment. The issue of communication barriers is discussed in more detail later in this book.

The interviewees confirmed that they had some connections within their community and gathered from time to time within their respective communities. Even Mr. Bazikian, who is not active in the community now, maintains contacts with some community members.

Vahe, for example, is involved in event organization, attends church services once or twice a month, and sees them as important community events. Participation at a similar level has also been mentioned by Vartan. Generally speaking, churches in both Sydney and Melbourne are considered places for gathering, which are seen as necessary beyond liturgy service and religious and spiritual needs. The Armenian Apostolic Church, thus, apart from performing its religious functions, serves as a social networking place for community members. The Church over the centuries, as argued by historian Sebouh Aslanian (Aslanian, 2006: 401-402), has performed a rationally-motivated social role of connecting diasporans within their communities, and also communities and their homeland (the Mother Church or the Holy See in Armenia).

Attending a church service, participation in various events, including sports in local Armenian teams, as in the case of Maria from Melbourne, are examples of engagement in the community. She, however, thinks there is a disparity in terms of the attention paid to different communities. For instance, to her, the Sydney community is stronger because it has more people in it. An important issue raised is related to the inferior perception of smaller communities from the homeland. Compared to the community in Sydney, the community in Melbourne with about 10,000 Armenians is still perceived as small. "If they bring an Armenian singer, he or she usually goes to Sydney, and the youth there is much more in numbers," complains Maria. She, therefore, feels that sometimes the Melbourne Armenians are disadvantaged. Maria disagrees that being a center of many events, in the case of Sydney, is only an outcome of better organization and points to uninterrupted church services and priests as an important factors. "My parents told me that shortly after I was born (in the 1980s), I was going to be baptized, and my parents had to go to Sydney because there was no priest in Melbourne then," said Maria, emphasizing that the church was an example of an active diasporic cultural connection her family had.

The frequency of community events and gatherings is not consistent. The daily routine of diasporans makes it challenging to find time for more involvement in diaspora affairs. Connection to the homeland, thus, may take the form of individual activity, often virtual, through the use of electronic communications, most importantly, the Internet. According to Helen, a new opportunity has now been created to be more active, mainly through the use of the Internet. She adds that it was obviously not the case before.

Overall, there are various types of events taking place in the communities. As mentioned above, there are even events jointly organized by the communities of Sydney and Melbourne, such as sports events. On the other hand, the year 2015 was of crucial importance since it was the 100th anniversary of the most significant calamity befalling the Armenian people, the Genocide of 1915, which was commemorated worldwide, including in Sydney and Melbourne. According to the Ministry of Diaspora of Armenia, approximately 20-30 major events take place every year in the Armenian community in Australia (Ministry of Diaspora of Armenia, 2010: 161-162, 2011: 193-195, 2015: 151-152). For example, in 2015, 18 events were specified (Ministry of Diaspora of Armenia, 2015: 151-152), with 15 of them somehow related to the centennial events – a television marathon, in which a number of political and cultural Armenian organizations participated, with the attendance of Ms. Hranush Hakobyan, Minister of Diaspora of the Republic of Armenia, as well as the installation of commemoration memorials, issuance of resolutions

At the Tsitsernakaberd Memorial, Yerevan, April 24, 2017

recognizing the Genocide by town councils, protests against the denial of the Genocide by Turkey.* There were also events related to the establishment of Armenian Studies (in the University of Sydney), publications on the Genocide, presentations on the tragedy and its implications. A notable achievement for the community has been the appointment of Ms. Gladys Berejiklian, a member of the Armenian community, in the position of Treasurer of New South Wales and, later, her successful election as the Premier of New South Wales – the highest-ever government position held by an Armenian in Australia.

Some participate in diaspora events several times a year, as in the case of Anahit; she says that her close friends are all Armenians, and once or twice

---

* The Gallipoli Campaign or the Gallipoli Battle was a major battle during World War I, where 58,000 allied soldiers and 87,000 Ottoman soldiers died. Anzac Day (April 25), in remembrance of the event, is one of Australia's most important national days. (The Guardian, *What Happened at Gallipoli?*) Ironically, the day of the disastrous amphibious landings at Gallipoli coincided with the beginning of the Armenian Genocide (24 April 1915). As many argued, the larger-scale commemoration of the battle in 2015 by the Turkish authorities was to undermine the Armenian Genocide centennial commemoration events in 2015.

151

a week, they gather together, mainly for social events. "I hope Armenia will be better, and I hope one day I will live there," said Anahit. She continued that while a teenager, she used to rule out the idea of living in Armenia but not any longer. "I was telling my mother, 'just let me be Australian,'" an attitude which changed later, especially after her first visit to Armenia in her late-teens, as mentioned previously.

Vrej says that a lot of people of his age (late 30s – early 40s) are hardly involved with the Armenian community, though "I have made a decision to be a member of the community. Sometimes I sacrifice my time but do so for the community," he adds. Sometimes there are sports events, dinners, a once-a-month barbeque evening... There are also presentations and performances. The gatherings are mainly in the Armenian club, in the Church, at the school. *

Religious and cultural events, subscriptions to Armenian magazines published in Sydney (*Armenia, Karoun, Miutiun,* and *Luys*), gatherings in social clubs and formal organizations, such as the AGBU, ARF, in a day school (Galstaun College), dance parties (known as *barahantes*). These are various types of activities specified by interviewees. One of them, a high school teacher, pointed to her involvement in one of the committees at a diasporic institution as a treasurer and emphasized her recent more active engagement in community affairs. Weekend schools – Mesrop Mashtots Mateosian Varzharan and Aginian Varzharan, which is by the Church, are also among the places of activity.

With a range of activities conducted in communities, over time, as Levon worries, they have become mainly dinner banquets and fundraizing event. He admits that there are sports events organized as well, even though he, as mentioned, did not participate in them. This point was similar to what Helen and Maria specified, both from Melbourne. Maria says that she is more into Armenian dances and art. According to her, the most common place for a gathering is the Church. She finds it interesting there since the priest researches information related to a particular topic and brings it to a discussion. For Levon, the main places for gathering are community halls, the Church, and also the AGBU. "Not me directly, but through the family, I am also linked to the ARF," he says. Aram, a lawyer from Sydney, finds it difficult to participate frequently. Due to his

---

* The Galstaun College (a day school).

commitments, he now participates in about two functions a year. "There were charity events, cultural events; we used to gather in pubs," he concludes about his earlier years.

In Melbourne, according to Garo, participation is through mass events in the Church, commemoration events, such as anniversaries of the Genocide, school concerts, or cultural-dance events. "There are few organizations in Melbourne where we gather," says Garo and mentions Hay Gentron [Armenian Center], the AGBU, and also Sahagian Sporting Club.

A more specific opinion was brought up by Vartan, a person with a rich diasporic experience, including as a diaspora institution administrator: "Usually they are anniversaries," he says and opens up,

> Unfortunately, the usual gatherings just to come together and have fun are not there anymore. There were theatrical events before, where I used to present as well. Today, if you try to organize similar events, there will be difficulties, and less people find time and are willing to be present and participate in such events. Nowadays, mostly there are anniversaries of organizations or events. Because the community is getting bigger and bigger, we used to gather in halls. It is not coffee and tea anymore, and when people pay money for an event, the organizers are obliged to give more, to hire bigger and better halls for particular events.

Diasporic connections are there, first of all, to satisfy diasporans' thirst for sticking to their roots. However, despite this self-centeredness, any participation in a diaspora event or organization, by default, assumes diaspora return, return to the roots. In many cases, the connection is with other diasporans who have a similar origin. Return, as argued, is a root-centered phenomenon. Connections with the homeland can become more effective, from the homeland's policy viewpoint, if the needs of diasporans and their communities are identified by the homeland (policy-makers), based on understanding the roots but also the routes of the communities' formation. The routes, which pass through various spaces, carry living experiences and place-centered, often nostalgic, memory. As argued, such experiences influence diasporans, and understanding those routes can help policy-makers in the homeland to reach diasporans more efficiently and connect them to their roots (the homeland or its cultural representatives) more effectively. As specified earlier in the book, understanding the routes can help them understand the nature of diasporans, their needs, and, possibly, expectations. Realistic expectations are what can strengthen trust between the two parts of a nation – the homeland and the diaspora.

Technological development, social changes, economic conditions, geographic distances, and other possible factors can affect the engagement of the diaspora in the homeland. What used to take place frequently is now considered an event, as some of the interviewees mention with feelings of melancholy. Over time, generation after generation, the communication frequency is changing. According to Vartan, "If it was two or three times a week, now is about once a month."[*] This decrease affects the quality of the relationship, and it suffers within society, including among family members, as Vartan observes. According to him, community events, once engaging whole families, now take place at individual levels with only part of a family engaged in them. Now, it is more difficult to have a whole family participating in or attending a community event, and fewer diasporans engage their whole families.

Several interviewees agree that the Armenian community in Sydney, being the largest in Australia, provides a broader platform for diasporic events. The number of diaspora institutions enriches that platform. On the one hand, it is easier for such a large community to maintain national identity. However, a large community size, arguably, can make the sense of responsibility each diaspora community member carries weaker. In smaller communities, participation of each diasporan is more visible and, thus, the sense of responsibility can push community members to be more involved in community affairs.

The frequency of community gatherings, among other factors, depends on people's involvement in diaspora institutions. Vrej, for instance, as a member of one of the largest and most influential organizations in the diaspora, the Armenian Revolutionary Federation (ARF), is involved in meetings "as a must." He says that he even takes his child to the Church, at least once every three months, as well as attending some gatherings around once a month. Vrej stresses that it is important to understand one's own identity and to keep the identity of the children strong. According to him, once children reach their youth and enter the real world, "they are alone to find their own identity." To him, the intimate connections and communications in the community are gone, and events now are

---

[*] The interviews were conducted before 2020 (before the COVID-19-related social and travel limitations).

becoming more formal and mainly attended by the older generation of the community.

Mateos, the crypto-Armenian, discloses that over time he has become more active as a community member. Even before, when living in Turkey, there were gatherings among the Muslim Armenian community members.

> A stranger cannot know whether the person is an Armenian; however, when you talk, you introduce yourself as an Armenian, they can say the same thing. In Turkey, you can identify somehow but cannot know for sure. We even participated in a university conference there called 'Armenians were forced to be Muslim,' where a lot of Muslim Armenians gathered.

After such an undercover diasporic experience, now in an open community in Australia, Mateos has become more engaged in the community, mainly in the Church.

> Here in Australia, I go to the Church, on average, once every other Sunday. In Australia, people do not know me, and I can go to the Church. My Turkish friends do not know I am Armenian. I even participated in Armenian groups, such as for 100 anniversary-related events,[*] a symposium, an art gallery.

Diasporic return means a connection within the nation. The homeland, indeed, is the cultural center for the diaspora. To a significant extent, it is also the political center or should become such. Understanding the connections diasporans maintain with Armenia is another aspect we aim to identify.

Connecting to Armenia: Barriers and Opportunities

Armenia is the territorial homeland nation-state for Armenians. The Armenian diaspora has developed into a globally-spread extraterritorial body, connection with which is seen as rationally beneficial for Armenia, particularly from the economic perspective. At the same time, the stronger the engagement of the diaspora to Armenia, the more the political sovereignty of the homeland may be challenged. Engagement of the diaspora assumes an unbiased connection with the whole diaspora, irrespective of the location of communities. This point implies understanding the needs of communities in different parts of the world

---

[*] Events to commemorate the 100th anniversary of the Armenian Genocide, held mainly in 2015.

and efforts to meet those needs, which, certainly, entails some sacrifice, including political. The opportunity cost of such engagement creates a paradox for the nation-state. As a territorial entity, the state comes to understand that national integrity could be different from territorial integrity. What anthropologist Arjun Appadurai emphasizes is that "loyalty often leads individuals to identify with transnational cartographies," and the efforts of a nation-state to accommodate diasporic groups "without giving up on the principle of territorial integrity" is less likely to continue (Low and Lawrence-Zuniga, 2003: 347).

Diasporans' connections to the homeland, even if cultural, at a distance, with no experience of physical connection to the homeland can still strengthen attachment to the homeland since the homeland is largely idealized. Language, probably, is the most powerful tool in communication with the diaspora. An ability to communicate in the homeland's language, as it logically sounds, can make the engagement of the diaspora in the homeland even more effective. Armenian is the official language in Armenia. However, it has two main dialects – Eastern Armenian, which is in use in Armenia, and among Armenians in countries of the former Soviet Union, as well as in Iran, in India and some parts of communities in North America and Europe, is carried by diasporans who have originated either from Armenia or historically from Iran (then the Persian Empire). In most other cases, the Western Armenian dialect prevails. The dialects, if spoken correctly, to a large extent, are mutually intelligible. However, the lack of understanding of certain cultural aspects of Armenia created by the Russian (Soviet) language-cultural influence has created a specific barrier for Western Armenian speakers in terms of their cultural integration in Armenia. This condition is a barrier to their effective communication with Armenians in Armenia. Many diasporans, to avoid any misunderstanding and as cultural resistance, use a foreign language (e.g., English) in their communication while in Armenia. The dual-dialect language system, arguably, has contributed to the weaker-than-expected level of knowledge of each other by the two sides of the nation, and as a derivative, to having their mutual trust challenged. Besides, certain stereotypes which prevent effective communication between the two spaces – Western Armenian-speaking communities and Armenia-based (or communities in the Eastern Armenian-speaking world), have contributed, to a certain extent, to the level of mutual intolerance. Such misunderstanding between the two sides of one nation further strengthens the communication barrier between them. As a step forward, in December 2016, the Minister of Education and Science of Armenia addressed the need to establish a Western Armenian cultural-language center in Armenia (168.am, *Centre for Western Armenian*). However, since then, no specific actions have been materialized.

Two-thirds of the interviewees have specified their frequent connection with Armenia. Reading news from Armenia, TV shows, articles online, watching movies have been specified as ways of connection. "I follow what is happening in Armenia," says Armen and adds that it is done on a daily basis. It is the same practice, several times a week, "quite often," say Garo and Levon. They read Armenian news, articles, watch movies, and also read the Bible. "I keep the connection alive," Levon stresses.

A permanent connection, in some form, has been established by Helen and Anahit. Helen, who has never been to Armenia, says she reads newspapers from time to time, including church news. She is also a subscriber to a magazine (*Armenian Life*) and reads it regularly. "I have no friends in Armenia, and going through the magazines once every two months keeps me in the loop of what is going on in Armenia." Possessing no formal connection with the homeland, nor relatives or friends, Helen thinks that direct participation in Armenia can be exercised mainly by providing material assistance For instance, she mentioned her husband's visit to Armenia long ago, after the earthquake of 1988, adding, "Such a tragedy helped to strengthen the identity." Anahit, whose country of origin is Armenia, underlines that she has relatives in Armenia and talks to them about once a week. She adds, "I follow news on Armenia, some Armenians on social networks, watch various shows on Armenian TV online."

Virtual communication as a connection, e.g., through Skype, was mentioned by Antonio and Aram. Listening to music, reading about Armenia, about politics in Armenia, according to Aram, are other ways he is in Armenia. "To some extent, I am aware of what is going on in Armenia, probably on a weekly basis," he stresses. "Calling Armenia is quite pricey, but calls are made regularly," says Michael Bazikian. As he describes, his advanced years do not allow him to be more flexible and use the Internet extensively. Instead, he relies on a more traditional means of communication – the telephone. Reading books, which he purchased in Armenia, to him, are also ways he feels himself in Armenia.

Bedros' connection with Armenia has been active for decades. Other than following the news on what is happening in Armenia, he reads diasporan newspapers, and a lot related to culture and science there; he keeps contacts with the Armenian Virtual College,[*] which he mentions as a very important educational institution. "I also have a connection with some people who are well-known in the political arena there," says Bedros. The years spent in Armenia, to him, have created a sound platform regarding diaspora-Armenia relations and, as Bedros says, he has always been in Armenia, and his presence in Australia has no relationship with his identity. This example is that of living in one space and physically residing in another.

"I have a higher-than-average communication with Armenia," Vahe says and adds that "many people do not know how to make the connection." In a broader sense, he sees strengthening the connection through the institute of citizenship. "Until you become a citizen, 'one nation, one people,' communication will not become a viable thing," Vahe stresses and adds that citizenship can help to strengthen that connection. He raises the point that many people do not even realize how citizenship can help to make the connection.

Regarding connection with Armenia, Vartan has identified problems that instigate communication among the younger generation. "The language sometimes is a very big barrier," he highlights. Despite TV and radio channels, among diasporans, "most of the reaction is that they cannot understand the language, especially as people in Armenia are talking so quickly, that it cannot be caught what they mean." The speech is very fast for many diasporans, as Vartan reflects, especially in "the case for the new generation... many speak Austral-Armenian," jokes Vartan and continues that they "have problems understanding pure fast Armenian language."

Another barrier that has been highlighted as a problem is the geographic distance between the communities in Australia and Armenia. Vrej points out that he is not connected to Armenia effectively, as geographical barriers stop him being there more often. He adds that his only connection with Armenia is as an advisor to a company he joined

---

[*] AGBU Armenian Virtual College (AVC) provides learners "with an opportunity to receive a full-fledged education in Armenian Studies" (AVC, *Mission*).

recently. The two interviewed teachers from Melbourne also stated that they were not well-connected with Armenia. "I do not know if there are any relatives in Armenia, other than my father's cousin, with whom there is no communication," Lily says sadly, and adds that she does not read anything from Armenia, unfortunately. Maria goes into more details. To her, the connection is mainly through culture. She likes to sing and remembers a lot of songs taught by her grandmother. Now, she says that living in Australia makes it "difficult to keep the identity, when the surroundings are foreign, while in Armenia everything is Armenian." As mentioned earlier, in Australia, Armenian tends to become the second language, unlike the situation in the Middle East, for instance, where it remains the first for most Armenians. "You have to find the balance to incorporate the Armenian language so that you do not lose it," summarizes Maria. The surroundings, to her, is the reason why so many ethnic Armenians (as she estimates, 60-70% of all) have lost their Armenian identity and are not diasporans but only ethnic Armenians. It is quite interesting that the number is opposite to what Helen specified in a separate conversation (out of about 10,000 Armenians in Melbourne, as subjectively estimated, 70% can be considered diasporan Armenians). Archbishop Najarian of Sydney reflects that, in Australia, the Armenian identity has been mainly preserved by second-generation Armenians [the second generation counted after the Genocide], while in the case of the U.S., in comparison, 3-4 generations have been the ones keeping their identity as Armenians. This statement assumes that there are many assimilated Armenians in Australia. His Eminence estimated that only about 10% as diasporan Armenians in Australia, with the rest being only "ethnic transnationals." At the same time, he also recognized that the sense of national identity among Armenians has increased, not only overseas in the diaspora, but also in Armenia itself.

Thus, with no attempt to derive a statistically-based conclusion, based on rough and subjective estimates of diasporans, still, about 1/3 to 2/3 of all ethnic Armenians can be considered 'ethnies' but not diasporans. With regard to the surrounding environment, Mateos, probably the most diverse interviewee in this study, brings an example from his real-life experience. In Turkey, as he said, there is an Armenian newspaper. However, it does not relate to Armenia but the Armenian community in Turkey. "Here too, in Australia, every day I read the same newspaper, so I know what is going on in the community," he adds. He is not much aware about what is going on in Armenia.

Communication with the homeland supports diasporans' stay in permanent return. Communication technologies have enabled the connection with the homeland to be faster and multi-faceted. They also provide diasporans with an opportunity to establish direct connections with the homeland, at the individual level, unlike in the old days, when a connection could be maintained through the community and its institutions. Due to communication technologies, geographic distance to the homeland or other communities stop being a major limitation since any diasporan from anywhere in the world can be connected to anyone, anywhere. It is the efficiency of networking that becomes the leading indicator for the effective engagement with the homeland.

Knowledge of Armenian Language

Only one interviewed diasporan in our study had no Armenian language skills. It is not a surprise, as he was the only one, who, most of his life, could not openly show his *Armenianness*, while living in Turkey. With some attempts made to learn the language in his late-teenage years, Mateos found the language difficult to learn and stopped. "In Turkey, we cannot learn Turkish as the second language in the school. So, we have to learn Turkish as the first language," said Mateos and continued that there was a local Armenian school; however, he could not go there, as he was not registered as an Armenian in Turkey. "In Turkey, I am a Muslim Turk," adds Mateos. To learn the language of his ancestors, for Mateos, is a double-challenge. To do so, he should overcome the difficulty of learning a language. Besides, experiencing the permanent crisis of identity (and of keeping his identity undisclosed) can act as a blocker on his way of learning the language.

All other interviewees have never had a problem with openly showing their Armenian identity. It is another point whether they speak Armenian, which is in use in the Republic of Armenia (the Eastern dialect). Lily shared her story that when visiting Armenia, she and her husband were mainly speaking English. It is not that they cannot speak Armenian, even though some diasporans face a psychological barrier, as the Western Armenian dialect, to a certain extent, is perceived socially foreign in Armenia. The problem was in understanding informal daily Armenian in

Armenia, with a lot of Russian words and phrases used, which are entirely unintelligible for speakers of Western Armenian. Overall, Lily marks her knowledge of the language at '5.5' out of '10,' and adds that such accuracy is judged based on her professional perception as a high school teacher. "I can communicate and make my points across, but the knowledge is not very strong," she says. Her communication in Western Armenian happens every day at home, but not 100% of the day:

> I speak it to my son. When directly speaking to him, then only Armenian. When the child is around, with my husband, we speak only Armenian. The child does not know any English; he can pick it up later anyway. He knows only Armenian. My father is a lot stronger among both parents, and I am weak in the written language, maybe '3' out of '10.' The reading skills are also limited. I read better than I write. I read slowly though.

It is interesting to note that Lily does not read Armenian often. A rhetorical 'chicken-and-egg' question could be asked whether this is because she is not good at reading Armenian or because she does not read often. Lily participates in the Hamazkayin cultural organization, so "when I need to read, I do, probably once a month," she says. "I have been in *Hamazkayin* as steps to learn the language and threw myself into it semi-selfishly because I wanted to become more Armenian."

The interviews made it clear that many pre-school children in diasporic Armenian families can speak Armenian only. It is later, after they go to a primary school, when they pick up English. Vahe emphasizes the strong role of the family environment in developing the sense of identity. He related in conversation that his language knowledge had been limited to Armenian only by the time he went to school. His parents thought, if not preserved, it would not be maintained, so they spoke Armenian at home. Vahe studied at a local school and also studied at an Armenian Saturday school in Sydney. Today, as he estimates, 90% of his conversations with relatives and friends are in Armenian. "When speaking Armenian, I think in Armenian," he stresses.

Vartan proudly stated that his communication is based on Armenian 70% of the time, as he estimates, due to his day-to-day involvement in diaspora organizational affairs. His knowledge of Eastern and Western Armenian allows him to speak Armenian both at home and also freely within the community, whatever dialect people speak there.

The environment where Armenian is in use has changed for most of the interviewees. Before, in the Middle East, where many of them come from, Armen emphasizes that, it used to be "at the household, in the school, with friends, kids in the street, even when shopping." The difference is that in Australia, at home, the language is Armenian with parents and family members, while it is English in the outside environment. At work, it is mixed, where the workplace is somehow related to *Armenianness*, clarifies Armen. However, even if the language environment is still Armenian, the language is mainly used verbally, with less written (formal) Armenian applied.

"I can speak and I think in Armenian when I talk to myself," Michael Bazikian says. He also mentions that he reads Armenian books, almost every day. However, he does not write often. Bedros emphasizes the need to use Armenian all the times at least in the two Armenian day schools (in Sydney). Anahit, who even went to a primary school in Armenia, has stopped reading and writing Armenian. "I have taken some steps toward recovering how to read and write, but I gave up, as I needed someone to help me," she says. However, Anahit speaks the language to all her relatives except for her daughter, because, as she explains, speaking English is essential for her to be ready for kindergarten. "If there is anyone from Armenia, I will speak Armenian," she says, even by shifting to the Western dialect, to overcome the communication barrier.

Garo, Levon, and Maria also specify that they speak Armenian in their families and with friends and relatives on a daily basis, as well as at Church. They can also read and write in Armenian. Levon's case is a bit special. Being the only one among the interviewees who has lived in both Melbourne and Sydney, he has studied at the St. Gregory School in Sydney for five years[*] and, after several years since then, he moved to Melbourne. Thus, Levon's view reflects his dual-city diasporic experience.

Helen also speaks Armenian within her family. Her case is also unique since she speaks Armenian with both parents, including her mother, who is ethnic Assyrian. "I speak Armenian with my Armenian friends. My dad took us to an Armenian weekend school," Helen said, and made it clear

---

[*] An Armenian Catholic school which does not exist anymore, and its site has been sold to the Australian Federation of Islamic Councils (ArmeniaOnline, *St. Gregory's Armenian Church*).

that it had not been enough. She reads Armenian but not often and adds that she made no effort to learn the written language.

Vrej has reflected on his Armenian language skills by saying that a balance is needed regarding speaking and reading. "From childhood, conditions were supporting it. I take steps to keep myself reading, and I do write, but very slowly and not well," he says and clarifies that his Armenian is exclusively Western Armenian, even though he can understand when he reads the Eastern dialect. Vrej used to go to a local weekend school during his school age, has grown up in an Armenian-speaking environment, and participated in sport and cultural events. "I speak Armenian with friends, with children; they do understand the language, even though their mother is not Armenian," Vrej says. He makes it clear that he has been taking conscious steps to maintain the language.

Aram and Antonio, the other two interviewees, speak the language at home. Aram uses Armenian to speak with his parents. His wife is a Lebanese Armenian; however, as Aram makes it clear, she does not speak Armenian, even though she understands some of it. Aram grew up in Jordan, where there were no Armenian schools and he had no opportunity to learn how to read and write in Armenian. Antonio, on the other hand, says that he speaks Armenian at home on a daily basis. With his education in Armenian, English, French, and Arabic, he confesses that his children predominantly use English, and the only other language they use is Armenian when they are at home.

Most of the interviewed diasporans, in both Sydney and Melbourne, have shown their determination toward maintaining at least the spoken Armenian language as a way of keeping their Armenian identity alive. In the absence of a supportive Armenian language environment, living in space, where assimilation is tempting, it becomes easier not to use the language. However, as seen, many diasporans have taken specific steps toward the preservation of the Armenian language, at least in the spoken form. At the same time, the use of written Armenian is limited. The communication problem between Armenia and its diaspora caused by a difference between the two main dialects and the limited use of Western Armenian, as argued, can be softened with more active physical connection with Armenia.

Physical Connection with Armenia

A stronger connection to the homeland assumes a stronger sense of national identity. Connections with the homeland space include reaching people and also places. In case it is hard to establish connections with people in the homeland – because of communication barriers, most importantly through language use – then, connecting to places becomes a shortcut for more efficient engagement in the homeland. Here in this book, physical connection to the homeland has been studied through the prism of the personal experience of the interviewees' – their physical presence in Armenia, be it in the form of tourism, work-related trips, experience of living there, or any other time spent there.

One out of every three interviewed diasporan has never been to Armenia. If we apply Nigel Thrift's classification of space to their case, the homeland space can be perceived in the form of any of the three kinds of spaces ('empirical constructions,' 'unblocking space,' and 'image space'), but not as 'place space.' This is because, without a first-hand (intimate) personal experience, it becomes virtually impossible to develop the perception of space as place. Even with a good knowledge of places, developed at a distance, perception is still limited to conceptual understanding, as Yi-Fu Tuan would describe it (Tuan, 2011: 6). Intimate knowledge, on the other hand, can strengthen the sense of belonging and, thus, as a derivative, the sense of national identity.

Helen, with her strong sense of *Armenianness*, as expressed during our conversation, imagines her possible visit to Armenia as "an abstract wish." She specified that she had never made plans to visit Armenia. If visiting it one day, she would like to go to churches, to Etchmiadzin in particular, and also to enjoy the food there. "I would like to go around Yerevan, to music places, concerts," she adds. Neither Helen nor any other interviewee had prior information on the questions asked, so that none of them had prepared answers, particularly related to places for possible visits in Armenia.

It is undoubtedly an issue of time and finance before making plans to visit the homeland. Diasporans' physical permanent return can be considered the ultimate goal of the diaspora's existence, of the meaning of 'diaspora' as a concept. At the same time, the wish to visit the homeland might not lead to a real physical return, even if there is no major barrier to doing so. For instance, in the case of Armenia, its independence in 1991 opened its borders to the diaspora, and many people became capable of repatriating to Armenia permanently. However, even if people often declared as a wish to go to the Hayrenik (Fatherland) before Armenia's independence was achieved, many never even visited it. Four other interviewees also expressed their willingness to visit Armenia and even made specific preliminary plans; however, for some reasons, the plans have not been fulfilled yet. "I do want to go to Armenia. I wanted to go this year for the Pan-Armenian Games," said Maria. For Mateos, the objective was to be in Armenia during the Genocide centennial commemoration events.[*] However, as mentioned, he, too, could not make the trip.

If visiting Armenia, Mateos would like to go to some historical buildings, "maybe museums, ancient buildings, churches…" However, he emphasized that he did not see Armenia as his homeland. "I do not see Armenia as my homeland. If I go to France, I will go to similar places," he emphasizes. Crypto-Armenians, as a segment of the global 'Armenian World,' have been understudied, and it is not certain if their perception of Armenia changes after their first visit there. This opens a large void for further study in the field.

For Maria in Melbourne, her priorities on a visit to Armenia would be the Cathedral of Etchmiadzin: "to experience looking at *khachkars*;[†] I want to visit Tsitsernakaberd,[‡] the main sightseeing places," she says, and adds that she would like to explore more and go to concerts to experience Armenian music, the arts, the zoo, and also to visit the Cascade in the center of Yerevan, "where the view on Mount Ararat opens." Even though some of the interviewees, who have never been to the homeland, have a certain perception of places there, their familiarity is not at the intimate but knowledgeable level. It is a concept or an image through which they perceive those places. Indeed, the meaning of places cannot be abstract and needs to be viewed within a complex of how migrants (diasporans, in this context) relate "themselves to the spatial by focusing on practices, social relations, different locations, etc.," specifies geographer Knut Hidle, who

---

[*] 100th Anniversary of the Armenian Genocide – the *Medz Yeghern*, commemorated in 2015.

[†] *Khachkar* (literally 'cross' and 'stone') is a type of Armenian medieval art. It is a sculpture of the cross in stone, placed vertically, facing the West (Armenian Encyclopedia, *Khachkar*).

[‡] The Armenian Genocide memorial in Tsitsernakaberd, in Yerevan (mentioned above).

emphasizes the need "to treat places in different meaning contexts" (Hidle, 2001: 11).

Four out of fifteen interviewed diasporans have visited Armenia twice, and one – only once. For all four of them, it was a short-term touristic visit. Vrej, being very specific about his plans, mentioned that he would like to visit Armenia once every two years and see, in particular, the post-100th anniversary Armenia. "I would like to go for a holiday trip, not work-related," he says. "We have driven all over the country, have seen the country, and would like to visit Karabakh (Artsakh) next time," as well as many churches, and go hiking and mountain climbing.[*] Such listing of places was quite abstract and did not reflect an emotional attachment to any particular place. A reason behind this, as argued above, could be a lack of any intimate perception of the homeland (Armenia) as a place space.

Armen mentioned that he visited Armenia twice, the second time with his family, fifteen years after the first visit, which was in 1986 when Armenia was still one of the republics of the Soviet Union. The first trip was to participate in a summer camp in Tsaghkadzor, one of the key resort destinations in the country, from which they traveled to various other regions in Armenia. When imagining his next visit to Armenia, Armen specified the country's regions far from the capital city, as well as Artsakh, "to see the country, the outskirts." His main reason behind such a visit was to go with the family, with children, so that they "will be educated by being a part of that, maybe to acquire property there, maybe one day even to decide to move there. I want to go for more connection to Armenia," specifies Armen.

For all the interviewees who have already been to Armenia, particular places have remained and continued to revolve in their memory. Garo visited Armenia twice within just three years. He specified that the first time it was an eight-day trip in 2012, while the second, for 16 days, was during the Pan-Armenian Games in 2015. This visit took place after our first conversation, before we met for the second time, already in Perth, where he moved for work from Melbourne. He shared that during his second visit to Armenia, he had been all-around Armenia, stayed in Yerevan, and traveled

---

[*] The conversation was held when the whole territory of the Republic of Artsakh was controlled by its government. The Second Artsakh War in 2020 has left a significant part of Artsakh's land under the control of Azerbaijan (as mentioned earlier in the book).

to many regions of the country. On his next visit, he plans to revisit monasteries and churches. "I would like to meet up with my friends, spend some time with them, to participate in a mass, let's say in Tatev."[*]

Antonio's case, probably, has been the most special in this regard. After his first visit to Armenia, he became determined for a big challenge, to fulfill a dream probably every Armenian thinks about. During his first trip in 2005, occasionally, he met two tourists, a British and a Norwegian, whom Antonio encouraged to watch an Armenia-Netherlands football match in Yerevan. Then one of the men told him about his recent climb to the top of Mount Ararat, where he went through Georgia.[†] Antonio became excited with the idea and expressed a strong desire to climb the mountain two years later, in 2007. However, earlier that year, Hrant Dink, a prominent Armenian journalist in Turkey, was murdered in Istanbul,[‡] and Antonio had to postpone the trip. In 2009, his wish came true and he climbed Mount Ararat. When talking about this experience, he turned quite emotional:

> There were stages with stays in a tent. I was climbing with a song, kept singing. I felt no pain, was the oldest person; there were two others, also Armenians – an Iranian medical doctor and a Canadian working in the United Nations. We were talking Armenian, Arabic, and Spanish, and the Kurdish tour guide was gentle. At the summit, I collapsed on my knees, it was my reaction, and I noticed the other two [Armenian] guys doing same.

---

[*] Tatev Monastery is a 9th century historical complex. During "medieval times Tatev Monastery was a vital scholastic, enlightenment and spiritual center and played a singular role in the country's history" (TaTever, *Tatev Complex*). Situated in southern Armenia, Tatev Monastery is now linked by the Wings of Tatev, the aerial tramway, which makes the historical site more accessible to the public and tourists (TaTever, *Tatev Complex*).

[†] The border of Armenia with Turkey has remained closed since the beginning of Armenia's independence, as part of the economic blockade initiated by Turkey, in solidarity with Azerbaijan, to support the latter in the Karabakh conflict. Therefore, it is not possible to travel to Turkey by land from Armenia.

[‡] "Dink, 52, managing editor of the bilingual Turkish-Armenian weekly *Agos*, was shot outside his newspaper's offices in Istanbul, on January 19, 2007. As the Committee to Protect Journalists (CPJ) reported, "Dink had received numerous death threats from nationalist Turks who viewed his iconoclastic journalism, particularly on the mass killings of Armenians in the early 20th century, as an act of treachery" (CPJ, *Hrant Dink*).

Antonio's engagement in Armenia involved three weeks of volunteer work building homes, a gift to a school in one of the regions in Armenia. He said that he was willing to continue his volunteer mission and to climb Mount Aragats, the highest peak in Armenia proper, on his next trip. A touching experience he shared was about an American Armenian he met during the more recent visit, who also brought by his daughters to Armenia. He confessed that wherever they went in Armenia, he was sprinkling his wife's ashes there. The whole of Armenia space, thus, had become a space of emotional attachment for that family. Antonio felt such regret that he had not met the person earlier and told him that, had he known about it, he would have taken some of the ashes to the top of Mt. Ararat.

Visiting Armenia for diasporan Armenians, however, does have barriers. For Lily, visiting Armenia was a stopover travel, on the way to the United States. "During the week-long trip there, I was excited to be closer to my heritage, felt extremely proud, especially when I saw Mount Ararat," Lily says and continues, "I thought I would be able to form many friends and communicate a lot. However, it did not happen." The main issue was the dialect barrier. Apparently, speaking Armenian within a diaspora community space can be a different experience compared to doing it in the homeland. In the diasporic space, arguably, any deviation (dialect) is more or less widely acceptable, on the background of the host country's language. Even if not, to a certain extent, the diasporans tend to find their communication niche and narrow their circle to people-carriers of the same dialect. However, the situation appears to be different in a very homogenous (language- or dialectwise) environment, such as Armenia. The perception of foreignness in the case of a dialect differing from the primary language can become a serious communication barrier. Generally speaking, even if both sides can comprehend each other, for the diasporans, the environment might not be motivating to speak the mother tongue (the homeland's language), and they shift back to their hostland country's language. It might not only be a matter of natural communication between the diasporans but also a measure to avoid being perceived foreign in their own homeland space.

This is a paradoxical situation. Usually, locals in every country tend to welcome visitors when they (try to) speak the local language, even if the visitors are not fluent speakers. Here the example shows that the visiting diasporans shift to English because they feel or believe (this might be even a subjective perception) that the way they speak, because of its difference from the local dialect, is less acceptable by the locals. Such perception (which might even be a misperception) can further strengthen the cultural barrier between the diaspora and the homeland.

Within this context, an interesting example was brought by Lily from her above-mentioned visit to Armenia. She remembered a lady who told her in her hotel, "Why speak English while you are in Armenia? How else could you have a perspective of your motherland? So, speak Armenian!" This was not only her opinion. Lily also remembered a five-year-old boy who told her that in Armenia, she should speak Armenian. "I felt if such a young boy accused us of speaking a foreign language, we felt more to speak Armenian." In Armenia, they went cross-country, covered from North (Gyumri) to South (Tatev Monastery), and Etchmiadzin – the Mother See of the Apostolic Church, went to the Opera House, the Cascade, the Vernissage[*] in Yerevan. A special emotional attachment was expressed about the Cascade – an example of a place-centric perception of space.

It is interesting to observe that the nature of the Armenians as a global nation (or a global tribe) is being "intensely place-conscious," and not "place bound," as Jivan Tabibian, a scholar and diplomat, specifies (Tabibian, in Ember et al., 2005: 46). This factor, on the one hand, enables the Armenians to be emotional and, therefore, attached to certain places and, on the other hand, allows them to create a new place in a newly settled space. Such possibility is enabled by the strongly localized nature of the Armenian diaspora, with "sedentary centers and a mobile population" (Ember et al., 2005: 46).

Michael Bazikian told a story about his first visit to Armenia, which initially became a big surprise to him. The visit, as he said, further strengthened his sense of Armenian identity, compared to what he had carried until he arrived in Armenia, even though, to him, his belonging to *Armenianness* had always been strong. The trip was a gift from Mr. Bazikian's son on his father's 80th birthday anniversary. After that visit, he has traveled to Armenia almost every other year and stayed there for nearly six months each time. These journeys to the roots opened room for thoughts and even disappointments related to the poverty cases he witnessed in Armenia, the living conditions, "wondering why such an old nation should

[*] The Vernisazh is the main souvenir market located in the center of Yerevan.

be in such a condition." He labeled the situation as a shame for diasporan Armenians "because, compared to their lives, we live in luxury." To Michael Bazikian, this fact led him to make a strong statement that such indifference toward "our brothers and sisters in Armenia" was an outcome of a loss of identity. By losing their national identity, according to Mr. Bazikian, the diasporans are in ignorance and do not care to know how Armenians live in Armenia, and they have lost the ability to appreciate the revival of the culture there. In particular, Mr. Bazikian mentioned the music field in Armenia. "Armenians love to have guests but lack money," it was his impression. "There is no courage to visit again," he says regretfully, in particular, by talking about his age as a barrier. Despite this, Mr. Bazikian speaks very emotionally about a possible perspective of living the rest of his life in Armenia. "I will be much happier there than anywhere else in the world," he says, but points to possible problems with medical services, which might not suit his needs at his age. Mr. Bazikian also highlighted problems of corruption in Armenia, as it was perceived in the early-2010s, when he was visiting Armenia. He emphasized the visibility of corruption and mentioned that probably that visible existence was a result of the small scale of the country and its economy. "Because Armenia is small, corruption is very visible and is the main obstacle," specifies Mr. Bazikian.

Vahe was 21 when he visited Armenia for the first time. Since then, his visits took place once a year, on average. As revealed, there were some expectations before his first trip to Armenia. Having visited several countries before that trip, Vahe had certain expectations of Armenia and even some hesitations. Dreams of Ararat and Armenia, and his ancestors' story, as he described his thoughts, he also knew of the hardships in the country, the resilience of the people, "with an experience of surviving a genocide, then decades of Soviet rule, the 1988 Earthquake, the war in Artsakh." However, as mentioned, "the exciting side was that there is a republic now, with all its problems, and it exists." Vahe spoke about his first shock, shortly after his arrival in Yerevan, relating to the language (dialect) barrier. Again, the difference in the dialects was specified as probably the main problem in communication between the homeland and its diaspora. The difference between Armenia and the diaspora is not seen just as a geographical split. Vahe touches on an essential point that, first and foremost, is the difference in the mentality of Armenians in Armenia and the diaspora. Among other possible factors, such a difference is related

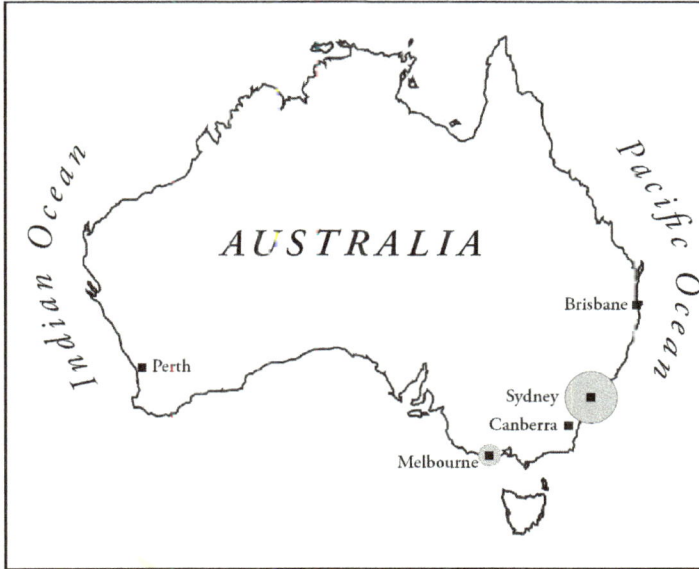

Armenians in Australia live mostly in Sydney and Melbourne

to knowledge about the diaspora among the local Armenians in Armenia. In particular, one of the causes can be a homogenous perception of the diaspora, and that is a major fallacy. For instance, the Armenian diaspora in Australia, being diverse in terms of its roots and structure, is often perceived as a homogenous community by the homeland nation-state.

Armenians can be found in many countries and cities around the world. However, it is only in Armenia, where, as Vahe stresses, "you come down the street, and when you buy something, you speak Armenian, everything is in Armenian." Apart from visiting Armenia as a tourist, Vahe had an opportunity to be there in an official capacity, too.

> There were two identities – Australian and Armenian. In the diaspora, a lot of people take Armenia for granted. We sat with the head of state, of an internationally-recognized state, for an hour-long discussion with the President, in an official capacity. Since a very young age, my attachment to *Armenianness* was very strong. This visit and the meeting led me to think that the diaspora could do more for Armenia. We also visited Artsakh.

Vahe underlines the difficulty of explaining in Australia (a country with no land neighbors) what problems Armenia, a landlocked country, has been facing. Then he goes further and speaks about the importance of effective communication between the diaspora and Armenia. As he believes, the perception of identity in Armenia changes and is being affected when non-Armenians visit them. The Armenia space is seen as unique to Vahe, who adds, "If we, the family, plan to visit Europe tomorrow, Armenia would be a destination on the way, even for some five days." He points at emigration from Armenia as a key national security challenge. "We need to build the infrastructure and the economy so that Armenians would not want to leave the country." In the near future, he would like to visit Gyumri, to go to (what is known as) 'Western Armenia' in modern Turkey, "to get as close as possible to see Ani."[*]

Vartan had a longer life experience in Armenia, where he studied for several years. For this reason, he does not plan to go there for sightseeing. Instead, he says, "I am not interested as a tourist and prefer to meet the locals, to visit churches, monuments, to visit specific places I have been before, also to go the far north."

Anahit, who was born in Armenia, had traveled there more frequently, after her visit in her teenage years. "I remember how excited I was before going to Armenia. I was talking to my mother about Armenia over and over." Anahit then got emotional about the following planned visit and stated that she expected to see everything remaining the same as before. There was a year she visited Armenia even twice, returning a month after the first visit. This second visit was quite challenging, considering the distance between her current home Australia and Armenia. "My daughter is four. Before, I did not even ask my parents to take me to places in Armenia. Now I plan to refresh what I have left there, plan to take my child to various places," said Anahit.

Aram, who has never been to Armenia, stated that he would like to visit historical places, as well as to go to 'Western Armenia,' "to go to Armenia in its broader sense." In general, plans to visit various regions in Armenia, not only Yerevan, have been specified by many interviewees. "I would like to go to Dilijan and Gyumri in the north, and, if permitted, to 'Western

---

[*] Situated on Turkey's eastern border with Armenia are the ruins of Ani known as "the city of a thousand and one churches" (The Atlantic, *The City of Ani*). It was founded over 1,600 years ago on several trade routes. This Armenian region was ruled by Byzantine emperors, Ottoman Seljuk and Turks, Armenians, Kurds, Georgians, and Russians. By the 1300s, Ani was in steep decline and was completely abandoned by the 1700s" (The Atlantic, *The City of Ani*).

Armenia' as well, for at least a month in Armenia," Levon, one of our interviewees says.

The story of visiting Armenia for the first time was probably the most fascinating in the case of Bedros, originally from the Middle East, who has been to Armenia 56 times (!!!). "I was calculating the stamps I have in my passports, so 56 times," he says proudly. The first time was in 1984 when he went to (then) Soviet Armenia with his family. "We took an Aeroflot flight,[*] with a stopover in Abu Dhabi, where we had to catch a flight to Moscow and then to Yerevan." He went into details and said that on the way to Moscow, the announcements were in Russian and English.

> Afterwards, we transferred to a domestic flight to Yerevan, and then, during the flight, the captain, captain Sarkisian, I remember, made an announcement in Armenian and welcomed the passengers. My kids, seven and five years old, jumped and said, "Did you hear, they speak Armenian?!" It was the first time for me as well in such a place to hear Armenian. I was shocked.

To him, that first trip was like a pilgrimage. "We went all over the country. I took 800 photographs, from the Haghpat-Sanahin complex and Haghartsin in the north to Khndzoresk in the south." Bedros said that the trip was later used as a learning tool, when he showed the photos to his students as part of a history lesson. In general, Bedros thinks that trips to Armenia, if they are short, can be used by diasporans, as opportunities for pilgrimages, as well as for part-time work. He expresses his strong willingness to revisit Armenia in the future. "I plan to visit it again and even to establish myself there, to move there," he says by adding that when in Armenia, every evening, he went to watch an event, a performance. Such a connection to the homeland plays an important role in strengthening national identity, as, arguably, it is the cultural connection, first of all, that keeps the identity alive.

Similar to the case of several other interviewed diasporans, the permanent return is there, even if it is not physical repatriation. It is essential to have more diasporans moving to the Armenian homeland permanently. However, having them being in permanent return, even on short-term trips, or even virtually or metaphorically, as argued, can strengthen their motivation to finally repatriate to Armenia for a longer term, even permanently. There might be various factors affecting the

---

[*] Aeroflot was the only air passenger company in the Soviet Union.

decision to move to the homeland on a permanent basis. As anthropologist Armine Ishkhanian emphasizes, the contemporary migration trends have been leading to the weakening of the myth of (physical) "return and patriotism," and that "most diaspora Armenians prefer to interact with Armenia transnationally and not as a one-way process," through "the transfer of ideas, cross-cultural exchange of materials, and know-how to a developing land, often making reference to their broader global aspirations" (Ishkhanian, in Darieva, 2011: 2).

Armenian Citizenship as a Connection

The acquisition of Armenian citizenship arguably is a tool that can potentially strengthen the sense of Armenian national identity. In general, as geographer Joe Painter argues, the concept of citizenship has been under pressure to be reconsidered as an outcome of contemporary processes of "globalisation, the development of supra-national polities, ethnic tensions, demands for group recognition and group rights" among other factors (Painter, 1998: 2). All our interviewees were asked whether, if they had an opportunity, would they choose to become Armenian by citizenship. Eleven interviewees answered affirmatively. One of them, Bedros, has even applied and acquired an Armenian passport. Michael Bazikian, who was almost 90 at the time of our conversation, added that despite his willingness, he thought acquisition of Armenian citizenship was not necessary for the duration of his stay in Armenia. "Acquisition of Armenian citizenship is a two-fold issue. Citizenship is useful when visiting Armenia. Every time I go to Armenia, I go through the formal procedure for a visa." On the other hand, as Mr. Bazikian specified, for diasporans, 'Armenia' and 'Motherland' mean something that must be defended, and having an Armenian passport would make one feel more attached to Armenia."

Other interviewees also spoke about possible advantages to acquiring Armenian citizenship and its potential of strengthening their links with Armenia. However, it has become clear that the interviewed diasporans had little knowledge about the procedure of citizenship acquisition in Armenia; in particular, the simplified process for ethnic Armenians.[*]

---

[*] The simplified procedure, as mentioned earlier, enables ethnic Armenians to acquire Armenian citizenship within a shorter period of time and with fewer requirements to meet (Embassy of Armenia to Canada, *Law of Armenian on Citizenship*).

Helen, for instance, became excited to know about that opportunity and added that she had no idea about the entry requirements for Armenia and stressed that the community did not know about the simplified procedure. To her, if more people know about it, many might take it up, and it will strengthen the Armenian identity. Vrej too thinks that the lack of information on citizenship acquisition is a barrier, which stresses the importance of communication between the homeland and diaspora communities. Even though the simplified procedure for becoming an Armenian citizen does not assume a visit to Armenia, the acquisition of citizenship raises the sense of responsibility of diasporans and becomes a motivating factor for their (following) visits.

The acquisition of Armenian citizenship is seen as an issue beyond doubt for Vartan. "Definitely without even thinking about it," he answers affirmatively and adds that any Armenian in the world should possess Armenian citizenship. Vartan gives a particular role to citizenship by saying that the only consolation Armenians, who lost their historical homeland, can have today is to have Armenian citizenship. Earlier, such an opportunity did not exist.[*] However, "now it is good the opportunity exists, and I will apply and will cherish the citizenship," Vartan says proudly. Armen also admits that one day he might apply to become an Armenian citizen, "maybe during our next visit to Armenia," he adds. On the other hand, in the case of the four interviewees, the responses have been quite different. Anahit, being the only interviewee born in Armenia, says that it is unclear to her what Armenian citizenship provides to citizens. "I haven't thought about that, and I do not know what citizenship will give me. I became an Australian not because I chose to do so. My parents chose," she says. Besides, Anahit added that, except for her, everyone else in her family (husband, parents, and brother) have Armenian citizenship.

For Lily, who is also not familiar with the simplified process, it is not a goal to acquire an Armenian passport, mainly because she has started a family in Australia and "just logistically that would not be feasible." Overall, she says that this question has never been of relevance to her. She thinks that the lack of information that prevails in the community is partly due to the absence of any representation from Armenia in Australia.

---

[*] An opportunity to become a citizen of Armenia without renouncing one's existing citizenship.

The view Mateos (the crypto-Armenian) has shared is that the acquisition of Armenian citizenship is not an attractive perspective for him. "I would like to say more yes than no, but it does not matter much," he says. Aram, on the other hand, admits that he would be willing to acquire Armenian citizenship; however, already possessing two passports, none of which he would like to renounce, the law prevents him from applying for a third one. "I would love to say 'yes,'" he says, "but I do not want to give up my current citizenship.* If I go to Armenia, it might be different; it is an uncertain expectation," he concludes. Strengthening the national identity is a process affected by many possible factors, among which it is essential to understand the connecting role diaspora institutions play by bringing homeland and its worldwide diasporans closer, as perceived by diasporans.

---

* According to Aram (a lawyer), Australia accepts dual but not multiple citizenships.

Chapter 7

HOMELAND-DIASPORA: INSTITUTIONAL DYNAMICS

Diaspora Institutions: An Overview

The diaspora-homeland relationship is evolving through the experience of each party. In the case of the Armenian diaspora, the relationship has gone through major transformations since Armenia's independence. The relations involve many strands, beyond the state apparatus, although state policies have broad-ranging effects on the nature of relations with the diaspora. For instance, the closed nature of the state during the decades under Soviet rule led to very limited relations between Soviet Armenia and the diaspora. The policies of the state since independence have been more inclusionary regarding the diaspora; however, we also need to understand how important non-state institutions have been to the homeland-diaspora relationship.

Anthropologist Tsypylna Darieva, in her work on the Armenian diaspora, stresses the weak ties between the diaspora and Armenia and argues that "the diaspora's support for Armenia is less institutionalized and less 'strategic,' but more individualistic and project-specific" (Darieva, 2011: 3). On the other hand, when comparing the Armenian diaspora with others, notably the Albanian and Chechen diasporas, Maria Koinova, a scholar of ethnonationalist conflicts and diaspora studies, argues that the Armenian diaspora shows high levels of institutionalization (Koinova, 2011: 340).

Nowadays, institutions undoubtedly play a crucial part in forging links between ordinary diasporans and the homeland, but they are now operating in the Internet era and socially-mediated connections, which allow diasporans to connect more easily with the homeland, without relying on particular institutions. It is also important to note that Armenian institutions overseas have to operate within the political, economic, social, and cultural milieu that sometimes impinge on their effectiveness or ability to reach out to particular place-based diasporans.

It is essential to understand how the homeland's (state-centered and non-state institutions) approach toward the diaspora is perceived by diasporans. This aspect is a focus here though a narrative study. Regarding diaspora institutions, some are directly related to the homeland, but there are also those which have originated and until now have been managed from the diaspora. Many of them have representatives in the Armenian territorial state.

There are two main types of diaspora organizations in Armenian communities: those which belong to a broader global network of institutions and those which are local with no branches elsewhere. Among the former are institutions which are parts of broader networks connected to it, such as those that work in collaboration with the ARF political party – the European Armenian Federation for Justice and Democracy (Brussels-based), the Washington, D.C.-based Armenian National Committee (ANC) of America, the Beirut-based ANC of the Middle East,* the Russian-Armenian Friendship Foundation (Moscow-based), the Centre for Armenian Studies (Tehran-based). The ARF also cooperates with such networks as the Armenian General Sports and Scouts Union (*Homenetmen*), the Hamazkayin Armenian Cultural and Educational Association (known more popularly as *Hamazkayin*), and the Armenian Relief Society, "all of which have chapters in Armenia and in almost all Armenian communities worldwide" (ARF – Dashnaktsutyun, Brief, 2011, 8).

The majority (80 percent) of interviewees stressed the role of the Armenian Apostolic Church as the most important diaspora institution, which is to be expected given the significance of religion within the context of Armenian national identity. Interviewees specify the Armenian Apostolic Church as one critical element to feeling 'Armenian.' Our oldest interviewee, Michael Bazikian, stated that, while he was baptized in the Church, he did not practice religion. Even so, he later revealed that he kept going to church because of his love for Church music and tradition – the ceremonial aspects. One interviewee, himself being an adherent of Roman Catholicism, also stressed the role of the Armenian Apostolic Church as the most important Armenian diaspora institution. He added that the Armenian Catholic Church also played an important role. "Visiting the Church is important, once a week, or even once a month. I have been here for 36 years," says Antonio. However, he added that there were problems in terms of maintaining such institutions. He noted that the "Armenian cemetery is neglected" because of budgetary limitations. Nowadays, "with

---

* ANC structures operate in Australia as well, called ANC Australia (ANC Australia).

people passing away, many do not pay and are careless," says Antonio. His main concern was about dwindling support and resources, and he stressed the role of the family in keeping Armenian language and culture alive. "All my efforts to educate my children to speak Armenian are being lost. My children and their spouses speak English with each other." This situation reflected the multi-faceted aspects of cultural identity and how identity could be transformed across the generations.

The role of the family in identity preservation was strongly emphasized by Margaret, a lady in her 60s, to whom I was introduced by Helen in Melbourne. Having heard about this research, Margaret was eager to share her views with me. The three of us met in a park close to the CBD in Melbourne and spoke for an hour or so. According to Margaret, the importance of passing family traditions for Armenians, including the connection between three generations in a family (grandparents, parents, and children), was the strongest support for maintaining the foundations of identity. For this to happen, she strongly advocated the extended family living as one household, where family members of several generations could learn from each other and become more tolerant toward each other's views.

According to Helen, the Church holds Armenians together. "It is like our second home, is the thing that unites the Armenians now," she said. Having a permanently appointed priest changes the whole organization in the eyes of community members. She points out that the increasingly active role of the recently-appointed priest in Melbourne made many community members excited. Another respondent argued that the Church should be the main institution that helped to "bring all Armenians together." However, there were also concerns about the ability of the Church to play such a role. Vrej, for instance, commented that nowadays, the services the Church provided were "close to nothing." He identified the role of the ARF as the most influential diaspora structure (he admitted his affiliation to it though). Regarding the Church, there were certain expectations from it and its role, which, to Vrej, was seen beyond pure liturgy and religious functions. "What value do I get from the Church, I do not know," says Vrej and adds that it should not only be liturgy-based. "For instance," he went on, "the Church in Singapore was not only a liturgy-based institution but also provided connections among community members." Vrej was mainly referring to the social contacts established and maintained by the Armenian Church in Singapore, and, by doing so, becoming the center of community life in Singapore. What is clear from the interviews is that the Armenian Apostolic Church, and to a lesser extent, the Catholic Church, played more than a ritual role, and served as important cultural and secular institutions in relation to the diaspora.

For Armen, who is engaged in education, the Church had always played a significant role, "the main sort of connection." He explained that political and benevolent organizations were important in particular fields – sport, culture, and education, but it was the Church that connected the whole community. "The Church, if not strong, will lead the rest of the community to also be weaker." Garo from Melbourne also considered the Church as the key institution helping to maintain the Armenian cultural heritage. A strong argument brought here was that it could invigorate those ties with other countries as well. "Both, from the government and cultural perspective, [the Church] should be kept alive," Garo said.

Bedros noted that the Church, schools, charity and cultural organizations played vital roles in maintaining the Armenian identity in the diaspora. To him, these institutions, together with state ministries in charge of culture, education, diaspora and foreign affairs in Armenia and its embassies abroad, "have to work in a synchronized manner and tolerate each other. Otherwise, it will be like a quadrangle wheel." He gave a special, bigger role to the motherland (Armenia). "I try to see the big picture. All have big roles. Like in a football match, you cannot say the defender is less important. They all have to be like one team," he said.

Thus, while recognizing the unique and significant role of the Church, other types of institutions are also seen as important. A particular significance is given to schools. Unlike the Church, the schools are not networks themselves but have been established as separate institutions, even though some are affiliated with various organizations. Garo, an engineer from Melbourne, for instance, sees the role of the Church as inseparable from the role of Armenian schools. Mateos, the crypto-Armenian interviewee, shares the opinion that the Church and schools are the most important institutions in the diaspora. Mateos points at the importance of the Church because it is the place where people can meet as Armenians. In addition to the role of the Church, Mateos also mentioned the crucial role of schools. He states: "I cannot communicate in Armenian," and adds that it is the school that helps to maintain the language. "You will be felt by the Armenians [at an emotional level] if you speak Armenian," he concluded.

Despite the substantial role given to the Church, many interviewees, such as Vrej, spoke about the role of other institutions. To him, other than the Church, the ARF is an organization providing a range of support through its structures.

Maria from Melbourne provided a balanced view by saying that all types of institutions were very important in different ways, be they educational, sport, or charity organizations. "Educational institutions are important because we have to educate the Armenians. Religious institutions are important for spiritual education; however, political and cultural institutions are all important." For Vartan, too, no institution has a unique role, and all are important in their own way. Unlike others, he sees the Church as divided.[*] He jokes that many things within the

---

[*] According to the Catholicosate of Cilicia, "The existence of two Catholicosates within the Armenian Church, namely the Catholicosate in Etchmiadzin (the Catholicosate of All Armenians or otherwise known as Holy See of Etchmiadzin), Armenia, and the Catholicosate in Antelias, Lebanon (the Catholicosate of the Great House of Cilicia or otherwise known as the Holy See of Cilicia), is due to historical circumstances. In the 10th century, when Armenia was devastated by Seljuks, many Armenians left their homeland and settled in Cilicia, where they re-organized their political, religious, and cultural life. The Catholicosate, the center of the Church, also took refuge in Cilicia" (Catholicosate of Cilicia Antelias, *The Origin of the Armenian Church*). It was later, in 1375, when "the Armenian Kingdom of Cilicia was destroyed. Cilicia became a battleground for Seljuks, Mamluks, and other invaders. In the meantime, Armenia was having a relatively peaceful time. The deteriorating situation in Cilicia, on the one hand, and the growing cultural and religious awakening in Armenia, on the other, led the clergy of Armenia to elect a Catholicos in Etchmiadzin. Thus, in 1441, a new Catholicos was elected in Etchmiadzin in the person of Kirakos Virapetsi. At the same time, Krikor Moussapegiants (1439-1446) was the Catholicos in Cilicia. Therefore, since 1441, there have been two Catholicosates in the Armenian Church with equal rights and privileges, and with their respective jurisdictions. The primacy of honor of the Catholicosate in Etchmiadzin, Armenia, has been recognized by the Catholicosate in Sis, Cilicia." After the Armenian Genocide (1915), the Catholicosate contributed significantly to the formation and organization of the Armenian Diaspora. The Catholicos, Sahak II, followed his flock in exile. After wandering in Cyprus, Syria, and Lebanon, he established the Catholicosate in Antelias, Lebanon in 1930. The Armenian Catholicosate of Cilicia has dioceses in the countries of the Middle East, Europe and in North and South America (Catholicosate of Cilicia Antelias, *The Origin of the Armenian Church*).

Armenian nation are double, including the Church, and mentions Mount Ararat with its two peaks, – Greater and Lesser Ararat (Masis or Sis, as many Armenians call it).

It is interesting to note that Michael Bazikian, through his nine-decade-long life experience as a diasporan, considers the Armenian General Benevolent Union (AGBU) as the most important pan-Armenian organization. Present in various parts of the world, to him, it is capable of being "the greatest stimulant" for the homeland. The diaspora is quite well-off and is capable of being of great help to Armenia, he argues and emphasizes the role of the organization in its capacity to help Armenia. "Without money, no major achievement can be achieved, including strengthening the national identity," he stresses.

The interviewees mentioned cultural organizations and community centers as important institutions in the diaspora. Schools were ranked the second, with four interviewees speaking about their significance. While 80% of the interviewees stressed the primary role of the Church for the diaspora, some pointed at other institutions.

Vahe's view, however, differs from the opinion of all the others. He sees the family as the most important institution. "No matter how many organizations exist, if a child is not engaged with Armenian culture in the family, preservation of the identity will not work," he says. He refers to those diasporans who think it is enough to send their children to an Armenian school, even to weekend schools. It will not help, Vahe thinks, to blame the environment when young Armenian parents cannot speak Armenian properly and cannot teach their children. "The language should be spoken in the home environment, as it is nearly impossible for any organization to do so without the support of the family," he argues. The point here is that with no promotion of *Armenianness* in the home environment, children will feel it is a burden on them to use their weekend to attend an Armenian school, just because they are Armenian. Among various organizations in the diaspora that have a strong role in carrying and strengthening Armenian identity, Vahe is sure that no organization can force a family to teach Armenian to a child. "If I do not do that, who will do so?" he adds at the end.

Educational institutions, charities, and political organizations, with affiliated educational, social, and sports branches form the diaspora's institutional network. Diaspora institutions pursue their goals, but they also serve as a mobilizing factor in terms of bringing the non-territorial diaspora to the homeland. The homeland nation-state has been trying to stay closer to diaspora institutions, as these organizations have a potential for strengthening and promoting the national identity and the homeland's development. Even though both sides show interest in facilitating the diaspora-state relationship, concerns over contested national leadership create certain reservations and prevent both sides from formulating and pursuing a unified policy toward the national development objectives.

The Armenian Apostolic Church

The role of the Church is related to the role Christianity plays in the history of the Armenian nation. Encyclopaedia Britannica mentions that "the Armenian Apostolic Church is seen by many as the custodian of Armenian national identity" (Encyclopaedia Britannica, *Armenian Apostolic Church*). As mentioned earlier, to the question "Who are Armenians?" it is common to hear from Armenians in various parts of the world, "The first Christian nation." The exclusivity in defining *Armenianness* is often limited to Christianity and, as its main carrier – the Armenian Apostolic Church. The Armenian Quarter in the Old City in Jerusalem is an example of such exclusivity of a Christian nation, which makes the presence of the Armenian Church among other titular religious representations special.[*] It is worth mentioning that the Church has a special recognition by the Constitution of the Republic of Armenia, which

---

[*] According to Tamar Boyadjian, the Armenian Quarter in Jerusalem makes the Armenians "the only people to have a quarter in the Old City along with the three monotheistic faiths: Christianity, Islam, and Judaism. The collapse of the Ottoman Empire and the Armenian Genocide led to the mass migration of Armenians from Cilicia to Jerusalem, with thousands of Armenians pouring into the Armenian Quarter. At this point, the Armenian Patriarchate of Jerusalem detached itself from the authority of the Istanbul Patriarchate and the Armenian National Assembly, to which it was subordinate during the period following the Armenian National Constitution in 1863. During the period under British Mandate, the Patriarchate kept amicable relations with British authorities, who largely maintained the Ottoman millet system and allowed administrative matters concerning Armenian refugees and local population to be handled by the Patriarchate. During the British Mandate period, over 10,000 Armenians lived in greater Jerusalem. Today, that number is under 1,000" (Boyadjian, *The Armenian Quarter*).

considers it as the "national church," recognizes its "exceptional mission" in Armenia and "in the spiritual life of the Armenian people, in the development of its national culture and in preservation of the national identity" (U.S. State Department, *Armenia*).

The role of the Church is that of the "cement that held the dispersed population together until the idea of Armenian nationalism very gradually began to spread in the eighteenth century" (Dufoix, 2008: 51). Anthony Smith stresses that "religious communities are often closely related to ethnic identities," and the nature of religious identity is "based on alignments of culture and its elements – values, symbols, myths and traditions" (Smith, 1991: 6). The Church, throughout the centuries, has arguably become the main prism, through which Armenian identity is perceived.

The Church, on the one hand, is a broad network of religious institutions worldwide, virtually in

Medieval Armenian Khachkar at Haghartsin Monastery

all the continents, where there are or have been Armenian communities. On the other hand, as a national church, the Church has been carrying out a unique mission of national identity preservation. The role of the Church has been seen as very important even by the secular Armenian nation-state.[*] For centuries, the Church has been trying to preserve the nation's identity and 'spiritual capital,' a concept defined as the "power, knowledge, influence, and dispositions an individual acquires by being in a social

---

[*] One of the most symbolic expressions acknowledging central role the Church has played in Armenian society was the awarding of the first passport issued in newly-independent Armenia to Vazgen I, the Catholicos of All Armenians, the head of the Church. He also became the first person awarded the Order of National Hero of the Republic of Armenia, the highest order awarded by the state (ArmTimes.com, *The National Heroes*).

Kecharis Monastery, cir. 11-13 century

group" (Berger and Hefner, 2004: 3). The Church played an important role abroad, "in the eye of the diaspora," and it was a factor that unified the life of the Armenian people and became a symbolic protector of the nation, culture, and language (Masih and Krikorian, 1999: 42). Over the centuries under foreign domination, the head of the Armenian Church was perceived as the head of the nation.[*] Despite the process of secularization of Armenia throughout seven decades of the Soviet atheistic rule, the Church continued in the diaspora to be a strong religious institution and preserver of national identity. Armenians, wherever they migrated and

---

[*] After the collapse of the Armenian kingdom of Cilicia in the 14th century, until 1828, Armenia was divided between the Ottoman and Persian empires. In 1828, a part of historical Armenia in the Persian Empire was transferred to the Russian Empire. As mentioned earlier in the book, the ('First') Armenian Republic was established on that part at the end of World War I, after the Russian Empire became Soviet Russia and Armenia was granted independence in 1918. In 1920, just two years after gaining independence, Soviet rule was established in Armenia, and later Armenia became a republic in the Soviet Union (the 'Second Republic') until it acquired its independence again in 1991, its 'Third Republic' (Parliament of Armenia, *History of Armenian Parliaments*).

wherever it was possible, used their opportunities to build churches.[*] It was of crucial importance for the people to practice their religion. Probably the main reason for an ethnic minority to do so is that "religion fosters stronger loyalty and commitment than other identities" (Stewart, 2009: 2).

Historically, other than being places for worship and cultural gathering, the Churches served as an efficient network connecting people, mainly merchants, many of whom have contributed to the Church through charity, as well as becoming part of the information flow. For example, regarding the Armenians who moved to the East from the Persian Empire, "the All Saviour's Cathedral in Julfa contained much information on the activities of merchants in the East, patrons and believers" (Aslanian, 2006: 392).[†] Based on his analysis, Aslanian concludes,

> It was rational for Julfans to remain loyal to their coalition, and in doing so to reproduce their community as a culturally defined and closed social network. Maintaining a Julfan Armenian identity was, in part, an economic concern that had more to do with generating social capital to compensate for other kinds of capital (political or military) that stateless Julfans did not possess, than with religious or cultural injunctions to maintain distinct identity (Aslanian, 2006: 401).

---

[*] The Armenian transnation of about 9-10 mln people worldwide has more than 1,000 churches, including more than 600 in Armenia. Among the churches, 933 are under the jurisdiction of the Mother See of Holy Etchmiadzin, with the rest being under the See of Antelias in Beirut, Lebanon. (Source: a conversation with Rev. Ter Paruyr, Head of Department of Interchurch Relations of the Mother See of Holy Etchmiadzin). A simple calculation results in one church for about 9,000-10,000 people. In South and South-East Asia (Asia to the east from Iran), where, as estimated, nowadays only hundreds of Armenians live, there are Armenian churches in India (Kolkata and the rest of West Bengal State, Chennai), in Myanmar (Yangon) and Singapore, where the churches have existed for hundreds of years (visited by the author personally).

[†] New Julfa was the point of origin for the Armenians and Armenian communities in Asia. According to Edmund M. Herzig, in the early-1600s, "it was the Safavid Shah Abbas I who settled them in a suburb of Isfahan," the district the Armenians called New Julfa, since they were re-settled from Julfa, a major trading city in the Persian Empire, "and the patronage of the court guaranteed their security and privileges as well as supplying them with goods (collected as revenue) for export..." (Herzig, 1991: 11). These arrangements, as argued, have contributed to the development of the trading diaspora communities in Asia significantly.

In this book, the objective is not to analyze the historic role of the Church in preserving Armenian identity. Instead, the identification of problems diasporans face relating to communication between the Church and the diaspora has been attempted. The Church is seen as the link between Armenia and the diaspora, between the nation's modern history and its pre-Christian past.[*] "The Church is the connection with the culture; most of the culture comes with the Church. It signifies our rich past," says Armen from the perspective of his diasporic life and career as an educator. The Church, it can be strongly argued, serves as the skeleton of the global Armenian nation, and, thus, problems associated with its current position and its role in the diaspora need to be identified.

For Anahit, it is not the Church that determines her Armenian identity. "It teaches, but not to form my identity. It has a minor role in my identity," she says. Lily's opinion is quite neutral, as well. Being baptized in the Church, "we pray before dinner and bed; we got an embroidered *Hayr Mer*[†] from Armenia and put on top of his bed." She thinks that the Church does not play a strong role in her family life, "even though we live a normal Christian life," she says. Lily explains that her home environment was an excellent example of an empirically constructed space, following Nigel Thrift's classification of space. Similar details have been specified by other interviewees as well.

Nearly all the interviewees emphasized the point that the Church not only performs the role of a religious institution, but it carries a broader mission. Vahe, who represents a diaspora institution, stresses in strong terms that the Church does not only preaches Christianity. To him, the importance of the Church is that "it preaches in Armenian, preserves the identity." Vahe specifies that the Church and the language are both interconnected and cannot be separated. Not being an expert of the divine liturgy, Vahe makes it clear that he can understand most of the *Badarag*; however, he thinks that it should transform into the modern language.

"I think the Church represents the nation," says Helen from Melbourne and continues by referring to a broader function of the Church, beyond its

---

[*] The connection between the Christian and pre-Christian past of the Armenian nation is also related to many (Apostolic Christian) church holidays, which are partly rooted in the pre-Christian past of the Armenians.

[†] *Hayr Mer* is the Lord's Prayer - "Our Father who art in heaven..." (Armenian Community Council of the U.K., *Our Father*).

divine nature. Armen sees the role of the Church in giving "the strength of the Armenian language and culture, and the identity." He adds, "it is the Church that kept the community growing." Garo from Melbourne also emphasizes that the role of the Church goes beyond its religious scope of activity. He elaborates by saying, "The Church is maintaining the identity; it connects the language, the history, it teaches the word of God, it enables us to preserve our identity." He expresses a concern that distance from the Church will lead to a loss of identity and culture. "It has been the Church that preserves it," Garo says and adds, "it maintains the language, the spirit, is important for educational institutions as well." Another interviewee from Melbourne, Levon, thinks that the Church "is tied to the identity of the Armenians. You can understand Armenia as a country just from the religion alone," he stresses, even though he has never been in Armenia. What Levon said was equating the history of the Church and Armenian nation over the past centuries, after the nation shifted from its Zoroastrian faith to Christianity.[*]

The Church is an independent institution and not part of another structure (for instance, of the Roman Catholic Church). Armen sees this as a strong point and justifies, "It is a national church, and if I go to church and I listen to a mass in Armenian, I feel different. In another church, I do not feel a sense of belonging. I am a Christian in that Church, not in the other one." Such a perception of the Church can lead to a thought that diasporans feel special in every Armenian church they visit since it is a part of the global Armenian Apostolic Church as an institution, and, as such, is a place of particular emotional attachment. As argued, the sense of belonging to the Armenian nation makes the Church space be uniquely perceived, even if it is only imagined and has never been visited before.

For Vrej, in Sydney, the Church as an institution in the diaspora and Armenia not only carries the Armenian national identity, but also "a responsibility for keeping the identity," for a nation spread all-over-the-world. A similar and more elaborated view was expressed by Aram, the lawyer from Sydney. He thinks it is the Church that keeps the identity alive, as it

---

[*] 301AD is considered the foundation year of the Armenian Apostolic Church when St. Gregory the Illuminator convinced King Trdat III (or Tiridates III) of Armenia to convert Armenia to Christianity (Santos and Contreras, BBC Travel, *First Christian Country?*)

teaches us the connection with Armenia; it keeps us Armenian, encourages us to be Armenian, and, to me, it is a cultural bridge. You may not like the teachings, the religious aspect, but it keeps us. It is more cultural than religious. The Church is a powerful institution that keeps the language. However, the language in use in the Church is not the modern one, and I do not understand it partly, but it is not the main problem.

Reflections shared by Mateos, the crypto-Armenian, are rooted in his heritage and hardship related to living many years with a hidden identity. To Mateos, the Genocide, along with its recognition is one of the most significant issues for Armenians. He questions whether he could have presented himself as a non-Muslim and elaborates that "the identity does not come without your religious identity." He reveals that he is not a religious person. However, "when you look what is happening in the world, religion comes with your identity. When you are born, they baptize you, when you die, it is in the Church as well. You carry it throughout your life." Speaking over various issues, Mateos came back to the role of the Church again and stressed its specific mission. "Even if you are against it, one day it comes back," and he concludes by saying, "the Church is not like any other one." His justification of such special perception of the Church is, as he says, "if I go there, I know that I can see some Armenians. It is a place for connections, for cultural connections, not just a liturgy place."

Bedros from Sydney thinks that by giving a unique role to the Apostolic Church, it "does not mean the Catholic and Protestant churches have no role" and emphasizes the importance of united efforts by different churches. Both Holy Sees of the Armenian Church, to Bedros, have a special role in this regard.[*] "They do not have to look at each other as enemy churches," he says, since both represent the Mother Church and should be as such, to be the driving force of keeping the Christian Armenian identity. Bedros gives a special role to Christian education and the media. The Church, he says, "does not reach the people effectively, the Church does not have religious programs or a TV channel in the Diaspora. The channel in Armenia is not accessible on TV in the diaspora," Bedros stresses and suggests that nowadays many people do not often go to the Church, and, provided there is a proper broadcasting channel, they can

---

[*] The seat of the Armenian Apostolic Church in Etchmiadzin, Armenia and the Catholicosate in Antelias, Lebanon.

listen to its program.[*] "With a Christian background, it will work like a fertilizer," he says. To be an effective communicator nowadays, and not mainly a carrier of the heritage, to Bedros, the Church has to go to the families and individuals, "to be accessible." He brings an example of an FM channel that broadcasts on Sunday evening; however, "it does not reach a broad range, while it could work with a radio station that reaches far," and more people could be involved. He even suggests having one channel for all the major Armenian traditional churches (Apostolic, Catholic, Protestant), which can be even for a longer duration. "This can be unified," Bedros says.

Michael Bazikian is more critical and sees the future of the Church in it being closer to the diaspora, through modernization. The Church, to him, "cannot carry on as it used to do over centuries and needs to be relevant to the life today." Mr. Bazikian's view is quite different from those of all other interviewees in the sense that he does not think the Church has any special role compared to other diaspora institutions. Along the same lines, the issue of modernization of the Church has been raised by others too. For instance, Levon, a company manager from Melbourne, thinks the Church theology and liturgy are correct. However, to him, "from the educational perspectives, it needs to change, to build more educational institutions." Probably the main change he suggests is to start advocating and not preaching.

Antonio, our only Roman Catholic interviewee, thinks the priests have to be in touch more actively within the community. "Meetings face-to-face are very important," he emphasizes and, half-joking, half-serious adds that Armenians "build a Church and forget about the rest." He specifies, "clubs are empty, the cultural center...; if no Armenian dance group, it would also be empty." Similar problems, he mentions, happen with other institutions as well, for instance, with the Armenian Catholic Church.

Vahe thinks that Church traditions, ceremonies, and sermons are what people need to know. To him, this will fill the process with "a sense of fulfillment," such as in the case of the symbolism used in weddings, which

---

* *Shoghakat* is a "spiritual-cultural TV company," founded by the Armenian Apostolic Church, which broadcasts in Armenia and via satellite TV (Shoghakat TV, *About Us*). Thus, the channel is accessible outside Armenia, which may not be known to many in the diaspora, as one of the interviewed diasporans has mentioned.

Holy Etchmiadzin in Armenia

"should be made clear and known for couples." Vahe also stresses the necessity for modernization of the Church by emphasizing, "whatever has worked for centuries might not work or be effective in modern days." Himself not being an overly religious person, Vahe attends the Church for various major events (Easter, Christmas, marriages, funerals, as he lists them). "If I need to relax, I will put the divine liturgy of the Church, not because it is a religious liturgy, but because it is a liturgy in Armenian," Vahe says. He added that going to the Church for him is like going to one's roots. "It maintains the identity," he concludes.

The Church has come a long way, Maria from Melbourne emphasizes and highlights a point not mentioned by any other interviewee. With prayers translated into English, there are non-Armenian neighbors now coming to the Church, as they are interested in it. Maria is optimistic but also suggests that "the Church should still do a lot in terms of educating the youth. I would like to see it being more involved in the school, so that they can talk about different topics with children, to be closer to the younger generation."

The Church is, first of all, a religious institution. Its existence is inseparable from its cultural-historical framework which goes back centuries. Language, music, architecture are all inherent attributes of the Church, which, as it can be argued, is the backbone of the metaphorical skeleton of the modern Armenian nation. It has been the space of the Armenian existence worldwide, with its churches serving as places for community life. Coming through the centuries, the Church has been carrying the Armenian identity, the language, and culture of the nation. The Church, at the same time, has remained a conservative structure, and that conservatism has arguably been helping the nation in its history, by preventing its culture from assimilation. Armenian language, as one of the core attributes of the Church, has become a focus of discussions, in particular, the necessity to change the language from *Grabar** to the language used nowadays. Levon, for instance, recognizes that the language is difficult to understand.

Vartan shares a similar view that the Church needs to change and to adapt to modern times. His primary concern is that the congregation is losing its followers-community members. Besides, he sees a paradox, as the Church, on the one hand, needs to preserve national traditions and the language, and on the other hand, it needs to modernize. This point might sound contradictory to the idea that it should maintain traditions and modernize, including keeping the language. "The new generation does not understand *Grabar*, and time requires change, and I wish the Church can change," says Vartan, who adds that in his opinion, as a community and a country, Armenians "are left a little bit behind in terms of the change."

How is the Diaspora Changing?

Understanding diaspora communities, among other aspects, assumes understanding the changes and transformations diaspora communities have been experiencing over time. The Armenian communities in Australia are relatively young. Most of the community members have settled in the country in the past three to four decades.

The Armenian diaspora has existed over the centuries. Before WWI, the Armenian diaspora, as mentioned earlier, was mainly composed of trade communities in various parts of the world. Some such communities were in India, most notably in Kolkata, older communities in Poland-Western

---

*   *Grabar* or Classical Armenian was the language in use until the 17th century when "Armenian developed into a modern form which has split into two varieties: West Armenian and East Armenian" (Krause and Slocum, *Classical Armenian Online*). Grabar Armenian is still the official liturgy language of the Armenian Apostolic Church.

Ukraine, and Crimea (Ministry of Foreign Affairs of Armenia, *Armenian Community in India*, Radio Poland, *650 years of Armenian Community in Poland*, Internet Encyclopedia of Ukraine, *Armenians*). Even philosopher Immanuel Kant stressed the commercial spirit of the Armenians and the strive to reach faraway regions and countries to "buy and sell" by knowing "how to obtain a peaceful reception from all the peoples they encounter" (Suny, 2015: 37-38). Over 1915-1918, the nature of the diaspora changed significantly, and it turned into a predominantly exile diaspora. After Armenia achieved its independence in 1991, a new wave of emigration took place. The Armenian Genocide was a "decisive 'break event'" in the history of the Armenian nation and its widespread diaspora, transforming the latter from a trade diaspora to a victim diaspora (Cohen, 1996: 5, 57).

During the last decades of Soviet rule, the Armenians had an opportunity, even with strict censorship by the state, to establish connections with 'compatriots abroad.'[*] During the seven decades of Soviet Armenia's existence (1920-1991), it can be argued that it was the diaspora that assumed the responsibility for the preservation of the Armenian national identity, most importantly, regarding the efforts for Genocide recognition.

The position of the Church has also been unique. The Mother See of the Church, located in Etchmiadzin in Armenia (Soviet Armenia then), had no choice but to abide by Soviet laws and the overall regulation of religious activities in the whole Union. Abroad, the Holy See in Anthelias, Lebanon performed (partly) the role of preserving the language (Western Armenian) and culture in the diaspora. Soviet Armenia, along with its limited power to reach the diaspora, had no real opportunity to lead the whole nation. The situation changed in 1991, with the establishment of the Republic of Armenia. Apart from its strongly positive role, this

---

[*] The Committee for Cultural Relations with Compatriots Abroad in Soviet Armenia was created in 1964. It was a unique case of such an institution in the Soviet Union and existed mainly because of the widespread nature of the Armenians worldwide. The Committee was mainly involved in the training of teachers and students in strengthening the ties between Soviet Armenia and the diaspora. After Armenia achieved independence in 1991, the Committee was dissolved, and a Department under the Ministry of Foreign Affairs was established. Later, in 2008, as mentioned above, the Ministry of Diaspora was formed (Interview of Ms. Hranush Hakobyan, Minister of Diaspora, in Russian).

decades-long commitment by the diaspora and, in particular, the Church in Antelias, led to a barrier in the relationship between the diaspora and the Republic of Armenia, because of contested leadership from both sides. If before 1991 the diaspora claimed to be the preserver of Armenian identity, and (Soviet) Armenia had a very limited political ability to question or limit that power, then, after 1991, the situation changed. Armenia, as a member of the UN, became a player in the inter-governmental arena, with a higher political status – that of a sovereign nation-state. Several interviewees in this study emphasized that the diaspora was caught unprepared for such transformation. "Neither Armenia nor the diaspora was ready for such a change," said Michael Bazikian. He stressed that the diaspora and Armenia "do not know each other well." The point that no matter where Armenians live, "Armenia should be seen or perceived as their cultural center," is the core of Mr. Bazikian's view of Armenia-diaspora relations in the future.

One interviewee, Armen from Sydney, agrees with the point that the main change he has observed in the diaspora is Armenia's independence. The following position is seen as essential, seeing that it expresses an overall perception of Armenia within the diaspora.

> Before, Armenia was a place we got connected, but we could not feel part of that. Every time I had to identify myself as an Armenian, I had to provide a long explanation what Armenia was (a part of Soviet Union). Now you can point to and say, 'this is our country.'

Thus, Armenia's independence not only transformed the relations between the two parts of the nation, but it also changed and strengthened the self-identification of diaspora Armenians. "Now, if people do not know about Armenia, it is their ignorance," says Armen.

With Armenia's independence, the attributes of a sovereign nation-state further enriched the Armenians' sense of identity. Armen explains, "it is easier to explain to my children when Armenia has its flag, its national attributes. In the past, it was the community that kept us together." As presented, since independence, the focus of diaspora engagement is on the transformation from the inter-community relationship level to relations with Armenia.

The transformation processes going on in diaspora communities throughout the past two decades have been of different nature, compared to those that took place earlier. Vrej, whose parents were born and grew up in Egypt and then migrated to Sydney, stated that he had a different experience compared to his parents, "for whom keeping the Armenian identity was easier." Vrej's position is that the parents maintained and lived that identity by themselves. "My parents' generation… they lived in the same area, among Armenians, so that they could keep it. Later, the identity is fading," says Vrej. As he explains, the fact that he chose to strengthen his identity is "a reflection of maturity," of the need to find his identity, his roots. Nowadays, he points out that many Armenians have lost their identity as a result of the work of many diaspora organizations and individuals, "they have contributed to the split," he says. Vrej emphasizes the lack of consistency and poor management that has led to such an outcome. He then refers to his earlier years, when growing up, he would regularly (once a week) go to play with Armenians of his age, which is not common among the youth nowadays.

Thus, the diaspora has acquired an opportunity to shift to a new system of relations with the homeland. However, over these couple of decades, as presented by several diasporans, the diaspora has experienced a weakening of its own Armenian identity. Is it because of the relaxation caused by the fact that, after independence, Armenia has been perceived to be responsible for leading (at least, representing) the nation, and the diaspora does not carry the same strong identity preservation responsibility as it did before 1991? Antonio from Sydney agrees with this point. "I have been attached more in order not to lose my identity," Antonio says and adds that he feels more responsible for not giving up on it. However, he reflects, "The diaspora is lacking the preservation of the identity." As an extraterritorial entity, the Armenian diaspora, being larger in numbers than the population in Armenia, depends on its ability to gain from relations with Armenia and vice versa. However, a question that probably sounds somewhat rhetorical is whether gains in relations mean acquiring more, such as stronger economic ties and mutual business interests, or not losing anything, such as the language and traditions? As argued, the first perception can lead to the strengthening of ties between the homeland and its diaspora, which can further promote the language, culture, and traditions. On the other hand, the fear of loss, as in the second case mentioned above, without being supported by strong mutual interests, can lead to a weakening of interest toward those attributes over time.

"Loss of language is the biggest challenge, and the loss of tradition," Vahe says. The main problem, to him, is that this trend affects all diaspora communities. At the same time, he is optimistic that the language will survive and will not perish, "because there will always be people who will support it." Vahe highlights that collective action is needed now, "as it will be late tomorrow." Kev Dertadian, Chairman of AGBU Youth (Sydney), strongly emphasizes the weakening trend and appeals to the community and the youth by encouraging the Armenians in the city to become part of the community. "Our communities are struggling," he says, and makes his point clear by adding, "the day-to-day activities of modern Armenian communities involve much more than mourning the losses of and demanding reparations for the events of 1915" (Dertadian, 2016).

For Lily, a high school teacher in Melbourne, the transformation of diaspora-homeland relations is two-fold. "I am coming out of two angles," she says and adds, "it is me and the community involved in the organization," which, to her, is progress. On the other hand, the diaspora is weakening, and Lily particularly specifies her generation of diasporans in their 20-30s, as many do not involve themselves in diaspora affairs. "After finishing an Armenian school at the age of 12, they do not get in touch with many Armenians and marry non-Armenians, and, as a result, lose their connections," she says. A reason for such transformation, she argues, is that "given the country they are in, this is inevitable." She even estimates subjectively that only about 20% of Armenians in the community have ever been to Armenia, which, to her, is a low number.

Aram identifies time as the primary factor that contributes to this process of weakening the Armenian identity in the diaspora. "We have become more enslaved to our work," he admits and brings an example of his recent life experience of several months in Dubai, "I met some Armenians there, and they said the same thing." The environment makes its change, and the lack of an Armenian environment does its job. Attending a local school, to Aram, makes it harder to maintain the Armenian identity in a broader social environment.

Garo, another interviewee from Melbourne, also admits that over the years, "it has become more difficult to preserve the Armenian language, history, culture." Vartan, on the other hand, sees personal wealth as the main destructive force. With it, he clarifies, the Armenians have started to forget the past and tried to do things differently; it is not very convenient for some people to remind themselves of their roots and identity, the need to give to the Church, to the community. I believe the only change is the wealth. Being good for individuals, however, has not been good for the whole. The late Alex Manoogian,[*] who once said that he knew that there were Armenians in the United States who were richer than the AGBU itself, but they did not give a cent to AGBU, Armenia, or the community.

Despite these alarming and pessimistic views, there have also been positive sides to the transformation shared by the interviewees. Bedros, for instance, points at the promotion of research on the diaspora and specifies work of the ANC, or the Zoryan Foundation in Canada. The study of the diaspora, to Bedros, is instrumental, a foundation of a research center, as specified. He added regretfully that, as he heard from a fellow diasporan, there used to be a research center at the Macquarie University in Sydney, an established center, which was lost, as "nobody cared of it so far."

* * *

A diaspora, being a dynamic phenomenon, with its structural diversity and geographical distribution, has no choice but to adapt to local realities and to transform with changes in local (host) environments and the homeland. "Diaspora is not outside the world. The world is changing, and the diaspora is changing as well," says Mateos. His perspective on changes in the diaspora is through the prism of pre- and the post-centennial anniversary of the Genocide. The main point brought by Mateos is that, before the 100th anniversary, the diaspora was trying to tell the world about the Genocide. With more countries recognizing it, "the diaspora had achieved what it wanted. Before [2015], many people in the world did not know what happened, but the 100th anniversary changed the situation," Mateos reflects on his observation. To him, in the Armenian community in Australia, people were trying to present the events that took place during the Genocide. Such efforts have led to a situation where people are more aware of the tragedy. Over time, "the change happened even in some Turkish people's mind." After the centennial events, more people accept

---

[*] Alex Manoogian (1901-1996), philanthropist, long-time President of AGBU, he has been widely known as the inventor of single-handled faucets, created by his company Masco Corporation (Gelder, *Alex Manoogian*).

"to live with others who are different," Mateos says. "Something has happened after the anniversary," he concludes.

For Anahit, "the community is more vocal." However, she also recognizes that more frequent communication, for instance, over social media, is often not productive enough. "Mostly, it is empty, just talks, nothing major happens," Anahit says and refers to the tragedy of Kessab,[*] when "nothing could prevent it." Maria, the teacher from Melbourne, sees the changes in Armenia-diaspora relations as positive at different levels. She has been the only interviewee, who mentioned the Pan-Armenian Games as a powerful tool that strengthens the ties between the two parts of the nation. "This is a good change," she commented.

Levon, who has lived in both Sydney and Melbourne, spoke about changes from the technology perspective. "A lot of young people bring new ideas," he said and stressed the importance of understanding differences. "Other diasporic communities are not similar to, let's say, what we have here." Levon points at the larger community in Sydney having more businesses, while in Melbourne, they are still developing. "I have lived in Sydney and have been living in Melbourne," he specifies, and then comments that Sydney, being much larger in terms of its Armenian community, "has even less segregation within the community, compared to Melbourne." Levon thinks the lack of a day school in Melbourne is a major drawback.

Among the interviewees, Helen's response was the most thought-provoking regarding the perception of the homeland space, shared by someone who has not experienced personal and intimate knowledge of that space. "I feel excited about going to Armenia and think if I go there, by feeling more comfortable with my people, I might not come back." Buying products from Armenia was seen as another way to connect to Armenia. Helen's expectation, being emotional even before any visit to the homeland, can arguably strengthen the position that diasporans' first visit to the homeland can become a significant cornerstone for maintaining

---

[*] On March 21, 2014, as presented, the Turkish authorities "armed and dispatched Al-Nusra terrorists to Kessab to loot, destroy and desecrate homes, farms, churches and businesses" in this Armenian-populated town, and, as *Today's Zaman*, the Turkish paper mentions: "Many Armenians have also drawn parallels with the forced expulsions which took place in 1915" (Azadian, *Kessab Tragedy*).

their sense of diaspora return. Certainly, there is a possibility that expectations might not materialize as a result of that visit. There will be diasporans who will also be disappointed. However, with the following visit – the "going back," as we use one of the interviewee's expressions, diasporans' attachment to the homeland can become permanent.

Does Community Size Matter?

Anthropologist Pnina Werbner describes diasporas as "communities of co-responsibility" (Werbner, in Wise, 2006: 14). Relations between Armenia and its diaspora are never static. Being spread all-over-the-world, the Armenian diaspora assumes connections with communities virtually in all the corners of the world. Naturally, the level of communication with some regions has probably been more effective, while some others have been left less attended. The reasons behind this can be different. It seems, among other factors, an important one might be the size of communities and the geographic distance from Armenia.

Diaspora return being a permanent process, by assuming interaction within communities, between communities, and with the homeland, also enables direct return on an individual level, especially considering the modern state of technology. The urban Armenian diaspora's every community has its specific sub-identity, with its different institutional structures. The point raised here is to what extent does the size of communities matter? Do numbers and critical mass play a role?

Vrej, an interviewee from Sydney, believes that the community size is important:

> Size does matter. At what size it matters is a question. Even though we are one community, in fact, we are not one. It is very split in terms of social and political alliances, mostly political associations. The size does matter, but even with 40,000 in Australia, we are not as one. The bigger the size, the more likely it will be split. Not so much economic or social factors, but, to some extent, geographic distribution, with the political being the most important.

A similar approach toward community size has been expressed by Lily, who thinks that it does matter, as a larger number of community members, the range of events becomes broader and richer. At the same time, she also points at the importance of effective organization in the community. However, eventually, she thinks "to be meaningful, you need numbers."

Antonio from Sydney gives a simple estimate that only some 300 diasporans are active in the large Sydney community, and also mentions the small number of students in both day schools in the city. "Something is wrong," Antonio says regretfully with regard to this situation. Several other interviewees, Aram, Armen, Garo, and Maria, who represent communities from both selected cities, all agree that community size is an important factor for keeping it active and well-connected. However, it is not seen as the most important one. Aram, for instance, remembers his time in Jordan, where, as he says, the community was smaller but stronger, while in Sydney, the city is big, and the Armenians are not that organized and close. He connects the effectiveness of the community to the environment as well. "In the Middle East, you feel more xenophobic and try to maintain your identity; you stick to each other more, while here, we are more relaxed and feel less responsible for preserving the identity," Aram says. Armen admits that the community has been growing and becoming more active "as more types of activities can be conducted." He specifies that usually, one sees the same people active in community affairs and events. Armen brings it out that there is a struggle regarding those who will lead events, as many community members are not actively involved. Garo shares a similar thought by saying that a larger community assumes more variety for the community life since it enables itself to be more vibrant, to have more children at schools, more community members attending the Church. Thus, to Garo, the community size does matter for the variety of events; however, for being active, "this does not matter."

One-third of the interviewees stated that the size of the community did not matter at all. "No matter what you believe in, action is the most important," emphasizes Michael Bazikian, from the standpoint of nine decades of being a diasporan.

"I don't think so. How people communicate with each other is what matters," Helen says. With her rich experience of living in the diaspora, she is confident that the larger community has more power, certainly. To her, one of the main problems that exist in the community, at least in Melbourne, is the "segregation among the Armenians." More specifically, she speaks about diasporans sticking to their own group of diasporans with a similar sub-cultural origin and dialect. Anahit, also speaks about the split and specifies that the size of the community does not matter as much as the united nature of the community. "In Australia, the community is not united, at least in Melbourne," she concludes.

The community size does not affect the results of community activity, Vartan emphasizes. "We are about 40,000-50,000 in Australia. To be active, the size does not matter," he says and specifies that to stay active and be in diaspora return, "the concentration and interests are to be there." Vartan raises the point that people are not that interested anymore; fewer parents are sending their children to Armenian schools. As a justification, the situation with the Armenian schools was raised earlier. A community of about 40,000-50,000 people in both Sydney and Melbourne assumes about 5,000 people of school age. However, the total number of students in both Armenian day schools in Australia equals to only about 400, or around 8% of the full capacity.

Mateos (from Melbourne) agrees that the size of the community does not matter since "it is about quality first of all." His main argument is that, if there is no unification and if a wide diversity of opinions exists there on certain issues, the nation is not strong. On the other hand, in a smaller community, which has stronger feelings and connections, especially when trying to achieve certain political goals, the community is stronger. Mateos brings an example of (open) Armenians in Turkey, who, according to him, are not relatively many, but "are trying to do something, for example trying to persuade Turkey to recognize the Genocide."

Vahe, with his daily involvement in diaspora-homeland affairs, looked at the community size issue from both sides and provided a balanced view. To him, it does and does not matter. He estimates that in a community, which is larger than any other in the Asia-Australia region, only about 1,500 people are active, which, to him, is a low portion. An example he brought was participation in the 100th-anniversary events – only about 1,200 people. Then he compared this number with that of a much larger Armenian community – in Los Angeles, U.S., with only about 2,000 people who participated in events. "It is a complex between quality and quantity," Vahe says and emphasizes a point that a smaller community can be alive and active. Levon from Melbourne also considers the size of the community not being important, as even larger communities can be passive. "Size is important for keeping something going," Levon says and adds that having a big community is great; however, "if the younger generation is not interested, then the community will be gone." Levon gives more importance to passion and active participation in the community. "People should care," he says.

By giving his preference to diaspora organizations, Bedros brings an analogical comparison with the Armenian community in Poland, where historically many ethnic Armenians live; however, "you do not find any." Nevertheless, Bedros considers community size important: "If you do not organize the community, it dies." He agrees that there are political differences, which are normal. However, he points out, "the most damaging is the perception of such a divide by the youth, as the youth starts not to care and to look for other nests." Bedros also emphasizes that ideological identity does not matter for many young diasporans. Political disagreements in the diaspora, to him, can carry a destructive potential, as diaspora organizations, to a large extent, are pan-Armenian in their nature and have deep historical roots. One of the main problems, thus, to Bedros is strengthening the community for a younger generation of Armenians. If the youth is closer to the community, then they will also have an opportunity to be directly involved in the homeland as well, to be in more active virtual communication with it and with the extra-territorial 'Armenian World'. Modern technological development has been transforming homeland-diaspora relations. If before the Internet era, community life was limited by physical communication between the community members at the local level, then nowadays, modern technology makes the diaspora return active on a daily basis. The question of the importance of community size, thus, needs to be viewed through another prism different from what has been done for decades. Diaspora institutions cannot be observers and, therefore, need to consider the new realities that modern technology creates and promotes.

Chapter 8

DIASPORA-ARMENIA RELATIONS:
OVERCOMING THE CHALLENGE

Challenges in Relations

The study of diaspora-homeland ties assumes thorough understanding of the potential benefits for both sides of the nation regarding the dynamics of their relations, identification of problems, and existing challenges between homeland and diaspora, as well as within the diaspora itself. In the discussion that follows, the focus is on the tensions between the geographically fixed homeland and a deterritorialized and multi-sited diaspora with its own notions of homeland. It reflects upon the potential for realizing a multi-sited and global sense of nationhood through closer connections between homeland and the diaspora.

It is worth stressing, as mentioned earlier in the book, that in the diaspora, people's lives are lived "not despite, difference; by hybridity" (Dufoux, 2008: 24). As nonagenarian Michael Bazikian points out, the diaspora's main challenge is "to bring Armenians together" in a sense that the diaspora views the homeland as a center, and the center sees the diaspora as a full part of a dispersed national body. Thus, being hybrid, diaspora communities deal with both the homeland and their hostlands, as well as other communities in an extraterritorial diaspora. Return to the homeland does not take a form of permanent physical repatriation only, but rather a collective sense of being united and belonging to a united nation in an extraterritorial and multi-sited sense. That national sense of space is not a separate-from-homeland entity, but involves the homeland, by transforming the latter into the center of the nation's political, economic, and socio-cultural existence. The diaspora, as largely perceived, is ultimately about helping the homeland, Armenia, and "spending money to support it," as Mr. Bazikian explains. His strong belief is that diasporan Armenians should be encouraged to move to or visit Armenia, as well as to teach the Armenian language.

In the diaspora it is not uncommon to find the viewpoint that diasporic engagement in the homeland can happen largely at a distance, with temporary (including frequent) visits there. Specified elsewhere in this book, the economic and emotional aspects are viewed as important motives, which can fuel the diasporic physical return. It can be added to the argument that remaining in the diaspora (or even withdrawing from it and becoming only an 'ethnie') or migrating to the homeland can be accelerated by the economic factor. Such a trend can be a derivative of positive expectations and business (investment) confidence in the homeland (Armenian) economy, sustainable development, and effective international integration, all of which, as argued, will only strengthen the trend with a snowball effect.

Maria in Melbourne stresses two issues: the lack of close connections within the Armenian community and the special role that the Church can play in forging a stronger community. She remembers how, years earlier, when the dismissal of a priest in her church resulted in weaker community cohesion and collaboration. She stressed that younger members of the local Armenian youth were not supported enough within the community. Stronger support would help to build a stronger sense of Armenian togetherness. An observation Maria shared was related to a particular case, when a group of diasporans wanted to initiate an event but were not encouraged, as it was a personal matter and not related to any formal organization. Maria is sure that feeling the Armenian identity is like feeling oneself at home, whatever community event it is, whether a dancing party (*barahantes*, as it is often called) or going to Armenia. During such events "you feel like you are home." Maria here emphasizes the role of particular places as objects of attachment. Even though she speaks only about places in the community and for the local community of Melbourne, the importance of perception and feeling of places in the homeland cannot be overestimated.

Dilution of the Armenian identity may lead to just keeping their '-ian' (or '-yan') ending surnames.[*] "We can't afford to lose our identity," says

---

[*] With few exceptions and, if not changed by a person, Armenian surnames end with '-ian' or '-yan', indicating their belonging to a particular family. For instance, Vardanyan signifies belonging to the family of Vardan (normally, the patriarch of a family a long time ago). The root of a surname can reflect a name, an occupation, or even a place. As a rule, western Armenians have the '-ian' ending, while the norm in Armenia is '-yan.' In Turkey, most Armenians do not have either of these endings, but those who do, use '-yan' to comply with modern Turkish orthography.

Vahe and gives a strongly pessimistic perspective while arguing, "at least we are fortunate that we have a nation-state, unlike the Assyrians or others in the region." He also emphasizes that there are strong connections between the largest Armenian communities in Sydney and Melbourne, and fewer links to smaller communities. Linkages within the broader region are also relevant; for instance, the Archbishop (from Sydney) pays visits to the Armenians in New Zealand and Singapore once or twice a year. Vahe specifies that he participates in pan-Asian Armenian meetings, usually through inter-personal connections and informal social networks, rather than through formalized institutional connections. "All is in an unofficial capacity, nothing formally organized," concludes Vahe.

The diaspora communication, as proposed here, has three dimensions:

- within the broader diaspora community;
- between the communities (either within the same or in another country); and
- between a given community and the homeland.

This classification can be misleading if the diaspora is perceived as a collection of physically separated communities. Such classification has a broader meaning if we can view diasporans (even though they are members of a particular community) as people who can be in independent communication within any of these three dimensions.

It can be argued that the global Armenian network has been broken. This is a paradox since the Internet seems to be able to unite, although it does not do so effectively. The Internet and social media have the potential to fix this break. Indeed, as a matter of coincidence, the Internet era matches almost perfectly with the history of independent Armenia. Diasporans in their mid-30s have seen Armenia as an independent country their entire conscious lives, simultaneously using the Internet as a media and communication tool for most of those years. Despite this profile, many diasporans still put their primary emphasis on community life in the diaspora, and see their community as an important connection to the homeland. It can even be argued that, if left to inertia and with no support of diaspora engagement by a homeland-led and mission-based rational policy, the Internet can even play a separating role. Psychologically, diasporans can perceive the homeland as not so remote, thanks to the advanced communications, even if their involvement in the homeland and, most importantly its economy, remains dormant.

One of the interviewees, Helen from Melbourne, stresses uniting the diaspora within communities, no matter where diasporans come from, as the main challenge. Irrespective of the roots and even routes, importance is given to bringing the community together. However, weakening links within communities, as many interviewees have stated, partly caused by increasingly stronger direct diaspora return practices (direct connections and links), arguably make diasporic communities less powerful, at least from the point of information flow and control. On the other hand, the existence of the Republic of Armenia as a sovereign political entity can influence the diaspora's power. The Internet has become a tool that enables the strengthening of communication between diasporans and the homeland, but also, as noted by several respondents, can make people less active within their respective Armenian communities, as there are faster and, sometimes, more efficient lines of communication with the homeland.

"We are in an environment that shapes us," says Garo and emphasizes the importance of teaching the youth to maintain their distinctive identity. At the same time, he recognizes that passing cultural knowledge from one generation to another is difficult. As for the ties between the diaspora and homeland, he sees economic relations as crucial. Commerce can improve links and understanding between diasporans and homelanders, with more businesses operating in Armenia, as some interviewees specify. Short trips, mainly to Yerevan, do not allow diasporans to see "the difficulties of people living there," according to Garo. This is an important point, and it can be argued that improved ties will only be forged with deeper knowledge and realistic perceptions of Armenia by diasporic communities. Garo makes it clear that there is a need for more involvement in both directions. He states that "there could be programs to encourage people to go and live in Armenia" and agrees that even temporary relocation or residence in Armenia would help diasporans develop a less conceptual and more intimate sense of the Armenia space. Furthermore, establishing businesses in Armenia can be an important step, which, as emphasized, could be encouraged from the Republic's side. While Garo was in favor of diasporans helping with things like financial aid and moral support, he recognizes that there are obstacles too; for instance, "you hear from other diasporans that they are not accepted in Armenia very well." He goes further and explains that the reasons behind such an attitude could be that

Statue of Mesrop Mashtots outside Matenadaran
Museum in Yerevan

"the locals in Armenia are going through tough economic times, and they might feel there is inequality between them and the diasporans."

Among challenges in diaspora-homeland relations, Anahit, a housewife in Melbourne, focuses on the lack of education by saying,

> For instance, I did not know much about 1915[*] until I met my husband, who told me much about the tragedy. If my husband was not an Armenian,[†] I would not know much about it. Maybe lack of interest will prevail, and the Armenians might lose the knowledge of their history. Maybe a major challenge is lack of funding, nobody is standing by us, we have lack of support, mainly financial support. Also, there is a lot of corruption in Armenia, even though there is corruption in many countries.[‡]

Such arguments suggest that the whole system of diaspora-homeland relations depend on the knowledge each has about the other, which, in turn, leads to expectations of each other. In-depth knowledge and realistic

---

[*] The Armenian Genocide.

[†] He is an Armenian from Armenia.

[‡] These interviews were conducted before the change of power in Armenia in April-May 2018, after which a large-scale campaign against corruption was declared by the new government.

expectations of each other can develop trust, which, arguably, is a necessary pre-condition for successful inclusion of diasporans in the homeland.

Vrej in Sydney asks a rhetorical about how the next generation will maintain its Armenian identity and continues,

> It is very difficult. I do not have an Armenian wife, but I try to communicate in Armenian. My wife understands some Armenian; I try to speak with my kids. They go to an Armenian Saturday school. I accept my responsibility of keeping the identity alive.

According to Vrej, the Armenian government's first responsibility is to preserve Armenia and its people. However, it is also seen to be responsible for protecting, preserving, and developing *Armenianness* for Armenians globally. "I am not sure how it can do so. It can achieve a level that can connect to Armenians globally; the government has a responsibility to create and promote Armenia's brand so that worldwide people will know it well." Overall, the diaspora is seen as a powerful participant which can help Armenia "with soft power" for development and promotion of the country's brand (Grigorian, 2016: 109). Such an intense devotion to the preservation of *Armenianness* and the 'Armenia' brand can become a motivating factor for Armenians to go to Armenia. This point, to Vrej, should be put as the highest priority for the Armenian government. Bedros in Sydney also stresses the importance of developing a strong brand for Armenia.

Aram, on the other hand, sees the challenges through the prism of multiculturalism, which, to him, is a challenge itself. As he explains, Australia "is such an inclusive environment, which makes it so hard not to be absorbed and makes it impossible not to be engaged by the Anglo-Saxon environment." His main point is that the environment in Australia does not encourage diasporans of other nations to enrich it (Australia) with their diasporan identities; to a large extent, the Australian environment absorbs these diasporans. Does this mean the environment supports assimilation rather than integration? "You lose your *Armenianness*," stresses Aram. As he specifies, interaction and intermarriages affect identity preservation, and this continues to be a major challenge. It is noteworthy to refer to James Clifford, who stresses that, even though in assimilationist ideologies or societies, of which Australia might be considered one (Clifford's example is the United States though), "immigrants may experience loss or nostalgia, but only en route to a whole new home in a new place." However, the local host environment "cannot assimilate groups that maintain important allegiances and practical connections to a homeland" (Clifford, 1994: 307). Moreover, as Nikos Papastergiadis, a scholar of cultural studies, emphasizes, diasporas are even as influential locally as globalizing forces with regard to the threat on nation-states (Papastergiadis, 2013: 21). These strong statements, it can be argued, underline the clear distinction between diasporans and non-diasporan 'ethnies,' and their different levels of vulnerability toward assimilation.

Keeping the culture and language alive is seen as the most significant challenge to Lily. She specifies, "in Australia, it is our identity, there is not much knowledge about Armenia here." With regard to the connections between communities, Lily also points out that across Australasia, there is no connection between the different Armenian communities. Antonio from Sydney, also identifies the preservation of the Armenian language as the main priority. According to him, "it is easier to speak English. I feel I have kept myself Armenian, but I have lost my family language-wise." He points at "something monotonous and routine" happening in the community life and considers the connection with Armenia a necessary means of preserving the Armenian identity. However, as he explains, "people who reach Armenia are somehow mainly same, mostly aged 60 years and older." Antonio's opinion is that the Armenians in Australia should do more in Armenia. He points at a problem of low youth participation in events organized by the community, for which, among other possible factors, is an ineffective way to get across the generational gap. As briefly mentioned above, the diaspora organizations are not united but split, as other interviewees have also noted. "People do not go [to events] because some others are there, etc.," as he emphasized.

Armen from the Sydney community sees "trying to stay Armenian" as the main challenge for the diaspora. Culture and language, as well as keeping people active within the community and strong are crucial. He states, "if they do not speak the language, they can eventually assimilate and lose their identity." Armen accepts the essential role of religion in opposing assimilation. However, he accepts that Armenia's position is not easy, especially as it requires financial expenditure which it cannot cover at this moment. "It is up to the community to establish connections to Armenia," Armen suggests. The other side of the issue Armen highlights is the willingness of communities to be engaged. "When the community is not interested, then it is a problem" he argues and adds that Armenia as a homeland for the diaspora can do a lot if a community is willing to cooperate. "It can provide the manpower, ideas, support for events, for instance, cultural performances." The relatively recent increasing activity has included cultural support from the Ministry of Diaspora, such as two visits by the Minister, seminars and language teachers, or artists for events. By recognizing the importance of efforts to support such far away communities from Armenia as those in Australia, Armen does not specify how the homeland can motivate its diasporic communities to be more engaged in the homeland.

Similar to Armen, Levon (in Melbourne) also thinks that the most significant challenge is "holding on to the culture." His view is that the 'millennials' are struggling to hold on to their identity because of the speed at which society is changing. "How to keep them engaged?" Levon asks rhetorically and argues that this is a big challenge at the moment. His points out:

> having new blood coming and doing work is very hard, especially in Melbourne. Here it is very difficult. In committees, many are 30+-year-old, 40+, and very few 20+. Engaging the younger ones is the biggest issue. On the other hand, the diaspora has good relations with the motherland Armenia. However, the initiatives are not reaching Australia (*Ari Toun*, etc.).[*] It is not much else here a young person of Armenian background hears. It is very hard to determine that link, especially when your parents are from outside Armenia. I think the link can be improved. What Armenia should be focusing on is more content in English language.

In the diaspora, many among the first- and second-generation Armenians still maintain Armenian language skills. Nonetheless, the younger generation has weaker Armenian language skills. By keeping them informed about the processes taking place in Armenia and the diaspora, the homeland can ignite interest among the youth, which, in turn, can

---

[*] *Ari Toun* (or 'Come Back Home' in English) was a program that encouraged young Armenians across the world to visit Armenia. According to the Ministry of Diaspora, over several years (by 2018-2019), nearly 8,000 young Diaspora Armenians visited Armenia through the *Ari Toun* (Hayern Aisor, *The Ari Toun Programme*). *Ari Toun* was replaced by other initiatives announced after the Ministry was restructured into the Office of High Commissioner for Diaspora Affairs in 2019 (Diaspora.gov.am, 2021)

motivate some of them to learn Armenian. Armen says that many in the diaspora do not know much about Armenia, and "when they want to know, the language barrier is becoming a problem." To him, this mainly happens because "they have become disenchanted and are not in schools anymore, are disconnected." As an educator, Armen's view is rooted in the developments of not only overall community-Armenia relations but also of those between the education systems and institutions of the two countries.

Challenges in the diaspora, to Mateos, the crypto-Armenian from Turkey, are different from the views of other interviewees. He admits that the diaspora does not know Armenia well and also reflects on the current situation by saying, "when the diaspora talks, it is always about the Genocide." Mateos suggested to also look at some progress, in particular, on the fact that "some Turkish people and political groups started to connect with the diaspora," some "started to talk about how we can connect, how we can improve the relations."

As suggested by some diasporans, this in-depth knowledge of each other from the diaspora's and the homeland's sides is necessary. It can be added that knowing each other better can benefit both sides of the nation and can make the process of engaging the diaspora in the homeland more effective. However, the whole inclusionary process, as argued, suffers from the problem of contested leadership. How can such a problem be overcome and what might be possible solutions?

The Diaspora and the Homeland: Knowing Each Other

Over the previous decades of Armenia's independent nation-state existence, much has been said that Armenia has not succeeded in effectively engaging its diaspora. Among the successful cases, it is worth referring to the case of Israel and the Jewish diaspora. Both Israel and Armenia are small countries having geopolitical problems within their region. Both nation-states are homes for only a portion of their global nation, with a larger part living overseas. The Armenian and the Jewish diasporas have often been compared with each other as classical cases. One of the key similarities is that both are 'victim' diasporas, as Robin Cohen classifies it (as mentioned earlier in this book). In the case of Armenians, the diaspora has been such throughout the 20th century, while the Jewish diaspora has been in exile and experienced persecutions for centuries, with the biggest tragedy taking place in the 20th century. At different times, the Jews "looked either on their homeland or to more local links" (Cohen and van Hear, 2008: 35), which, to some extent, can be said about the Armenians as well. To a certain extent, both diasporas have been economically or professionally successful. Cohen writes that even "long-settled in peaceful settings, it was difficult for many Jews in the diaspora not to 'keep their guard up'" (Cohen and van Hear, 2008: 35).

When conducting an analogical comparison, an important difference is noteworthy. In the case of Armenians, before or after the Genocide, they have not been under threat in their hostlands. Thus, by looking at their homeland, they have followed the ultimate dream of permanent physical return, not caused by a threat of forced relocation or another exile, as was the case of many Jews, particularly in Europe.

Following the foundation of the State of Israel, in its relations with its Jewish diaspora worldwide, the State "did not work in partnership with Israeli immigrants due to the inherent tension between the phenomena of Israeli immigration and Zionism" (The Reut Institute, 2013: 7). However, as emphasized, the situation has changed, and the two sides "increasingly realize that the Israeli diaspora can be a political, economic, social, and cultural asset" (The Reut Institute, 2013: 7). As such, Israel assists its diaspora in their "efforts to develop pride in Jewish identity" and "offers opportunities for real engagement with Israeli society and can be mobilized against the assault on Israel's legitimacy" (The Reut Institute, 2013: 7).

Thus, it can be concluded that in the case of relations between the homeland (Israel) and its diaspora, the shift in relations has been an outcome of a pragmatic approach. In turn, Israel has been playing a key role in preserving Jewish identity in its diaspora, which is "manifested through various means of engagement with the Jewish State" (Ben-Moshe, in Ehrlich, 2009). The existence of Israel is so important to the Jewish diaspora that, as presented, "87 percent of Canadian Jewry believes Israel is "important to being a Jew"; more than 80 percent of American Jews in the 2000 National Jewish Population Survey were very or somewhat familiar with social and political events in Israel, and over 80 percent strongly or somewhat agreed that Israel is the spiritual center of the Jewish people; 81 percent of British Jews were, according to a 1997 survey, strongly or moderately attached to Israel; and 86 percent of respondents to a 2002 survey of French Jews said they felt 'very close or close' to Israel" (Ehrlich, 2009).

Despite even ideological tensions and political disagreements, with signs of contested leadership, the Jewish diaspora "has had a distinct role to play with developing the homeland, raising funds, mobilizing political activity, and providing immigrants," and "Israel continues to play an unequivocally essential role in Diaspora Jewish identity," which is "expressed through many areas of Jewish life, such as education, community, philanthropy, and political activism" (Ehrlich, 2009). Such inclusion of the diaspora in the homeland life of Israel has resulted in "growing rates of *aliyah*,[*] participation in Israel programs, and visits to the Jewish state" (Ehrlich, 2009). Closer cooperation assumes that the nation-state and its diaspora have come to realize the importance of preserving the global Jewish identity, irrespective of ideological and political differences, and differing opinions.

"We are disorganized," says Bedros, whose travel experience to Armenia is the richest and, in order to be more organized as an extraterritorial nation, he suggests having a national program or plan by bringing analogical comparisons with Pan-Turkism and Zionism, as examples of national plans of the Turks and the Jews, respectively. In comparison with Zionism, for instance, the Armenian diaspora, as anthropologist Tsypylma Darieva argues, "does not have an ideological foundation for supporting Armenia" (Darieva, 2011: 3). The absence of ideological support, arguably, is the main barrier to effective engagement, or better to say, mobilization of diaspora with homeland Armenia. As proposed, such mobilizing processes can take place if they are based on ideological foundations. In turn, ideological foundations need a basis, which is the presence of an idea, a national idea (Vardanyan, Aravot.am, 2021).

Diaspora-homeland relations, as argued, depend on mutual expectations. Indeed, knowledge of each other and trust toward each other are essential for forming realistic and mutually-beneficial expectations. In this regard, Armen's opinion is that the diaspora does not expect much from Armenia. "My personal expectation would be to have an opportunity to develop Armenia without being shut down. For instance, I have certain skills which I have developed in Australia and would be more than happy to help the country to develop," he states categorically. Armen expresses a concern that the country "might be shut down" because of inefficient

---

[*] Immigration of the Jews from the diaspora to Israel.

bureaucracy, "by people who feel they do not need help or who think we are the best and it does not matter." This factor might be a serious barrier in diaspora-homeland relations since it prevents the diaspora from being effectively engaged in the homeland, at least in its economy. "This is something I have seen over the past few years," says Armen and refers to examples when, offering free help, he sometimes faces barriers, when "many [people] think they can do it on their own."

Diaspora is a broader, dispersed, extraterritorial entity, while the territorialized homeland is in one location. The rationality of engaging the diaspora assumes that the homeland bears the responsibility to understand its diaspora and its needs and expectations. When referring to the Armenian diaspora, larger and more established communities are usually the focus, a point also raised by several interviewees in this study. However, there are also diasporans in smaller numbers in other parts of the world.[*] For the homeland, it becomes important to have an up-to-date estimation of the number of diasporan Armenians, i.e., those who are in permanent return. Reaching diasporans effectively, strengthening their return, even at the virtual level, which is possible nowadays from the technological viewpoint, can motivate many non-diasporan 'ethnies' to transform into diasporans.

"If Armenia opens up its doors a little bit more to the world... There are lots of opportunities," says Armen, and adds that he does not know what Armenia expects from the diaspora. "I think it expects us all to repatriate eventually," he guesses and adds that, at this stage, the main expectation is "in terms of financial help." Here, Armen shares his understanding of the expectations the two sides have from each other by stating, "I think the diaspora distrusts the homeland in general, but I do not think Armenia distrusts the diaspora." He sees little substance in

---

[*] A small number of Armenians can be found in many countries or cities, which are not considered diaspora communities as such. For instance, the number of Armenians in various parts of South and East Asia is so small that the Ministry of Diaspora of Armenia (in 2008-2018) had no specialized unit (department) dealing with them. Instead, the department in charge of CIS countries (former Soviet Union), especially the Division of Relations with Communities in Central Asian countries, covered those small communities of South and East Asia – in India, Singapore, Malaysia, Thailand, Korea, China, Japan, etc. (Ministry of Diaspora of Armenia, *Department of Armenian Communities of the CIS*).

relations, to begin with, "because of lack of information and understanding, because of ignorance, rumors, the general culture of spreading lies and rumors, propaganda." The lack of sufficient knowledge about Armenia in the diaspora, to Armen, is partly related to the language barrier of the millennium generation. Thus, before Armenia's independence, there had been different problems and barriers between the two parts of the nation. Later, with the development of the Internet era, the problems, as stated, are being shifted to another level. Armen's view of millennials is connected to their differing understanding of the geopolitical situation in Armenia, compared to how older generations see it. "Having an understanding of the geopolitical situation in Armenia is a very hard task for the millennials," says Armen and points at the inability of many "to articulate about foreign issues, etc., in Armenia. And that is where trust comes from." The diaspora, to him, feels segregated and even perceives a closed-door attitude or corruption, which diminishes their trust. Even if there have been some positive results of the post-2018 government's anti-corruption campaign, it will take time before Armenia's business environment is perceived stable and favourable. Armen stresses that it is important for the diaspora to understand the policy in Armenia, "even if they [diasporans] do not agree with it." Another point raised, similar to what has already been mentioned earlier, is that Armenia perceives the diaspora as a homogeneous entity, a major problem since even within a certain country communities are diverse.

The Armenians are "a large diaspora connected to a small country," says Aram in Sydney. This point can be instrumental regarding the self-perception of Armenians and their identity as a global nation and as a sovereign nation-state. Aram sees the fact that a lot of people outside Armenia are considered as diasporans, while they do not connect to Armenia and do not know much about it. His point is an indirect justification of the rationale behind the idea proposed in this work to the homeland's (Armenia's) government about differentiating the diasporans from non-diasporan 'ethnies.' Aram provides a realistic view that many in cities with large diaspora communities "do not experience what is happening in Armenia and cannot dictate anything" and also stresses the need "to accept the fact that we are not living in Armenia." Aram makes a comparison with some other classical diasporas. For instance, when talking about the Jewish diaspora, he expresses a wish that Armenians could be more like them in assisting each other financially, "or to tell what to do." On the other hand, he refers to the Irish diaspora, which "has completely integrated within the local environment. They think of themselves as Irish, but, to a large extent, do not care what is happening in Ireland."

Aram argues that 1991 became a cornerstone regarding understanding each other by the homeland and the diaspora. "There have been changes in challenges," he stresses and gives an example of, for instance, ARF's role, which shifted since 1991. He speaks about change as something widespread within the diaspora.

> In the diaspora, we have thought of ourselves as either Dashnag, Ramgavar or Hnchag. You go to Armenia, and it has its criminals, its people, its socialists, etc. You cannot put them in three categories. This is what the diaspora does not understand. We in the diaspora thought of imposing our cultural beliefs onto Armenia proper. It does not work. The Armenians over there have gone through a different experience, much different from what the diaspora has gone through. There is a lack of knowledge, understanding, empathy. For instance, when Armenia decided to open up the borders with Turkey, a lot in the diaspora did not accept it.[*]

This is a fascinating description of the situation by a diasporan who has never been to the homeland. It is a reflection on the needs and priorities of Armenia as a sovereign political entity. The state should take care of not only issues and challenges related to the preservation of culture, language and, to a more significant extent, its global nation, but also of day-to-day situations and challenges associated with the maintenance of law and order, of ensuring the provision of vital necessities to its public, and securing safety and peace within its borders.

---

[*] The question of opening the border with Turkey has been controversial in Armenia. Patriotic feelings and the sense of national identity preservation prevent many from considering some possibly positive outcomes of the border opening. Besides, a significant part of the population worries that following the opening of the border, there will be an inflow of cheaper Turkish products into the Armenian market. Many businesses in Armenia, as worried, will need protection by the (Armenian) state, as they cannot compete with the economically more attractive Turkish products. The talks about opening the border have become more pressing after the 'Second Artsakh (44-Day) War' in 2020.

Aram admits that there is a lack of empathy from the diaspora toward Armenia. "The economy is of greater importance for Armenia," he clarifies and continues, "It is beautiful and easy for us to think from the idealistic perspective." Aram provides an interesting view on the difference between the diaspora (mainly Western Armenian speakers) and Armenia. "There is the *akhpar* and *akhper* distinction," he stresses,[*] and sadly makes it clear that being an Armenian, he thinks he (and many others) are perceived as outsiders in Armenia. "We go to Armenia as tourists, while going to live there will help," he concludes.

This situation demonstrates a two-fold problem. On the one hand, the Armenians in Armenia still find it difficult to accept the differences between them and the diaspora. Many would agree that the Armenians in Armenia are born and live with a permanently-felt threat of being conquered and even exterminated. Recent history remains in their memory, and it is difficult to change this perception even over decades or a century. Thus, the local population may subconsciously see outsiders, to some extent even diasporans, as foreigners and show intolerance. The other side of the problem can be related to the self-exclusion of the diasporans from the 'Armenia' space. It is a typical differentiation in the diaspora to distinguish between Armenians with a foreign origin and those from Armenia by using an Armenian word *hayasdantsi*, which underlines the background from Armenia.[†] "This is a shame to have such a label in use," says Bedros from Sydney. Such differentiation contributes to further self-exclusion of diasporans and, at the same time, promotes the split between the two parts of the nation. The power of words cannot be overestimated. The use of differentiating words and phrases makes communication between the two less effective and even less tolerant of each other (homeland and diaspora). By existing under the two different cultural umbrellas, the homeland and the diaspora have already been affected by differences, and having the differences widened will only strengthen the

---

[*] In Western Armenian 'akhpar' used to be a popular address, compared to 'akhper' in Armenia. Literally, it means 'brother,' while it is used in a broader sense to address a person in an informal way (like a 'guy' or 'man' in an informal address in English). The difference is mainly related to Western Armenian pronunciation. The real point is different. It is a common word to emphasize the difference in identity of Western Armenian speakers, an impolite reference a mean way of differentiation and exclusion.

[†] The word literally means 'a person from Armenia.'

split in communication between them. Engagement of the diaspora with the homeland assumes going beyond the tourist-sightseeing relationship format. It is logical to assume that the concept of 'imagined community' is present in the perception of the homeland, which can be further strengthened by visiting the homeland. No matter whether they are short- or long-term visits, they are essential in building an intimate knowledge of the homeland. Moreover, diasporans, if emotionally attached to specific places, and not merely having a more general perception of the Armenia space, can still be included in the homeland more effectively.

Vartan in Sydney suggests that Armenians "have to find a solution to attract wealthy people, not only famous ones, and to change the mentality of the wealthy in order for them to give for the benefit of the community and the Republic of Armenia." Attracting wealthy diasporans to Armenia can arguably be useful if they decide to be closer to Armenia by investing there and are motivated to do so. This initiative can strengthen the sense of diaspora return. Investments, in this sense, can be in any form, as business, social enterprise, or even education for themselves or their families.

Foreign investments are beneficial for any economy. Regarding Armenia, investments can be seen in three categories:

- local investors (including of returned diasporans),
- diasporans from abroad (so-called investments of Armenian origin), and
- other foreign investments.

Non-Armenian-origin (foreign) potential investments, taking into consideration the scale of the Armenian economy, are limitless. However, before non-Armenian (non-diasporan) foreigners invest in Armenia, the homeland should first focus on encouraging the diasporans to do so. They could become a bridge and motivating factor for non-diasporan investors. Local potential investors in the homeland (Armenia) have intimate knowledge of the local (Armenian) business space. On the other hand, knowledge of the homeland by diasporans puts them in an advantageous position, compared to non-diasporic foreigners, in terms of their awareness of Armenia and its political-economic-social environment. As argued, it can be difficult to motivate non-diasporan foreigners to invest in Armenia if they see diasporan Armenians not investing sufficiently and not connecting the Armenian economy with the rest of the world. In turn, the diaspora will not stay active as investors unless potential local investors invest actively in Armenia. Then, non-diaspora investors will follow the trend of investments in Armenia. (Vardanyan, 168Finance, 2019).

Perspectives of Engaging the Diaspora in the Homeland

A rhetorical question can be asked whether there is a need to change anything in the diaspora-homeland relationship? A simple reason for change is that in the contemporary world, diasporas are becoming more integrated into host countries, and this development is becoming a "permanent phenomenon," as Khachig Tölölyan would describe matters (Tölölyan, 2000: 108). In this way, the diaspora might not even be fully included in the homeland. Higher than an emotional level, the inclusion of the diaspora in the homeland is, first of all, driven by pragmatism and rationality. The reasons behind this engagement are in the actual and potential benefits such inclusion can bring to both sides, not only culturally but also financially and politically. In the modern world, where globalization processes seem to continue, the national perspective is giving way to a globalized one; however, there are tendencies that show a strengthening of nationalism and pan-national endeavors. The attempt to include the diaspora in the homeland is a process of a bordered homeland nation-state engaging with its exterritorial diaspora space. The most recent crisis-driven diaspora mobilization was during the 'Second Artsakh (44-Day) War' of September-November 2020 which demonstrated a potential for such pan-national unity. However, it also stressed the importance of maintaining trust and transparency in homeland-diaspora relations. The massive aid provided by the diaspora to Armenia during the War, including more than US$170,000,000 of financial support, or approximately $17-18 for every Armenian worldwide, to the Hayastan All-Armenian Fund (Vardanyan, Aravot.am, 2021) was followed by criticism for the lack of accountability from Armenia's side.

* * *

According to our interviewee Michael Bazikian from Melbourne, the Armenian diaspora has got unlimited abilities and opportunities to promote Armenia and to improve life in Armenia, working conditions, hospitals and education. His main view is that everything, for all the changes in Armenia, needs money, and the diaspora has the money. However, trust is the major problem in relations, and there is a need to overcome it. For Mr. Bazikian, everything possible needs to be done for every Armenian to realize *Armenianness* and strengthen their sense of belonging to "the ancient, proud and educated nation."

Robin Cohen sees a big difference in diaspora politics when it is stateless and state-linked (Cohen, 2005: 180). Thus, compared to the pre-independence period, when the diaspora was the mobilizing force in pan-Armenian initiatives, the Armenian diaspora, after Armenia's independence, has been more engaged in "benign activities," as Cohen would describe such situations when analyzing the diaspora's effectiveness in general (Cohen, 2005: 181). All the activities before independence were seen as essential for maintaining Armenian identity and supporting the creation of the national state. There was no claimed or contested leadership from the homeland in such circumstances, as it did not have the strong political weight of a nation-state. After independence, however, the diaspora, not able to transform and adapt to the new realities, found itself in a situation where it could not dictate its expectations, as the other side was a sovereign nation-state.

In diaspora-homeland relations, Khachig Tölölyan emphasizes, there is competition in the diaspora, at all levels, "to control institutions and funds; to recruit loyal constituencies; to attract cultural producers to one vision or another of diasporic identity" (Tölölyan, 2000: 109). Understanding homeland-diaspora relations needs to be based on the grounds that the homelanders and the diasporans have a clear perception of their belonging. Anthony Smith argues that people belong to their homeland as much as it belongs to them (Smith, 1991: 23). "Armenia and diaspora is a partnership," says Bedros and adds that partners should trust each other, and "it is extremely important to reinforce the trust." He thinks that the diaspora, in general, does not trust Armenia – a similar thought also expressed by Armen (as mentioned above). "It [the Diaspora] loves Armenia, but that's it," he says. Again, similar to Armen's opinion, Bedros also specifies that Armenia trusts the diaspora more. Does this mean that Armenia has more realistic expectations of the diaspora than the latter has of Armenia? If expectations are less realistic in this case, then relations tend to be based more on emotional aspects, which can lead to disappointment in case they do not materialize.

Vartan from Sydney sees the situation differently and argues that Armenia sets higher-than-real expectations, which are mainly finance-related. At personal levels, he agrees that contributions can be made if the attitude, expectations, or as he says, "the modus operandi is different." Vartan perceives cooperation between the diaspora and Armenia not only through the prism of financial contributions. He states that many cannot give money, but they can work in Armenia; economic facilities should be provided to diasporans to establish business with tax holidays, let's say, no taxes for three years. Many Armenians will go and invest in Armenia. Today the expectation is 'just give me.' This does not work. In business, it is 'give and take.' Incentives to people are needed. When you have high expectations, you start doubting, and the mistrust comes then. Because of those expectations, even if they are real, and because of mistrust developed earlier... But if you announce the benefits and advantages, guaranteed, protected, you will see the difference.

Diasporas, Khachig Tölölyan emphasizes, "have been idealized as open, porous, circuit-based, cosmopolitan not parochial, deterritorialized, exemplary communities of the transnational moment, and therefore capable of offering – not of ascribing to or imposing upon, as nation-states do to their citizen-subjects – flexible, multiple identities." (Tölölyan, 2000: 112). It can therefore be proposed that such idealized misperceptions of diasporas become a determinant of misleading expectations.

The diaspora-Armenia relationship is not bilateral. On the one hand, there is Armenia, the homeland, while the other side is made up of many units. These units are composed of not only communities but also many individual diasporans. Vartan, for instance, stresses the multi-unit nature of the diaspora, in contrast to the one-unit nature of Armenia as the homeland, by emphasizing that every single community in the diaspora is not the same. "This is the same in language," he says. His main point is not that the Armenian language is different, but that from one environment to another, the language mentality changes as well. Vartan brings a comparison between different mentality in Spanish-speaking countries (the broad Latino environment) and mentality of the Armenians (the differences), for instance, in the Middle East or in France. The space the diasporans are surrounded by or are a part of, as suggested, affects the community, its perception of self, and every diasporan in the community. "The diaspora is a multi-level building," says Vartan and continues, "you should go up and down to check what is there, on every level." The above-mentioned point can mean that that same approach may not work for every diaspora community, and expectations should also be differentiated.

Vahe from Sydney strongly advocates thinking bigger. "Armenia has challenges which not Armenia alone, but Armenians need to deal with," he says and identifies two issues that should be addressed to improve the inclusion of the diaspora in the homeland. First, the divide between Armenian and the diaspora should be removed. It is a generational change, Vahe clarifies. "I would want to see the perception. Unfortunately, this idea exists in Armenia that the diaspora left Armenia and went to the diaspora without generally understanding why the diaspora was formed." His second point is that the diaspora should become an active participant in Armenia,

> to have a direct connection with Armenia, other than just saying 'I speak the language,' 'I go to a Saturday school,' 'I am an ARF member,' 'I am an AGBU member,' 'I am whatever...' How do you make that person have firm roots back in the Motherland? On the way to do so, Armenia, as the homeland, should encourage the right to return to Armenia, similar to what Israel does.

The existence of regulations that encourage the diaspora to return to Armenia, including the simplified procedure of citizenship acquisition, is expected to be better known in the diaspora – an opinion raised by interviewees in this study. Potential benefits of inclusion in the homeland, other than the emotional aspect, are not well known, as emphasized earlier. With about seven million people living in the diaspora, Vahe's wish is to have everyone visit Armenia at least once in a lifetime. He continues by stressing the importance (for Armenia) to understand that the diaspora is not there for Armenia to just ask for money:

> The diaspora is not a bank account to withdraw money from. The diaspora can be a huge benefit to Armenia, but if Armenia can open itself and guarantee the safety of investments... Armenia takes the diaspora for granted as a pool of money. They think they know everything without anybody's help. I would say those communities that need help from Armenia are a minority, not a majority. The majority can help Armenia. Inclusion is a two-way street. The government of Armenia and the citizens of the Republic must understand the importance of the diaspora and their role in the development of Armenia, and the diaspora should understand its role in it as well.

Inclusion in Armenia assumes participation in its political, economic, and social life and processes. As Vahe explains, "we want Armenia to be a free society, a democratic society." He sees the important role of the post-Soviet generation in this process of building a new society. "However, you cannot sit and just talk about it, but be an active participant, to have a mass of people involved in it," stresses Vahe. 'Being engaged' is seen as being marketers for Armenia, for the 'Armenia' brand abroad. "The diaspora has the biggest role to play in promoting 'Armenia,'" and, as specified, even though Armenia has its own challenges, it needs to be promoted "from the positive sides, through influential networks."

Arguably, the most important achievement of branding will be the non-Armenians speaking about Armenia, promoting it among non-Armenians. Thus, for the diaspora's inclusion in Armenia, the economic interests are emphasized. The emotional side can, indeed, help; however, it needs to be motivated by long-term economic expectations. The diaspora, as a global network, is capable of providing financial support to help Armenia, to enrich Armenia with necessary skills. It is essential to engage the diaspora for any of these reasons, with a particular emphasis on importing skills from the diaspora. Some early signs of such 'brain gain' have been announced by the new initiatives launched by the Office of High Commissioner of Diaspora Affairs, such as the *iGorts* project (Diaspora.gov.am, 2021)

By elaborating on the interviewed diasporans' ideas, one can conclude that the Armenian diaspora, at least most of it, has existed with established business practices for decades. By possessing essential business skills, the diaspora can apply them in Armenia, provided there are favorable conditions created there. Another point is whether Armenia, especially its businesses, are ready for such an inflow of 'foreign talent' from the diaspora. The recent immigration of Syrian Armenians has proven to be such a success.[*] If the diaspora can inject financial and political support into Armenia, as well as business skills, then Armenia can use its relations with the diaspora to export its culture there and, through it, to the rest of the world. This cultural support to the diaspora will contribute to branding 'Armenia' by promoting the country for foreign investments, be it in the

---

[*] Many refugees from Syria established themselves in Armenia recently. Among them are many in the food service industry who have opened restaurants. They have contributed to further improvement of quality and assortment of food in restaurants, as well as to the improvement of restaurant service in the country. (The Guardian, *The Syrian Refugee Restauranteurs*).

form of direct business ventures, tourism, an inflow of students or simply by raising awareness about the country overseas, which can strengthen Armenia's political position in the world arena.

Levon from Melbourne strongly insists on providing economic incentives to those who are willing to move to Armenia and open a business. As he justifies confidently, "on the one hand, people come and open businesses in the country and, on the other hand, people are not leaving the country." Garo, an interviewee also from Melbourne, stresses the importance of motivating diasporan Armenians economically. "Economic interests are to be promoted, and economic cooperation should be facilitated," he says.

Armen, an educator from Sydney, thinks that an essential step toward reducing barriers between the two parts of the nation is through changes in the language system. To "feel more as one, it would be the writing and spelling that will show uniformity," he suggests and specifies that the Armenian government and the diaspora have to work together "so that a person in Armenia or the diaspora can read a book the same way, without feeling it's two." An analogical comparison in this regard can be made with other languages, which are spoken in different parts of the world or by different countries, for instance, English, Spanish, French, or Arabic. However, if in the case of any of these languages, it is spoken by different peoples in different countries and territories worldwide, in the case of the Armenian language, it is spoken by one nation but split into two parts, with the second one being extraterritorial and everywhere. Armen, himself being a speaker of Western Armenian, proposes that it does not matter which direction the problem is solved, whether the Western or Eastern Armenian dialect is selected as the only formal one. "This should be solved, in whichever direction, as it is more important that the decision is made," he says. Provided such a major problem is solved, or, at least, is in the process of its solution, a diasporan in Armenia will feel less foreign and would be perceived as less foreign by the locals. For Armen, it is essential to build an effective economically motivating system that would include the diaspora in the economy of Armenia:

> Why I am here is an issue of opportunity. If a diasporan goes to Armenia with the family, he should feel the opportunity is there, can build financial stability, and build that country instead of living in different parts of the world. Everything there is still quite young and inexperienced. With more opportunities provided,

more Armenians will go and live there. For many, the next step is to go and live in Armenia. However, they also need some kind of security and will not think about moving out again, but will consider it a permanent location, where they will spend their life there.

Armen explains that the distrust that has developed between the diaspora and the homeland over the past decades – since independence – is a result of the transformation in the relationship. The problem of emigration from Armenia and other significant issues of national importance are seen relating to the capability and willingness of the leadership in Armenia to solve it. "For diasporans, the business environment is important," says Armen and specifies that knowing more about what is going on in Armenia will help. Similar to several other interviewees, Armen also admits that Armenia and the diaspora do not know each other well, but also stresses an alarming point that they "are not that willing to work with each other." As a justification of his opinion, Armen refers to the community in Australia. It has been formed by people coming from different parts of the world, and they "are not in active relations with Armenians who have come from other parts of the world, who are not 'theirs', and they might not support them that much." Thus, Armen raises an argument that even sub-identities matter.

Anahit, from Melbourne, is also not sure if both sides of the nation know each other well, and adds that this may be the main problem in their relations. Speaking in overall terms, full utilization of the potential from diaspora-homeland relations is possible, as proposed, if the diaspora maintains relations with the homeland in these dimensions:

(a)   intra-community relations;

(b)   inter-community relations;

(c)   community-homeland relations;

(d)   individual diasporan-community relations;

(e)   individual diasporan-individual diasporan relations; and

(f)   individual diasporan-homeland relations.

Neither of these dimensions should be underestimated, as the full potential of diaspora-homeland relations includes the dimensions specified above, and, if any of them are weak, the overall potential of relations will be underutilized.

Development of homeland-diaspora relationship should be seen through the prism of understanding what happened to the people, the reasons that have led them to become diasporans, what their life was, as Mateos suggests. In other words, what he proposes can be interpreted as a necessity to identify the roots but also the routes of diasporans. As a crypto-Armenian, with his most recent years spent in Melbourne, Mateos stresses the importance for Armenia to reach its diaspora communities and specifies the main problem in homeland-diaspora relations by saying,

> Armenia is a country; it is assumed to be more powerful than a community. We see Armenia as a country. However, we do not live there and do not actually feel what Armenians feel about what is happening in Armenia. This is the beginning of the problem.

Visits to Armenia, according to Mateos, are essential for the country. He suggests opening schools and facilitate education as a way to strengthen mutual relations between the two sides of the nation. Mateos is confident that the diaspora can be active in the process by encouraging diasporans to go and study in Armenia.

Improvement of relations between Armenia and its diaspora assumes, first of all, improvement of communications between the two, which can raise the level of knowledge about each other. The creation of an active channel of communication is seen as something crucial, for instance, by Levon in Melbourne, who thinks that diasporans should be aware of how they might reach Armenia over issues they experience or information they need. "Having someone in Armenia you know, you can talk to for a diasporan... be it an information hub, an organization, a department maybe, that is completely transparent, that you can talk to and understand what is going on, how you could help or vice versa, not corrupt, a legitimate organization," argues Levon. He sees physical return, particularly by bringing skills to Armenia as critically important. Here it should be mentioned that such unawareness can be attributed partly to weaker willingness to find information about ways to connect to the homeland (Armenia) and also to the (so-far) weaker effectiveness of major diaspora-related government structures in Armenia.

Physical return, in general, can be of temporary or permanent nature, and each type has its advantages. For instance, a temporary return can facilitate businesses, as well as such industries as health care (medical tourism), culture (tourism), education (study in Armenia, short- and long-term), etc. Even if trips are not long-term, the most important aspect is the established connection between the diasporans and Armenia. Such a connection has a potential for strengthening and extrapolating onto a larger scale by bringing more diasporans to the country. Longer-term return, undoubtedly, provides more opportunities for the utilization of skills in Armenia. Immigration of young and mid-age diasporans makes it possible to benefit from positive externalities created through the import of brains, a practice already successfully applied by some countries.[*]

Diaspora-Homeland Relations: The Problem of Contested Leadership

Political scientist Kristin Cavoukian argues that diasporans are 'constructed' by Armenian state elites according to the ability of those elites "to navigate a political culture and wield a symbolic vocabulary that the RA [Republic of Armenia] has recently institutionalized in its 'diaspora management' institutions" (Cavoukian, 2013: 722). This ability, being dynamic, as it is argued here, imposes pressure on the diaspora with regard to its perception of the 'rules of the game' set by the homeland's side.

The development of Armenia into an economic powerhouse is seen as one of the ultimate objectives of Armenia and the diaspora. Aram stresses this point and makes his thought clear by stating, "I would like to see us organizing ourselves as the Jewish diaspora is and would love to see Armenia more in regional politics." Certainly, proper organization is needed for that, and Aram refers to the Israeli lobby, underlining that it has not achieved its strong organization overnight. "It is a long process, through centuries, and lobbies abroad helped create Israel," he says. His view is based on the necessity of strengthening the political power of Armenia. "Our job in the diaspora is to help Armenia itself; for better or worse, that is our homeland," he stresses. He speaks about looking at the past and demanding reparations for the Genocide. "If that happens, I am for that," he says proudly; however, he also strongly promotes looking

---

[*] A comparatively successful engagement has been in progress by the Indian state "due in part to the return of some highly-qualified Indians to their native country" (Giordano and Terranova, *The Indian Policy of Skilled Migration*). Engagement of the diaspora in India is "slowly, but visibly, yielding results in terms of economic benefits and in the context of 'soft power'" (Rajan, 2014: ch. 3, p. 2).

forward and states, "our job in the diaspora is to help Armenia itself, not the historical Armenia but the Republic itself." As a lawyer, who has been living a life of an active diasporan, Aram does not underestimate the significance of recognition of the past. However, his forward-looking view tends to identify potential for improvement of communication between the diaspora and Armenia and, thus, strengthen the relationship the diaspora has with Armenia.

> Armenians in the diaspora will be more effective to help Armenia from the outside. It is ideal to go and live there, but I think it is more effective to help from outside. Legal help, investments, not just charity money. Unilateral transfers are also important, but investments are more needed. Helping to improve the infrastructure is important. Tax breaks, making Armenia attractive not only for Armenian investors is what is needed since the return on investment is important.

The diaspora's extraterritorial existence all-over-the-world, as argued by Aram, makes it invaluable to the homeland. Thus, Aram's view can be considered as an indirect justification of the diaspora's existence without its ultimate goal of permanent physical return.

Lily, an interviewee in Melbourne, strongly emphasizes the need to strengthen education in Armenian, similar to what several other interviewees underlined as well. "Because we are so scattered and have immersed ourselves in so many countries, I would wish Armenian education to be stronger," says Lily. She clarifies that by insisting on the importance of education, she is trying to be unbiased and not affected by her profession as a teacher. In particular, Lily stresses that education in the Armenian language "should not be limited to weekend schools, for instance." As mentioned earlier, there is no full-day Armenian school in Melbourne. At the same time, her opinion is quite pessimistic with regard to what is going on in the diaspora nowadays. She says,

> I do not think I have seen much progress with regard to the development of Armenia-diaspora relationship. It has been fairly stagnant. We in the diaspora have the numbers, have the resources, have the knowledge, enthusiasm, but we are not going anywhere with that.

A wish, a dream among the diasporans, is to see Armenia more powerful and able to take care of its people so that they would be happy to live and work in Armenia. Unlike many other interviewed diasporans,

Anahit from Melbourne disagrees that there is a problem of low awareness about Armenia among the diasporans. This opinion can be probably related to her stronger connections with Armenia and the fact of being originally from there. For Anahit, the problem is deeper at the perception level and is about an "arrogance toward Armenia and the situation there."

Maria from Melbourne wishes that Armenian diasporans will "stick together" and refers to the Assyrians or the Egyptian Copts as examples of very connected diaspora communities. Maria also points at the lack of information. She adds,

> fresh new minds, with more fresh and diverse mind in the leadership of diaspora organizations will help. We can make the change and can have the transformation happening. The need is to communicate and collaborate better. Whatever is happening in Australia, in the community. I am not sure if Armenia knows about it. The lack of information is an issue. Communication is not effective. There need to be meetings aimed at further improvements. Someone from Armenia should come from time to time; someone from here needs to go there, to facilitate communication and knowledge of each other.

Perspectives of diaspora-homeland relations, to Maria, fall in three areas: "Getting together as a nation, coming together as a community, and communicating what we are lacking here." Maria's experience as a diasporan has led her to think that Armenia expects the diaspora to continue preserving Armenian identity. She also adds that, "if someone from there comes here, and I have met a few, they get shocked in a sense that our 'Armenianism' is not what they expected." Expectations of the diaspora should be realistic, Maria insists. She makes it clear that, after migrating to Australia, Armenians from Armenia have the experience of "seeing 'Armenia' Armenia in their daily life."* While in Australia, "it is not that much" and makes it clear that new immigrants from Armenia might be disappointed to see the situation. An example she refers to is a sizable number of Armenians from Turkey, who have forgotten the Armenian language and converse in Turkish, a fact not well received by many Armenian speaking Armenians, for whom the memory of the Genocide continues to be a pillar of national identity and heritage preservation.

---

* As if they see Armenia reflected in everything, everyone, and everywhere.

Maria and Helen, both Melbourne Armenians, emphasize the importance of organizing tours of Melbourne for youth groups coming from Armenia and ask whether the Church could organize trips to Armenia. With reference to this, Helen thinks that, as a smaller community, Melbourne Armenians feel less privileged with regard to the attention paid to them by the far-away homeland. Maria also expressed the same concern. In this regard, smaller communities in Perth, the Gold Coast-Brisbane area, and other cities in Australia are even more disadvantaged. It is a paradox that more attention is paid to a large community, which itself is richer and has access to more resources to organize more events. There has been a visit by His Holiness the Catholicos of All Armenians to Melbourne.[*] Helen also remembers the visit of the President of Armenia to Singapore, an event she attended there.[†] "We were so excited to have the President going to Singapore, but they never come to Australia," she says regretfully.

Diaspora-homeland relations are seen as inseparable concerns of diaspora institutions. A special role attributed to the Armenian Apostolic Church emphasizes its unique potential to mediate in communities and unite the two parts of the diaspora, Eastern and Western Armenian speakers, as well as its two Sees, and through that, the whole diaspora. Making one seat of the Church is seen as vitally important. Antonio, who himself is not a member of the Armenian Apostolic Church (he is Roman Catholic), firmly believes that this unification would be a significant milestone. He accepts that such a union had been attempted two decades earlier but failed.[‡] Unification of the Church, to Antonio, is not a task that

---

[*] His Holiness Garegin II, the Catholicos of All Armenians, visited Melbourne on November 23, 2002. He arrived in Melbourne from Sydney, which he visited on November 21-22, 2002 (Asbarez, *Karekin II Official Visit*).

[†] This event has been mentioned earlier in this book.

[‡] Karekin II (or Garegin II) was the Catholicos of the Great House of Cilicia in Antelias (Beirut), when Vazgen I, the Supreme Patriarch and Catholicos of All Armenians, passed away in 1994 (Agadjanian, 2014: 135). Karekin II participated in the elections of the next Catholicos of All Armenians and became Catholicos Garegin I in 1995, "and his pontificate lasted until his death in 1999" (Agadjanian, 2014: 135). With Garegin I elected as Catholicos of All Armenians, there was a hope that the two Sees would finally unite and the Mother See of Holy Etchmiadzin would eventually become the only See of the Church. However, history has proved otherwise, and for over two decades, the two Sees have remained separate as before.

only the Church and its two Sees should be involved in. As suggested, this problem of contested leadership between the two needs the involvement of the three major political organizations in the Diaspora – the *ARF*, *Ramkavar*, and *Hnchak* political parties, who "should work together as one diaspora, one people, one nation." On the way to achieve this ambitious goal, which was also proposed by Armen from Sydney (he was mentioned earlier in this chapter) Antonio stresses the unification of the language by bringing the two main dialects closer to each other. "The perception of 'us' should prevail. Once you do, the followers will come."

The responsibility of the Church has been stressed by other interviewees too. For instance, Vrej from Sydney thinks that the Church should take some responsibility for the further improvement of Armenia-diaspora relations and in overcoming barriers, including the problem of contested leadership. "It should not be just a religious organization; it should be a community institution," he suggests in strong terms. Thus, for the Armenians, who have a communal rather than territorial identity, the role of the Church is seen as one that can further strengthen the communal sense of identity in the diaspora. Vrej does not undermine the role of other diaspora organizations; however, to him, the role of the Church is special. As he clarifies:

> If the Church is to take responsibility to build schools, social community organizations, you no longer segregate people by their political ties. Some communities might help, but some might need help. Before the 1990s, there was no role of the state to include the diaspora, as the state was not sovereign. Since the early 1990s, not much was done by the state, and in particular, by the Ministry of Diaspora, with regard to strengthening inclusion.

As a barrier to overcome, Vrej suggests establishing a representative office of Armenia in Australia (embassy or, at least, a consulate), which is home for such a large Armenian community. He stresses that it will help in the long-run if the Armenian state is physically present in Australia. In this regard, a recent development gave some hope, after Mr. Zorhab Mnatsakanyan, the Minister of Foreign Affairs of Armenia, announced (in 2019) the intention of Armenia to establish an embassy in Australia in the distant future (Aravot.am).

Improvement of diaspora-homeland relations, first of all, assumes an improvement in communication between the two sides. For the particular case of Armenians, Vrej points to the ineffective connection of

Statue of Mother Armenia dominating the Yerevan skyline

communities in the broader region (Australasia). His business, as specified, covers four distinct markets (Australian and New Zealand, South-East Asia, India and North Asia), "all different markets across the larger region, where small pockets of communities live, with different requirements, compared to those in Australia." He says that when traveling in that vast region, he does connect to Armenians, but only through his personal connections, a point also mentioned by Vahe above.

In the case of Armenians, the diaspora, due to historical circumstances, was active in the process of identity preservation and, for many decades, as argued, was the leader of the nation. In the year 1991, the political independence of Armenia changed the whole framework of Armenia-diaspora relations. Since then, the nation has had its sovereign political entity – the nation-state – which has tried to show its superior position[*] and shifted to a more inclusionary approach to relations with the diaspora. Such positioning is noticeable even in verbal expressions (announcements). As a vivid example, when praising the U.S. Senate for its recognition of the Armenian Genocide on December 12, 2019, Armenia's Prime Minister Pashinyan made an announcement "on behalf of the Armenian nation" and not Armenia or the people in Armenia (Radio Liberty, 13.12.2019).[†] This is an example of Armenia's claim to lead pan-Armenian processes, which can also assume readiness to become a political and cultural (and, possibly, economic) center of *Armenianness.*

The roots of such contested leadership can be found in the nature of objectives both sides have set. Khachig Tölölyan makes it clear that "homeland and diaspora leaderships both recognize that the transnation's different segments, though temporarily united by crisis, do not share the same political goals and principles" (Tölölyan, 2000: 123). Such difference makes contradictions inevitable. With established political structures and goals, the diaspora, naturally, tries to maintain and preserve them and to remain relevant – despite the fact such a stance may contradict the ultimate goal of diaspora's existence – permanent physical return. Is this a dead-end then?

---

[*] One example was the exclusion of the ARF from the internal politics in Armenia in the 1990s, as mentioned earlier in the book.

[†] The U.S. Senate, following the House of Representatives (30.10.2019) on 12.12.2019, unanimously recognized the Armenian Genocide (*The New York Times*, 12.12.2019)

One reason behind such tension caused by pan-national leadership claims in both Armenia and the diaspora can be related to having one part of the global nation residing within a particular territorially-bound area (Armenia) and the other area – the non-territorial diaspora – being dispersed globally. Managing relations between the territorial homeland and its extraterritorial diaspora is not a project. It is a continuous process, which assumes, in-depth knowledge and understanding of the other side, and can build and strengthen trust between the two sides of the nation. It is only through mutual trust that both the homeland and the diaspora can obtain an opportunity to establish clear and realistic pan-national and homeland-centered goals and expectations, driven by rational motives of the homeland's inclusionary policy toward its diaspora.

CONCLUSION

Armenia as the cultural homeland for the global Armenian nation has experienced drastic and dramatic transformations throughout the past hundred years. The processes include the Armenian Genocide, the establishment of the nation-state in 1918 (after losing statehood more than five centuries before it), the loss of sovereignty in 1920 and the establishment of Soviet rule accompanied by a significant loss of its territory, rapid industrialization, environmental problems (with a 20% decline in the level of its main freshwater resource – Lake Sevan),[*] World War II,[†] the revival of the Genocide issue in its wider political context, the Artsakh unification movement, the 1988 devastating earthquake, the collapse of the Soviet Union, the independence and the establishment of the modern Republic in 1991, the Artsakh wars paused by a cease-fire, a three-year long energy crisis, a three-decade long transportation blockade (by Turkey and Azerbaijan), mass emigration and, as a result, large gender disparity, internal political conflicts (but not military or civil wars, fortunately, as in case of several other post-Soviet republics), resignations of political leaders, political terrorism (the murder of the Prime Minister, Chairman of the National Assembly, and six other MPs and government members during a parliament session in October 1999), numerous mass political protests (with a violent one following the presidential elections in February 2008), and a peaceful change of power in April-May 2018 (popularly called the 'Velvet Revolution.')

Changes in post-1991 Armenia, particularly after the 2018 political transformation, have not yet resulted in the physical return of diasporan

---

[*] Over several decades, starting from 1933, Lake Sevan lost 42% of its water volume, and the maximum depth was reduced from 98.6m 79.8, mainly as a result of water used for hydroelectric power generation (Hovanesian and Bronozian, 2009: 178).

[†] During World War II, Armenia was one of the constituent republics of the Soviet Union. There were also hundreds of thousands of ethnic Armenians living in other republics of the Union. Thus, it is estimated that around 500,000 ethnic Armenians fought for the Allies, among whom some 200,000 were killed or classified as missing, including 100,000 from Soviet Armenia (or 1 out of 15 people in Armenia). (Sanjian, 2005: 1).

Armenians to Armenia. Many diasporan Armenians have been pointing at economic and political factors as barriers to their return. Is this delayed return because of a hope of improvement, adaptation to the 'diasporic comfort zone' in hostlands, or a result of a permanent blame-game, which is an end in itself? It can be argued that, in the Armenian case, the diaspora's physical return is blocked by the lack of a political agenda and ideology in the homeland toward the diaspora. The Second Artsakh War has further deteriorated the prospects of a large-scale physical return to Armenia from the diaspora. Unlike successful examples of mass migration, based on ideology (as in the case of Israel) or economic benefits and expectations (as in the case of the Indian diaspora), Armenia has not demonstrated its potential for effective engagement of the diaspora. Yet.

Both the diaspora and its homeland possess inherent values that can benefit the other. Each side should understand the clear benefits of effective communication and connection with the other. The potential value of one side to the other is not a guarantee that possible benefits will be well-understood and, more importantly, materialize. Promotion of knowledge about each other, as argued, empowers the two sides of the nation to develop realistic demands of each other, supported by an ability and willingness to enrich the other side, rather than simply to expect benefits from it, or, at a purely emotional level, to wish unity and engagement without rational, concrete steps.

'Diaspora,' as an area of study, is directly related to discussions of nationalism and global political and cultural dimensions of nationhood. As discussed in this book, homeland states have become more interested in engaging diasporans, among other ways, through attempts to strengthen their cultural influence abroad, to attract foreign investments, and to increase their political power internationally. There have been successes and failures regarding the effectiveness of the diaspora's inclusion in the homeland. In the case of Armenians, the subject of study here, it is common to hear that the homeland Armenia, so far, has not succeeded in utilizing its diaspora's potential and has not engaged diasporans effectively (Dinnie, 2008: 228-229). Relations between homeland and diaspora are not easy. As mentioned by diasporan Armenians who were interviewed as part of this study, intra-community and diaspora-Armenia ties are far from being effective. Both communities where the study was conducted (Sydney and Melbourne) were in the same country and relatively young, as they were formed over the last 40 to 50 years. During the first half of that period, homeland Armenia, as part of the former Soviet Union, was less accessible for the diaspora. However, relations between Armenia and its global multi-city diaspora have seen significant transformation following Armenia's independence.

In this book, an attempt has been made to identify diasporans' experiences, their sense of national identity, and their perception of the space of belonging. As a study of diaspora-homeland relations and the transformation of this relationship, this book has led to findings in the following three dimensions.

Institutions: The Role of the Armenian Apostolic Church

Historically, and to a lesser extent even now, the Armenian Apostolic Church serves as the main network connecting the nation worldwide. It has been seen as a link between Armenia and the diaspora, a representative of the nation, and, arguably, its skeleton. Many Armenians, as discussed here, attend liturgy services because they are in Armenian. However, the use of the ancient Armenian language (*grabar*) is seen as a barrier to communication because it is less intelligible. As proposed by some interviewed diasporans, there is a need to modernize the Church to make it "become closer to the youth."

The Church is seen as responsible for the preservation of the identity and traditions of the nation. The Internet, arguably, has become the essential tool which can contribute to the transformation of the homeland-diaspora relationship, with a substantial role of the Church within it. The global Armenian diaspora, in reality, is broader than the traditionally regarded network of 70-80 cities with a relatively large Armenian population. As such, it includes communities and even separate diasporans in various parts of the world where the Church is not represented. Historically, building a church could serve two key purposes – to satisfy the spiritual needs of local Armenians and to strengthen the network of Armenians globally (Aslanian, 2006: 401-402). Nowadays, the historical influence of the Church as a spiritual skeleton of the nation is in the process of transformation.

Widely perceived as one of the most important, if not the most important Armenian institution in the world, the Church is seen as a key player that can take action for continuous improvement of Armenia-diaspora relations. Furthermore, as specified by some of the interviewees, the Church is responsible for improving communication between the homeland and the diaspora.

The position of the Church places it higher than political differences existing between various diasporic institutions, even between those institutions and the Armenian state. The Church, traditionally perceived by many as the most powerful pan-Armenian network-institution, is viewed as a potentially effective mediator between various parts and institutions of the global Armenian nation. The Church, as a national institution, is seen as a broader organization than a religious structure; it is responsible for strengthening the ties between Armenia and the diaspora. It is above politics and can help overcome probably the most significant barrier which exists in relations between Armenia and the diaspora – the problem of contested leadership.

Problems of Inclusion: Challenges Under Contested Leadership

Armenian national identity was strengthened by the Armenian diaspora decades before the modern Armenian nation-state was established in 1991. Is the diaspora a symbolic representative of the nation, or does it possess a real capacity for mobilization?

A separate in-depth study can provide more insight into Armenia's ability to mobilize its diaspora. Ulf Bjorklund stresses the strength of Armenians "to build relatively mobilized diaspora communities with a fair degree of pan-diasporic integration" (Bjorklund, 2003: 352). The most recent political-military crises – the Four-Day cease-fire break in Artsakh in April 2016 and, especially, the Second Artsakh War in September-November 2020 – have become the most extreme events, the study of which can uncover the effectiveness of diaspora mobilization.

The modern stage of technological development, the bridging role of social media and social connections, and the increasingly active migration of people from country to country have continuously raised the significance of understanding diasporas and their importance to their homelands. Modern technologies, including transport and communication, as James Clifford emphasizes, contribute to diasporas being closer to their "old country," or the homeland (Clifford, 1994: 304).

Armenian diaspora-homeland relations are multi-dimensional and have an impact on a broader range of stakeholders, not only on the two sides of the nation, but also on the host country and even beyond it. Social media and the internet have transformed the diaspora into a space where diasporans can regularly interact with each other, with other communities and, most importantly, with their homeland, as communities abroad, as social groups, or individually. They can physically be in one community but virtually in another one or many communities at the same time. Another side of this relationship is that the homeland has the potential to reach every diasporan in any corner of the world.

The inclusion of diasporas into their homeland nation is a challenge. As a dynamic process, it needs to be based on realistic expectations and effective communication. Advanced communication technologies provide a compelling opportunity for homelands to effectively reach their diasporas. However, to utilize such opportunities, homelands need to adapt to new realities and modernize their old communication and engagement strategies towards their diasporas.

The inclusion of diasporas in homeland affairs is primarily a rational choice. In the case of Armenians, diaspora communities do not always share the same perception of Armenia in terms of their space of belonging, or the homeland's and diaspora's roles. There is a broader perception of Armenia, with modern Armenia not being a historical homeland, but the cultural/ethnic representative of such a homeland. For many in the diaspora the broader area on the Armenian Highlands is the historic homeland, with the Armenian nation-state today only a part of the larger whole. Concerning its role as of a symbolic representation of *Armenianness*, compared to the diaspora, Armenia, with its higher political status of a nation-state, as viewed by the interviewed diasporans, is expected to be the cultural center for the Armenian people globally. The interviewed diasporans, who were in their 40s or above, provided their insights on the diaspora's relations with Armenia before and after its independence. The transformation of Armenia into the center of the 'Armenian World' assumes that Armenia is not perceived as a competitor in its relations with the diaspora. This argument or view, in turn, can help to overcome the problem of contested leadership between the two sides, though in a two-way process.

If there is a need to shift the diaspora's perception of Armenia, the policies of the Armenian government toward the diaspora requires a more differentiated understanding of diaspora communities, aimed at encouraging diaspora return, be it in the form of physical, virtual, or only an imaginary return. As argued throughout this book, not all ethnic Armenians are diasporans. As proposed, the ultimate goal of the homeland's policy toward its diaspora is to strengthen the diaspora return process among the diasporans and to transform all non-diasporan 'ethnies,' who live outside Armenia, into diasporans.

Based on this study, it is also argued that the development of a sense of belonging among diasporans can become a cornerstone of the engagement process, which will reduce the impact of the problem of contested leadership. Possession of a sense of belonging to Armenia, as argued, to a significant extent, is an outcome of emotional attachment to it, even if Armenia's boundaries do not match those of the historical homeland. The homeland itself needs to adapt to the new realities and modernize its historically-formed communication and engagement strategy in relations with the diaspora. Trust and realistic mutual expectations from both sides are essential conditions for the inclusion of the diaspora in Armenia and for strengthening diaspora return – an essential condition for effective inclusion and integration.

Permanent Return: A View from the Diaspora

Nowadays, the Armenian diaspora, according to Khachig Tölölyan, "no longer consists of a series of exile communities, fragments of the nation awaiting real or even symbolic repatriation," which has "necessarily and inevitably developed local, host country-specific, 'ethnic' features" (Tölölyan, 2000: 108). This strong argument identifies the contemporary nature of the Armenian diaspora. The diaspora has remained organized, with its institutions being the skeleton of their communities. At the same time, these institutions help diasporans to become even more attached to their hostlands; it is a paradox that "the more successful a transnational diasporic organization is, the more it is likely to have developed local branches and services" (Tölölyan, 2000: 114). Hence there is a contradiction: the diaspora, driven by permanent return and acting predominantly through its institutions, deviates from its mission of permanent physical return (more known as repatriation) through the 'help' of those institutions. At the same time, Tölölyan points at a unique phenomenon, a critical behavioral feature of the Armenian diaspora. To him, rather than changing their local environment through efficient integration in the local cultural and social environment, the Armenians can simply emigrate (Tölölyan, 2000: 112). This historical behavior, as argued here, has been an essential factor that facilitates the migration of Armenians from Armenia and prevents them from their physical return there, even though many remain in permanent virtual or imaginary return. Emigration from Armenia, as Noubar Afeyan, an Armenian-American businessman and philanthropist suggests, can even take place in the diaspora. When speaking about the ongoing assimilation process in the diaspora, Afeyan calls it 'emigration from the Diaspora' (R. Vardanyan and N. Alekyan, 2018: 63). However, it can be argued that the assimilation process is more of a case of withdrawal than emigration. Emigration assumes moving to another space (including within the extraterritorial space), while assimilation means abandoning the diasporic sense of identity and belonging. Such abandonment can be reversed by transforming 'ethnies' into diasporans by the diaspora's homeland nation-state in its inclusionary policy toward the diaspora.

The inclusion of the diaspora in the homeland is a complicated endeavor. Diaspora, as a phenomenon, has dual characteristics. Living in an extraterritorial space and making homes in faraway places, diasporans are in a position of permanent return in relation to their territorially-bounded homeland, even if this is a form of virtual or metaphorical return.

Rooted in the sense of geographic belonging, diasporans' perception of national identity in this book is examined within the framework of homeland-diaspora relations, viewed through the prism of key political and geographical concepts of 'nation', 'space', and 'place.' Even with a strong sense of belonging and return to Armenia, many interviewees stress the point that they are still in need of a consistent inclusionary approach from Armenia.

Armenians, for decades, have sought to see an independent Armenia. Maria Koinova emphasizes that "the strength of a strategic center and the strength of the diaspora institutions matter in relation to each other" and provides a comparison of a strong diaspora institution (she uses ARF as a particular case) and a weaker Armenian state, resembling a strong Jewish lobby and a weaker Israeli state (Koinova, 2011: 352). Israel experienced mass immigration of more than one million people in the early 1990s (Ministry of Aliyah of Israel, *Aliyah from the Former Soviet Union*). Unlike in the case of Israel, there has been no such immigration wave of diasporans to Armenia since it achieved independence in 1991 (the number of Syrian Armenians migrating to Armenia after 2011 was incomparably small), which, as argued, can also be a reflection of the uncertain perspectives of relocating to a weak homeland.

Accompanied by the sense of belonging to the homeland (Armenia) and by being in permanent return, diasporans, nevertheless, live normal local lives in their host countries. Staying physically in hostlands and having established lifestyles there, over time, it becomes more difficult for diasporans to migrate to their homelands. Not only limited to the Armenians, but in a general sense, many of those diasporans, who even have such a chance, never physically return to their homeland (Kenny, 2013: 21), even though physical return seems to be the diaspora's ultimate goal. With regard to the Armenian diaspora, as argued in this book, such an outcome is related to what Khachig Tölölyan describes as the diaspora's nature as a "permanent phenomenon" in their host lands, with structures and established institutions and traditions, where each community has developed host country-specific features and organizations, which "address local needs" (Tölölyan, 2000: 108). This transformation into a permanent phenomenon in the hostland, thus, creates a barrier for permanent physical return. This trend of "very little 'return'" (physical repatriation) is a "particular kind of 'sojourning,'" as Sossie Kasbarian would say. She also argues that, to a certain extent, this phenomenon can be explained by the gap existing between the lost (mythical) homeland and the "step-homeland" – the Republic of Armenia (Kasbarian, 2009: 358).

Among the questions the interviewees in this study were asked, "where do you belong?" became the most difficult one. "Being a diasporan is a feeling" - this idea was expressed in multiple interviews. Diasporans feel they 'live' in the homeland even if they have never been there. Return, as the main driving force of any diaspora and its ultimate goal, arguably, tends to be more effective when it is based on place-centric intimate perceptions of the homeland, which is a complex dynamic cultural environment, where places are the elements of that dynamic environment. Based on interviews and observations, the Armenian diasporic return is viewed as a three-dimensional phenomenon: within the community, between communities, and with the homeland. Detailed identification and analysis of diasporic 'routes' are needed for a more effective inclusionary policy by the homeland's agencies. By routes, in this context, one means the ways forming the whole path of becoming a diasporan in a particular space. The distinction between the two views of (cultural) identity, as Steward Hall suggests, makes it essential to consider the 'routes' and even prioritize them often as more important than the 'roots.'

It is interesting to observe that citizenship as a marker of national identity is not placed on top by the Armenian diasporans, compared to other markers – blood, culture (and family), language, and religion. The sense of national identity, as argued, is not related to citizenship in the case of many diasporic Armenians – a phenomenon that can be explained by their strong communal identity. The study of diasporans' feedback has revealed that a key factor is the impact of visits to the homeland, which have strengthened the revival of identity. Physical return, even if it is temporary or only of a touristic nature, strengthens the emotional side of the perception of the homeland, by making knowledge of it intimate and place-centric. Otherwise, if staying at the level of virtual or imaginary return, the homeland space remains at the 'conceptual' or 'knowledgeable' level, which is mostly based on images and imaginaries, if we use Yi Fu-Tuan's classification. The place-centric approach of Armenia's inclusionary policy toward the diaspora is seen as the key to strengthening the homeland as the cultural center of the whole nation before it moves to the next level of becoming the political and economic center.

* * *

'Diaspora' and 'national identity' are interdisciplinary areas of study. Therefore, there is a wide range of studies of diasporas, and the Armenian diaspora and identity, in particular. At the same time, many Armenian diaspora communities have remained understudied. This book is an attempt to fill a gap, to some extent, in the study of the Armenian diaspora by focusing on faraway (from homeland) diasporan communities, from the perspectives of geographic concepts of 'space' and 'place,' and by identifying the connection of the extraterritorial diaspora as a part of the global Armenian nation with its diasporic territorially-bounded homeland nation-state of Armenia. Identification of diasporans' national identity and sense of belonging is seen as of particular significance for a better understanding of geographically remote diasporic communities and their perception of the homeland and connections with it.

Some of the issues considered as important in this work are related to the transformation of the diaspora's role following a significant geopolitical shift in the homeland – acquisition of sovereignty by homeland Armenia. This book has attempted to identify problems inherent in the inclusion of the diaspora into the homeland nation (Armenia) such as a lack of adequate knowledge about each other, unrealistic expectations, lack of trust, and the presence of contested leadership. Many of these themes are relevant to not only Armenians but also other diasporas as well.

Before the establishment of its homeland nation-state, the Armenian diaspora was very engaged in preserving its Armenian identity and claimed to be responsible for identity preservation. It can, therefore, be argued that national identity has long had global and extraterritorial dimensions. Detailed studies concerning the historical background of our Armenian diaspora communities (Sydney and Melbourne) can only contribute to the enrichment of evolving diaspora-homeland relations and how these relations are perceived by diasporans.

This focused approach and its findings, to an extent, can be applied to other Armenian diaspora communities and even non-Armenian diasporas. At the same time, specific considerations should be made when working with other diaspora cases. Community size, location, and social-cultural environments, as discussed in this book, can have a significant impact and suggest a different approach in policy formulation and implementation from the homeland's side. Regarding other diasporas, their origin, dispersion in the world, among other factors, should also be considered carefully.

Diasporans, a narrative study of whom is included in this work, represent a wide range of professions and differ in terms of their diasporic roots and routes, generational differences, places of residence, and connection to Armenia. In many cases, answers and opinions provided by the interviewees have coincided, and many other responses have complemented each other. Future studies of communities can delve even deeper into specific aspects raised in the book.

As this study has highlighted, by living in a different ethnoreligious environment, such as the Middle East, Armenian communities have experienced different challenges regarding the preservation of their national identity. That is why the framework of this study may not be entirely applicable when working with communities in other distinct social and cultural environments. As some examples in this book have demonstrated, diasporans tend to develop a stronger need for identity preservation in diverse environments, even if they are located on a shorter distance from the homeland (e g., the Middle East). The approaches to diaspora-homeland relations highlighted in this book can assist scholars and policymakers in forming a better understanding of the main challenges diasporic communities may experience.

Transformation of identity (perception of identity and sense of belonging) is a dynamic process, and it will be interesting to observe how it changes in different communities over time. More studies focusing on the development of diasporic institutions also can complement the views analyzed here.

The phenomenon of 'diaspora' has become a center of attention not only in academia but also among policymakers in homeland nation-states. Policies pursued by homeland countries, to be effective, assume thorough knowledge of the homeland and its diaspora, their mutual expectations, and the extent to which they trust each other. There can be a diversity of views regarding national identity and belonging in the diaspora, and studies at the micro-level can reveal much about political, cultural, and economic dynamics within the diaspora, in different regions, countries, and even individual cities within single countries.

The Armenian diaspora, as a global phenomenon, can be found in tens and even hundreds of cities in the world, many of which are on a shorter distance from the homeland (Armenia). Therefore, among other possible factors, distance to the homeland can have its implications on such aspects as the perception of belonging to space, connection to the homeland space, or preservation of the language. Studies focused on these aspects of identity can provide comparative insights into communities, including small ones, which are located in different parts of the world. Such exploration can lead to a better understanding of the impact of geographic distance on diasporans' identity perception.

In the increasingly globalized world, strengthening national identity for nation-states is becoming a task of strategic importance. Regarding diasporic nations, both sides, diasporas and homelands, share the responsibility for maintaining and strengthening their unique identity. Return, as the main driving force and existential condition of any diaspora, as well as its primary objective (with permanent physical repatriation being the ultimate one), as repeatedly stressed in this work, tends to be more effective if it is based on a place-centric and intimate perception of the homeland. Strong trust and realistic expectations, as presented, are decisive factors that can keep diasporans in permanent return and can transform non-diasporan Armenian 'ethnies' into diasporans – an essential goal for the homeland, Armenia, which is home to only a third of the global extraterritorial nation.

Due to ongoing technological progress, it has already become possible for the homeland to reach every diasporan anywhere in the world and for diasporans to stay directly connected to the homeland and the rest of the diaspora. Considering the financial cost of reaching the whole diaspora physically, Armenia, through the efficient use of communication technologies, can strengthen connections with its global diaspora, with particular significance given to smaller and less connected communities. Diaspora studies addressing the potential of communication technologies in diaspora-homeland relations can provide insights into the opportunities of using technology for diaspora engagement more effectively.

The inclusion of the diaspora in the homeland, as argued, should aim at transforming the latter into the core, the center of the global transnation. First of all, this process assumes making the homeland (Armenia) the cultural center of global *Armenianness*, a role Armenia has already been performing to a certain extent. Considering the fact that Armenia (the Republic) is not the historical homeland of many diasporans, especially those living in the West (since their historic homeland has been lost after the Armenian Genocide), present-day Armenia, as proposed, should become the cultural representative of all Armenians in the diaspora (Vardanyan, 2021). The next level is the transformation of the homeland into the political center for the global nation, an aim, which, among other achievements, assumes making it attractive to acquire Armenian citizenship and actively participate in the country's life (Vardanyan, 2021). The greatest achievement would be the transformation of the homeland (Armenia) into the global nation's economic center. Applying emotional motivation for the diasporans' return without addressing economic factors (economic interests) cannot be effective as an inclusionary measure. The establishment of certain and stable 'rules of engagement,' i.e., a stable and predictable political and economic environment, is a key precondition for the effective inclusion of the diaspora in the homeland (Vardanyan, 2021).

The homeland's policy aims should maintain and develop relations with its diaspora, and such engagement should open new opportunities for action. It is not a project with a beginning and an end; it is an ongoing and never-ending process. As stated, the Armenian diaspora is a broader-than-traditionally-perceived network of 60-70 cities with large Armenian populations. Detailed identification and analysis of the main diasporic routes of diasporan Armenians will enable homeland Armenia to shape its inclusionary policy more effectively in its pursuit of becoming the cultural, political, and economic center of the global Armenian nation.

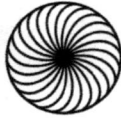

BIBLIOGRAPHY

100 Years - 100 Facts Project

San Lazzaro in Venice was established as the island monastery of the Mekhitarist Congregation in 1717. Accessed on June 13, 2017. http://100years100facts.com/facts/san-lazzaro-venice-established-island-monastery-mekhitarist-congregation-1717/.

The First Armenian Republic was declared on the 28th of May, 1918. Accessed on June 13, 2017. http://100years100facts.com/facts/first-armenian-republic-declared-28th-may-1918/.

The Republic of Armenia declared its independence on the 21st of September, 1991. Accessed on March 30, 2018. http://100years100facts.com/facts/republic-armenia-declared-independence-21st-september-1991/.

168.am news agency. *The Momentum is Approaching to Establish a Western Armenian Cultural-Language Centre in Armenia.* Accessed on December 08, 2016. https://168.am/2016/12/07/726431.html.

Adalian, Rouben Paul, *Musa Dag, Armenian National Institute.* Accessed on March 29, 2018. http://www.armenian-genocide.org/musa_dagh.html.

Adamson, Fiona. *Constructing the Diaspora: Diaspora Identity Politics and Transnational Social Movements.* Paper, the 40th Meeting of the International Studies Association. San Francisco. March, 2008.

Adamson, Fiona. *The Growing Importance of Diaspora Politics.* Current History. 115(784):291-7. New York. November 2016.

Agadjanian, Alexander. *Armenian Christianity Today: Identity Politics and Popular Practice.* Routledge. 2014.

Agnew, John. *Revisiting the Territorial Trap.* Nordia Geographical Publications. 44:4. pp. 43-48. 1999.

Agnew, John, *The Territorial Trap: The Geographical Assumptions of International Relations Theory.* Review of International Political Economy. 1:1 Spring 1994.

Aikins, Kingsley. Diaspora Matters. *TEDxTalks.* February 25, 2014. Accessed December 12, 2016. https://www.youtube.com/watch?v=yQ_y5LgM7D0.

Alonso, Andoni and Oiarzabal, Pedro J. *Diasporas in the New Media Age.* University of Nevada Press, 2010.

America: the Jesuit Review. *Pope Francis Will Visit Armenia, the World's First Christian Nation.* Accessed on June 13, 2017. http://www.americamagazine.org/content/dispatches/pope-francis-visits-armenia-worlds-first-christian-nation.

Anderson, Benedict. *Imagined Communities.* Verso. 2006.

Antonsich, Marco. *On Territory, the Nation-State and the Crisis of the Hyphen.* Progress in Human Geography. 33(6). 2009.

Antonsich, Marco, Mavroudi, Elizabeth, and Mihelj, Sabina. *Building Inclusive Nations in the Age of Migration.* Identities: Global Studies in Culture and Power. Vol. 24, No. 2. 156-176.

Appiah, Kwame Anthony. *The Ethics of Identity.* Princeton University Press. 2005.

Ararktsyan, Babken, Sargsyan, Ashot and Khachatryan, Gohar. *25th Anniversary of Independence of the Republic of Armenia*. Antares Publishing Co. Yerevan, 2016.

Aravot.am, *We intend to open Armenia's embassy in Australia* (in Armenian). Accessed on October 05, 2019. https://www.aravot.am/2019/10/02/1069715/

Armenian Apostolic Church

Catholicos of All Armenians. Accessed on April 15, 2018. https://www.armenian-church.org/index.jsp?sid=1&id=16769&pid=1&lng=en.

Mother See of Holy Etchmiadzin. Accessed on June 13, 2017. http://www.arme-nianchurch.org.

Armenian Church Catholicosate of Cilicia Antelias – Lebanon, The Origin of the Armenian Church. Accessed on June 13, 2017. http://www.armenianortho-doxchurch.org/en/history.

Armenian Community Council of the United Kingdom, Our Father (prayer, in English). Accessed on June 13, 2017. http://www.accc.org.uk/the-lords-prayer/.

Armenian Diaspora News Forum

'Armenia' Ship Arrives in Singapore. Accessed on June 15, 2017. "http://www.armeniandiaspora.com/showthread.php?257727-Armenia-ship-arrives-in-Singapore

Kolkata Community Hosts Armenia Vessel. Remembers Makar Ekmalian. Accessed on June 15, 2017. http://www.armeniandiaspora.com/show-thread.php?262329-Kolkata-Community-Hosts-Armenia-Vessel-Remembers-Makar-Ekmalian.

Armenian Encyclopedia (online), in Armenian. *Khachqar*. Accessed on June 29, 2017. http://www.encyclopedia.am/pages.php?bId=1&hId=1221.

Armenian General Benevolent Union (AGBU). Our History. Accessed on June 29, 2017.https://agbu.org/about/our-history/.

ArmenianHouse.org electronic library (in Russian). *Aghasi Ayvazyan*. Accessed on June 29, 2017. http://armenianhouse.org/aivazyan/aivazyan-ru.html.

Armenian National Committee of America (ANCA). *Diaspora Donors Pledge $350,000 to Match UNHRC's Syrian Refugee Program in Armenia*. Accessed on July 2, 2017.https://anca.org/diaspora-donors-pledge-350000-to-match-unhrcs-syrian-refugee-program-in-armenia/.

Armenian National Committee of Ausralia (ANC Australia). Accessed on June 29, 2017.http://www.anc.org.au/community.

Armenian National Institute, Washington, D.C.,

Frequently Asked Questions about the Armenian Genocide. Accessed on June 22, 2017. http://www.armenian-genocide.org/genocidefaq.html.

Monument, Museum, and Research Complex at Tsitsernakaberd, in Yerevan, Arme-nia. Accessed on June 21, 2017 http://www.armenian-genocide.org/Memo-rial.28/current_category.52/offset.20/memorials_detail.html.

ArmeniaNow.com news portal. Accessed on June 25, 2017. https://www.arme-nianow.com/genocide/60808/armenia_forgetmenot_symbol_genocide_cen-tennial.

ArmeniaOnline portal, *St. Gregory's Armenian School Site Sold to Islamic Group.* Accessed on June 25, 2017. http://www.armenia.com.au/news/Australia-News/English/1945/St-Gregory-s-Armenian-School-site-sold-to-Islamic-group .

Armenian Revolutionary Federation – Dashnaktsutyun (Armenian Socialist Party). *Brief,* Yerevan, 2011. Accessed December 11, 2017. http://www.arfd.info/wp-content/uploads/2011/11/ARF_Brief-A5-updated_October-2011.pdf.

Armenian Revolutionary Federation – Dashnaktsutyun. *Background.* Accessed on June 25, 2017. http://www.arfd.info/background/.

Armenian Travel Bureau

General Information. Accessed on June 25, 2017. http://www.atb.am/en/armenia/geo/.

Khor Virap Monastery. Accessed on June 25, 2017. http://www.atb.am/en/armenia/sights/christ/khorvirap/.

Armenian Virtual College (AVC). *Mission.* Accessed on June 29, 2017. https://www.avc-agbu.org/en/about/aboutAVC.html.

ArmTimes.com, *The National Heros of RA: Who and Why Has Received the Award.* Accessed on March 29, 2018. http://www.armtimes.com/hy/article/121024.

Asatryan, Garnik and Arakelova, Victoria. *The Ethnic Minorities of Armenia.* With assistance of OSCE Office. Yerevan. 2002.

Asbarez newspaper online. *Karekin II Official Visit to Australia,* 26/11/2002. Accessed on June 10, 2017. http://asbarez.com/48088/karekin-ii-official-visit-to-australia/.

Aslanian, Sebouh. *Julfa v. Armenians in India,* Encyclopaedia Iranica, XV/3, pp. 240-242. Accessed on June 16, 2017. http://www.iranicaonline.org/articles/julfa-v-armenians-in-india.

Aslanian, Sebouh. *Social Capital, Trust' and the Role of Networks in Julfan Trade: Informal and Semi-Formal Institutions at Work.* Journal of Global History. 2006, 1.

Avagian, Grigor. *Armenia And Armenians In the World.* Omega-N. 1994.

Ayvazyan, Armen. *Armenia's Conversion to Christianity,* Ancient Histoty Encyclopedia, 2015. Accessed on June 29, 2017. http://www.ancient.eu/article/801/.

Ayvazyan, Hovhannes and Sargsyan, Aram. *Encyclopedia of the Armenian Diaspora* (in Armenian). Armenian Encyclopedia. 2003.

Azadian, Edmond Y. *Kessab Tragedy Still on World Agenda,* The Armenian Mirror-Spectator, April 10, 2014. Accessed on June 9, 2017. http://www.mirror-spectator.com/2014/04/10/kessab-tragedy-still-on-world-agenda/.

Babkenian, Vicken and Stanley, Peter. *Armenia, Australia and the Great War.* NewSouth. University of New South Wales. Sydney. 2016.

Badalyan, G., *Armenian Highland,* Institute for Armenian Studies, Yerevan State University. Accessed on June 25, 2017. http://www.armin.am/en/Encyclopedia_Armency_Haykakan_lernashxarh.

Baser, Bahar and Swain, Ashok. *Stateless Diaspora Groups and Their Repertoirs of Nationalist Activism in Host Countries.* Journal of International Relations. Vol 8. Number 1. 2010.

Baubock, Rainer and Faist, Thomas (eds). *Diaspora and Transnationalism: Concepts, Theories and Methods.* IMISCOE Research. Amsterdam University Press. 2010.

Baumann, Martin. *Exile.* In Knott, Kim and McLoughlin, Sean (editors). *Diasporas: Concepts, Intersections, Identities.* Zed Books. London-New York. 2010.

BBC News

Nagorno-Karabakh Profile. Accessed on June 29, 2017. http://www.bbc.com/news/world-europe-18270325

Timeline: Armenia. Accessed on March 28, 2018. http://news.bbc.co.uk/2/hi/europe/country_profiles/1108274.stm.

Beck, Jan Mansvelt. *Geopolitical Imaginations of the Basque Homeland.* Geopolitics. Volume 11. 2006.

Ben-Moshe, Danny. *Jewish diaspora engagement with Israel,* in Ehrlich, M. Avrum (ed.). *Encyclopedia of the Jewish diaspora: origins, experiences, and culture,* ABC-CLIO, Santa Barbara, California, 2009, Deakin University library. Accessed on June 10, 2017. http://dro.deakin.edu.au/view/DU:30060356.

Ben-Rafael, Eliezer. *Diaspora.* Current Sociology. SAGE, 61 (5-6) 842-861 (2013), pp. 842-861.

Berger, Peter L. and Hefner, Robert W. *Spiritual Capital in Comparative Perspective,* Boston University, 2004.

Bjorklund, Ulf. *Armenians of Athens and Istanbul: the Armenian Diaspora and the 'Transnational' Nation.* Global Networks 3,3 (2003). pp. 337-354.

Blunt, Alison. *Cultural Geographies of Migration: Mobility, Transnationality and Diaspora.* Progress in Human Geography (2007) 31(5). pp. 684-694.

Boyadjian, Tamar. *Lamenting Jerusalem: The Armenian Quarter in the Old City,* Asbarez Newspaper online. Accessed on June 29, 2017. http://asbarez.com/109128/lamenting-jerusalem-the-armenian-quarter-in-the-old-city/.

Brah, Avtar. *Cartographies of Diaspora: Contesting Identities.* Routledge. 1996.

Brockhaus and Efron. *Small Encyclopedic Dictionary.* Saint Petersburg. 1899. Volume 1.

Brubaker, Rogers. *The 'Diaspora' Diaspora.* Ethnic and Racial Studies. Vol. 28 No. 1. January 2005. pp. 1-19.

Bunnell, Tim. *Re-positioning Malaysia: High-Tech Networks and the Multicultural Rescripting of National Identity.* Political Geography 21. 2002. pp. 105-124.

Callard, Felicity. *Doreen Massey.* Chapter 40 In Hubbard, Phil and Kitchin, Rob. *Key Thinkers on Space and Place.* SAGE. 2011.

Campbell, Lisa M., Gray Noella J., Meletis, Zoe A., Abbott, James G., Silver, Jennifer J. *Gatekeepers and Keymasters: Dynamic Relationships of Access in Geographic Fieldwork.* The Geographical Review. 96 (1) pp. 97-121. January 2006.

Campt, Tina Marie. *Other Germans: Black Germans and the Politics of Race, Gender, and Memory in the Third Reich (Social History, Popular Culture, and Politics in Germany).* University of Michigan Press. 2009.

Carnegie Europe. *Unfinished Business in the Armenia-Azerbaijan Conflict.* Accessed on February 23, 2021. https://carnegieeurope.eu/2021/02/11/unfinished-business-in-armenia-azerbaijan-conflict-pub-83844.

Cavoukian, Kristin. '*Soviet Mentality?' The Role of Shared Political Culture in Relations Between the Armenian State and Russia's Armenian Diaspora*. Nationalities Papers: The Journal of Nationalism and Ethnicity. 41:5. pp. 709-729.

Chakrabarty, Dipesh. *Habitations of Modernity: Essays in the Wake of Subaltern States*. University of Chicago Press. 2002.

Clifford, James. *Diasporas*. Cultural Anthropology. Vol. 9. No. 3. Further Inflections: Toward Ethnographies of the Future. (Aug. 1994). pp. 302-338.

CIA The World Factbook: Armenia. Accessed on April 08, 2018. https://www.cia.gov/library/publications/the-world-factbook/geos/am.html.

CIA The World Factbook: Azerbaijan. Accessed on June 29, 2017. https://www.cia.gov/library/publications/the-world-factbook/geos/aj.html.

Cohen, Robin. *Diasporas and the State: from Victims to Challengers*. International Affairs. 72 (3). July 1996. pp. 507-20.

Cohen, Robin. *Global Diasporas: An Introduction*. University of Washington Press. 1997.

Cohen, Robin. *Global Diasporas: An Introduction*. 2nd edition. Routledge. 2008.

Cohen, Robin. *New Roles for Diasporas in International Relations*. Diaspora: A Journal of Transnational Studies. University of Toronto Press. Diaspora 14:1. 2005.

Committee to Protect Journalists (CPJ). *Hrant Dink*. Accessed on June 29, 2017. https://cpj.org/killed/2007/hrant-dink.php .

Constas, Dimitry C. and Platias, Athanassios G. *Diasporas in World Politics: the Greeks in Comparative Politics*. Palgrave Macmillan. 1993.

Cowe, S. Peter. *Church and Diaspora: the Case of the* Armenians. (Chapter 18, pp. 430-456). In Angold, Michael (editor). *The Cambridge History of Christianity*. Chapter 18, Cambridge University Press. 2014.

Crippen, David. *The World Trade Centre Attack: Similarities to the 1988 earthquake in Armenia: time to teach the public life-supporting first aid?* Crit Care, 2001, 5(6), 312-314. Accessed on June 29, 2017. https://www.ncbi.nlm.nih.gov/pmc/articles/PMC137377/.

Council on Foreign Relations, *Nagorno-Karabakh Conflict. Accessed* on June 16, 2017. https://www.cfr.org/global/global-conflict-tracker/p32137#!/conflict/nagorno-karabakh-conflict.

Darieva, Tsypylma. *Come to More Mountains! Diaspora and Development in a Transnational Age*. Causasus Analytical Digest. No. 29. 29 September 2011.

Delano, Alexandra and Gamlen, Alan. *Comparing and Theorizing State-Diaspora Relations*. Political Geography 41(2014) 43-53.

Department of State of the United States of America. *Armenia*. Accessed on December 05, 2017. https://www.state.gov/documents/organization/171681.pdf.

Dertadian, Kev, *Let's talk about community (in the Armenian Diaspora)*. Accessed on 08 September 2016. http://agbu.org.au/lets-talk/.

Diener, Alexander C. and Hagen, Joshua. *Borders: a Very Short Introduction*. Oxford University Press. 2012.

Dinnie, Keith. *Nation Branding: Concepts, Issues, Practice*. Elsevier. 2008.

Douglas, Craig M., *Greater Boston Gains Population, Remains 10th Largest Region in U.S.*, Boston Business Journal, 24 March 2010. Accessed on June 13, 2017. http://www.bizjournals.com/boston/stories/2010/03/22/daily22.html.

Dufoix, Stephane. *Diasporas*. University of California Press. 2008.

Earle, Carville, Mathewson, Kent, and Kenzer, Martin. S. *Concepts in Human Geography*. Rowman and Littlefield Publishers. 1996.

Ebaugh, Helen Rose Fuchs and Chafetz, Janet Saltzman. *Religion Across Borders: Transnational Migrant Networks*. AltaMira Press. 2002.

Embassy of the Republic of Armenia in Canada, *Law of the Republic of Armenia on Citizenship of the Republic of Armenia*. Accessed on March 11, 2018. http://canada.mfa.am/en/citizenship/.

Embassy of the Republic of Armenia in India, *About Community*. Accessed on June 1, 2017. http://india.mfa.am/en/community-overview/.

Ember, Melvin, Ember, Carol R., Skoggard, Ian (editors). *Encyclopedia of Diasporas: Immigrant and Refugee Cultures Around the World*. Volume I: Overviews and Topics. Volume II: Diaspora Communities (v. 1). Springer. 2005.

Encyclopaedia Britannica

Armenia. accessed on November 15, 2019. https://www.britannica.com/place/Armenia

Armenian Apostolic Church. Accessed on June 11, 2017. https://www.britannica.com/topic/Armenian-Apostolic-Church

Armenian Language. Accessed on July 8, 2017. https://www.britannica.com/topic/Armenian-language

Buenos Aires. Accessed on June 11, 2017. https://www.britannica.com/place/Buenos-Aires

Cilicia. Accessed on January 10, 2018. https://www.britannica.com/place/Cilicia

Krasnodar. Accessed on June 11, 2017. https://www.britannica.com/place/Krasnodar-kray-Russia

Los Angeles. Accessed on June 11, 2017. https://www.britannica.com/place/Los-Angeles-California

Mount Ararat. Accessed on June 11, 2017. https://www.britannica.com/place/Mount-Ararat

Paris. Accessed on June 11, 2017. https://www.britannica.com/place/Paris/People

Engelhart, Katie. *The Unrecognized Nation of Nagorno-Karabakh Republic Faces an Uncertain Future*. Vice News. Accessed on June 29, 2017.https://news.vice.com/article/the-unrecognized-nation-of-the-nagorno-karabakh-republic-faces-an-uncertain-future.

Erhkamp, Patricia. *Placing Identities: Transnational Practices and Local Attachments of Turkish Immigrants in Germany*. Journal of Ethnic and Migration Studies. Vol. 31. No. 2. March 2005.

Esman, Milton J. *Diasporas in the Contemporary World*. Polity. 2009.

Fedorov, Gleb. *Old Believers Preserve Rare Russian Dialects in South America*, Russia Beyond the Headlines, 01 July 2016. Accessed on June 26, 2017. https://www.rbth.com/education/2016/07/01/old-believers-preserve-rare-russian-dialects-in-south-america_607167.

Foreign Policy. *The Syrian Refugees Coming Home to Armenia*. Accessed on March 29, 2018. http://foreignpolicy.com/2017/03/20/the-syrian-refugees-coming-home-to-armenia-migration-syria/.

Fowler C., 2002. *A durable concept: Anthony Smith's concept of 'National Identity' and the case of Wales*. In PSA 52nd Annual Conference: "Making Politics Count" University of Aberdeen 5-7 April 2002.

Gatens, Moira and Lloyd, Genevieve. *Collective Imaginings: Spinoza, Past and Present*. Routledge. 1999.

Gelder, Lawrence van, *Alex Manoogian, 95; Perfected Design of Single-Handled Faucet*, The New York Times. Accessed on June 7, 2017. http://www.nytimes.com/1996/07/13/us/alex-Manoogian-95-perfected-design-of-single-handled-faucet.html?src=pm.

Georgiou, Myria. *Diaspora, Identity and the Media: Diasporic Transnationalism and Mediated Spatialities*. Hampton Press. 2006.

Ghanalanyan, Tigran. *Armenian Protestant Communities in South America*, Noravank Foundation, 21 April 2011. Accessed on June 13, 2017. http://noravank.am/eng/articles/detail.php?ELEMENT_ID=5722.

Giordano, Alfonso and Terranova, Giuseppe. *The Indian Policy of Skilled Migration: Brain Return Versus Diaspora Benefits*. Journal of Global Policy and Governance. Volume 1. Issue 1. December 2012 (pp. 17-28).

Goenjian, A. K., Karayan, I., Pynoos, R. S., Minassian, D., Najarian, L. M., Steinberg, A.M., and Fairbanks, L. A. *Outcome of Psychotherapy Among Early Adolescents After Trauma*. The American Journal of Psychiatry, 154:4, April 1997, p. 536. Accessed on January 10, 2018. http://ajp.psychiatryonline.org/cgi/reprint/154/4/536.pdf.

Gottschlich, Pierre. Book Review: *Jurith M. Brown, Global South Asians: Introducing the Modern* Diaspora, in Roots and Routes, Vol.1, No.7, October 2012.

Government of the Republic of Armenia (official website)

General Information. Accessed on June 26, 2017. http://www.gov.am/en/official/.

Nikol Pashinyan's Official Visit to the Republic of Singapore. Accessed on September 13, 2020. https://www.primeminister.am/en/foreign-visits/item/2019/07/07/Nikol-Pashinyan-visit-to-Singapore/#prettyPhoto

Office of the High Commissioner for Diaspora Affairs. Accessed on November 02, 2019. https://www.gov.am/am/diaspora-affairs/head/966/.

Global SPC, *Invest in Armenia*. Accessed on June 29, 2017. http://www.investarmenia.am/en/regional-position-climate-and-natural-resources.

Gregory, Derek. *The Colonial Present: Afghanistan, Palestine, Iraq*. Blackwell. 2004.

Gregory, Derek, Johnston, Ron, Pratt, Geraldine, Watts, Michael and Whatmore, Sarah. *The Dictionary of Human Geography*. Wiley-Blackwell. 2009.

Grigorian, Sassoon. *Smart Nation: a Bluprint for Modern Armenia*. Gomidas Institute. London. 2016.

Guibernau, Montserrat. *Anthony D. Smith on Nations and National Identity: A Critical Assessment*. Nations and Nationalism 10 (1/2). 2004. 125-141.

Hakobyan, Hranush, *Interview*, 03/13/2014, Ministry of Diaspora of the Republic of Armenia. Accessed on June 8, 2017. http://www.mindiaspora.am/ru/Interviews/3505.

Hall, Stewart. *Cultural Identity and Diaspora*. Theorizing Diaspora. 2003. 233-247.

Hamazkayin Armenian Educational and Cultural Society, History of Hamazkayin in Brief. Accessed on June 29, 2017. http://www.hamazkayin.com/en/history/.

Hansen, Randall. *The Poverty of Postnationalism: Citizenship, Immigration, and the New Europe*. Theory and Society (2009). 38:1-24.

Hayern Aysor, **Periodical of the Ministry of Diaspora of the Republic of Armenia**

Australian-Armenian political scientist says Armenia has all the preconditions to become one of the leading countries in the world. Accessed on June 26, 2017. http://hayernaysor.am/en/archives/date/2017/01/12.

National Identity Issues Discussed at the Ministry of Diaspora of the Republic of Armenia (in Armenian). Accessed on June 28, 2017. http://hayernaysor.am/archives/158627.

Hetq.am news portal. 100 Churches Have Been Built in Armenia and Artsakh After Independence. January 11, 2017. Accessed on December 08, 2019. https://hetq.am/hy/article/74539.

Herzig, Edmund M. *The Armenian Merchants of New Julfa, Isfahan: A Study in Pre-Modern Asian Trade.* PhD thesis. St. Antony's College. University of Oxford. 1991.

Herzig, Edmund M. and Kurkchiyan, Marina. *The Armenians: Past and Present in the Making of National Identity.* Routledge. 2005.

Hidle, Knut, *Place, Geography and the Concept of Diaspora – a Methodological Approach*, Geografi – Bergen, 244–2001. Accessed on March 19, 2018. https://brage.bibsys.no/xmlui/bitstream/handle/11250/162328/knut%20hidle244.pdf?sequence=1.

Hindustan Times, *The Case of the Vanishing Armenians.* Accessed on June 26, 2017. http://www.hindustantimes.com/brunch/the-case-of-the-vanishing-armenians/story-SSAPjXzSx4XS96qY4hdS8N.html .

Ho, Elaine L. E. *Claiming the Diaspora: Elite Mobility, Sending State Strategies and the Spatialities of Citizenship.* Progress in Human Geography. 35(6). 757-772. 2011.

Ho, Elaine L. E. and McConnell, Fiona. *Conceptualizing 'Diaspora Diplomacy': Territory and Populations Betwixt the Domestic and Foreign.* Progress in Human Geography. 1-21. 2017.

Hobsbawm, Eric J. *Nations and Nationalism since 1780: Programme, Myth, Reality.* 2nd edition. Cambridge University Press. 2012.

Holding, Deirdre. *Armenia: with Nagorno Karabakh.* Bradt Travel Guides. 2014.

Hovanesian, Rafael and Bronozian, Harry. *Restoration and Management of Lake Sevan in Armenia: Problems and Prospects.* Lake and Reservoir Management, Volume 9, 1994, Issue 1. Published online in 2009. Accessed on October 31, 2019 https://www.tandfonline.com/doi/abs/10.1080/07438149409354754.

Hubbard, Phil and Kitchin, Rob. *Key Thinkers on Space and Place.* SAGE. 2011.

Hughes, James and Sasse, Gwendolyn. *Ethnicity and Territory in the Former Soviet Union: Regions in Conflict.* Routledge. 2001.

Huntington, Samuel P. *Who Are We? America's Great Debate.* Free Press. 2004.

Institute of Demography of the National Research University, Higher School of Economics. *All-Union Census: Race Streucture of the Population by the Union Republics (Armenia).* N. 831-832, 21 October – 03 November 2019. Accessed on 06 November 2019. http://www.demoscope.ru/weekly/ssp/sng_nac_89.php?reg=13

Internet Encyclopedia of Ukraine, *Armenians.* Accessed on June 8, 2017. http://www.encyclopediaofukraine.com/display.asp?linkpath=pages\A\R\Armenians.htm.

Jacobsohn, Gary Jeffrey. *Constitutional Identity*. The Review of Politics. 68. 2006.

Kalra, Virinder S., Kaur, Raminder, and Hutnyk, John. *Diaspora and Hybridity*. SAGE Publications. 2005.

Kasbarian, Sossie. *The Myth and Reality of 'Return' – Diaspora in the 'Homeland'*. Diaspora 18:3(2009). Published in Fall 2015.

Kenny, Kevin. *Diaspora: A Very Short Introduction*. Oxford University Press. 2013.

Khachikyan, Armen. *History of Armenia: A Brief Review*. Edit Print. Yerevan. 2010.

Kidd, Warren. *Culture and Identity*. Palgrave. 2002.

King, Victor. *The Sociology of Southeast Asia*. Copenhagen. Nias Press. 2008.

Kleist, Nauja. *In the Name of Diaspora: Between Struggles for Recognition and Political Aspirations*. Journal of Ethnic and Migration Studies. 34:7. 1127-1143.

Knight, David B. *Identity and Territory: Geographical Perspectives on Nationalism and Regionalism*. Anahitls of the Association of American Geographers. Vol. 72. No. 4 (Dec., 1982).

Koinova, Maria. *Conditions and Timing of Moderate and Radical Diaspora Mobilization: Evidence from Conflict-Generated Diasporas*. Global Migration and Transnational Politics. Working Paper no. 9. October 2009.

Koinova, Maria. *Diasporas and Secessionist Conflicts: The Mobilization of the Armenian, Albanian and Chechen Diasporas*. Ethnic and Racial Studies. 34:2. pp. 333-356. 2011.

Kolossov, Vladimir and O'Loughlin, John. *New Borders for New World Orders: Territorialities at the Fin-de-Siecle* GeoJournal. March 1998. Volume 44. Issue 3. pp. 259-273.

Kong, Lily. *Globalisation and Singaporean Transmigration: Re-imagining and Negotiating National Identity*. Political Geography 18. 1999.

Kotkin, Joel. *Tribes: How Race, Religion, and Identity Determine Success in the New Global Economy*. Random House. 1993.

Krause, Todd B. and Slocum, Jonathan. *Classical Armenian Online*, The University of Texas at Austin. Accessed on June 8, 2017. https://lrc.la.utexas.edu/eieol/armol.

Kuzio, Taras. *Borders, Symbolism and Nation-State Building: Ukraine and Russia*. Geopolitics and International Boundaries. Routledge. 2007.

Lenta.ru news portal (online)

Getting Rid of the Colonial Yoke (in Russian). Accessed on October 1, 2019. https://lenta.ru/articles/2019/09/21/araday/.

Nagorno-Karabakh Will Be Given a New Name (in Russian). Accessed on November 13, 2019. https://lenta.ru/news/2016/11/05/artsakh/.

Ley, David. *Transnationalism*. Elsevier. 2009.

Libaridian, Gerard J. *The Challenge of Statehood: Armenian Political Thinking Since Independence* Blue Crane Books. 1999.

Longley, Paul A, Goodchild, Michael F., Maguire, David J., and Rhind, David W. (editors). *Geographical Information Systems: Principles, Techniques, Management and Applications*. 2nd Edition. Abridged. Wiley. 2005.

Low, Setha M. and Lawrence-Zuniga, Denise. *The Anthropology of Space and Place*. Blackwell Publishing. 2003.

Manucharyan, Ashot. *Karabakh Movement: First-Ever 'Anthropocentric' Movement in the World* (in Armenian). Tert.am news portal. Accessed on June 26, 2017. http://www.tert.am/am/news/2015/02/12/manucharian/1587748.

Mansbach, Richard and Rhodes, Edward. *The National State and Identity Politics: State Institutionalisation and 'Markers' of National Identity.* Geopolitics. 2007. 12:3.

Marshall, Tim. *Prisoners of Geography.* Elliott and Thompson. 2019.

Martirosyan, Susan, *Armenians in the World Today: The Formation of the Big Diaspora.* 2014. Accessed on October 31, 2019. http://www.oikonomia.it/index.php/it/48-oikonomia-2014/febbraio-2014/219-armenians-in-the-world-today-the-formation-of-the-big-diaspora.html.

Massey, Doreen. *For Space.* SAGE. 2012.

Masih, Joseph R. and Krikorian, Robert O. *Armenia: at the Crossroads.* Harwood Academic Publishers. 1999.

Mavroudi, Elizabeth. *Contesting Identities, Differences, and a Unified Palestinian Community.* Environment and Planning D: Society and Space. 2010. Volume 28. pp. 239-253.

Mavroudi, Elizabeth. *Deconstructing Diasporic Mobilisation at a Time of Crisis: Perspectives from the Palestinian and Greek Diasporas.* Journal of Ethnic and Diaspora Studies. 2017.

Mavroudi, Elizabeth. *Diaspora as Process: (De) Constructing Boundaries.* Geography Compass. 1 (3). 2007. pp. 467-479.

McKittrick, Katherine. *Diaspora.* Elsevier. 2009.

Ministry of Aliyah and Integration of Israel, *Aliyah From the Former Soviet Union (1990).* Accessed on July 22, 2017. http://www.moia.gov.il/English/FeelingIsrael/AboutIsrael/Pages/aliyaUssr.aspx.

Ministry of Diaspora of the Republic of Armenia. *Armenian Diaspora Yearbook* (in Armenian). Yerevan. 2010. 2011. 2015 (separate editions).

Ministry of Diaspora of the Republic of Armenia

About Us. Accessed on June 15, 2017. http://www.mindiaspora.am/am/About_us

Conferences. Accessed on June 15, 2017. http://www.mindiaspora.am/en/Conferences/3418

Dual Citizenship. Accessed on June 15, 2017. http://www.mindiaspora.am/en/erkqaghaqaciutyun

Profile of the Armenian Community in Australia (in Armenian). 2017.

The First Five Years of the Ministry (in Armenian). 2013.

Ministry of Economy of the Republic of Armenia. *A Report on the Study on International Travel Through Borders of the Republic of Armenia in 2013.* 2014.

Ministry of Foreign Affairs of the Republic of Armenia

Citizenship. Accessed on June 29, 2017. http://www.mfa.am/en/citizenship/.

Who Needs a Visa to Travel to Armenia? Accessed on October 31, 2019. https://www.mfa.am/en/visa/

Ministry of Foreign Affairs of the Republic of Singapore, Press Room, 27/03/2012. Accessed on June 10, 2017. https://www.mfa.gov.sg/content/mfa/media_centre/press_room/pr/2012/201203/press_20120327_01.html.

Mishra, Anadi. *Getting Out of Marsh, Italy Awakening* (interview with Rakesh Ranjan). Roots and Routes. Vol. 2. No 10. October 2013.

Mitchell, Don. *Stuart Hall.* Chapter 28. In Hubbard, Phil and Kitchin, Rob. *Key Thinkers on Space and Place.* SAGE. 2011.

Mohamadi, Asal. *Representing Iran's 'Self' and 'Other': The Politics of National and Regional Identity.* Political Geography. 30 (2011).

Mohan, Giles. *Making Neoliberal States of Development: the Ghanaian Diaspora and the Politics of Homelands.* Environment and Planning D: Society and Space 2008. Volume 26. pp. 464-479.

Moisi, Dominique. *The Geopolitics of Emotions: How Cultures of Fear, Humiliation, and Hope Are Reshaping the World.* Doubleday. 2009.

Morley, David and Robins, Kevin. *Spaces of Identity: Global Media, Electronic Landscapes and Cultural Boundaries.* Routledge. London and New York. 2002.

National Assembly of the Republic of Armenia (official website), *The History of Armenian Parliaments.* Accessed on June 11, 2017. http://www.parliament.am/parliament.php?id=parliament&lang=eng.

Nations Encyclopedia: Armenia. Accessed on June 29, 2017. http://www.nationsencyclopedia.com/economies/Europe/Armenia.html.

National Statistics Office of Georgia, *General Population Census 2014, Total population by regions and ethnicity,* 2013. Accessed on June 27, 2017. www.census.ge

National Statistical Service of the Republic of Artsakh (Nagorno Karabakh), *Main Demographic Indicators.* Accessed on June 11, 2017. http://stat-nkr.am/files/yearbooks/2003_2009/8_Nasl_31-49.pdf.

National Statistical Service of the Republic of Armenia, *Demographic Database.* Accessed on June 11, 2017. http://www.armstat.am/en/?nid=420.

Nee, Patrick W. *Key Facts on Armenia: Essential Information on Armenia.* CreateSpace Independent Publishing Platform. 2014.

News.am news portal

Armenia Marks the Day of the First Republic (in Armenian). Accessed on June 29, 2017. https://news.am/arm/news/392325.html.

Forensic Examination Conducted Over Bodies of 3,577 People. Accessed on February 23, 2021. https://news.am/eng/news/629364.html

Newland, Kathleen. *Voice after Exit: Diaspora Advocacy.* Diasporas and Development Policy Project. Migration Policy Institute. 2010.

Ong, Aiwa. *Flexible Citizenship.* Duke University Press. 1999.

Office of the High Commissioner for Diaspora Affairs of Armenia. *About iGorts 2021.* Accessed on October 04, 2021. http://diaspora.gov.am/en/programs/25/fellowship.

Organization for Security and Co-operation in Europe (OSCE). *OSCE Minsk Group.* Last accessed on February 19, 2021. https://www.osce.org/mg

Ortmann, Stephan. *Singapore: The Politics of Inventing National Identity.* Journal of Current Southeast Asian Affairs. 28, 4.

OST Armenia, *The Armenian Diaspora.* Accessed on March 23, 2018. http://ostarmenia.com/en/armenian-diaspora/.

Oussatcheva, Marina. *Institutions in Diaspora: The Case of Armenian Community in Russia*. Transnational Community Programme. Working Paper Series. WPTC-01-09. Accessed on April 01, 2018. http://www.transcomm.ox.ac.uk/working%20papers/WPTC-01-09%20Marina.doc.pdf.

Ozinian, Alin, *Armenia's Security Dilemma Brings it to European Union*, Views-Week. Accessed on June 29, 2017. http://viewsweek.com/world/armenias-security-dilemma-brings-it-to-eurasian-union/.

Page, Ben and Mercer, Claire. *Diasporas and Development*. In Knott, Kim and McLoughlin, Sean (editors). *Diasporas: Concepts, Intersections, Identities*. Zed Books. London-New York. 2010.

Painter, Joe, *Multi-Level Citizenship, Identity and Regions in Contemporary Europe*, 1998, Colloquium on The Possibilities of Transnational Democracy, University of Newcastle. Accessed on March 21, 2018. http://community.dur.ac.uk/j.m.painter/Multilevel%20citizenship.pdf.

Pan-Armenian Games (in Armenian), *History of the Games* (in Armenian). Accessed on June 26, 2017. http://www.panarmeniangames.am/hy/extras/2014-08-12-06-40-20.

PanArmenian.net news portal

Armenia Among Most Religious and USSR-Nostalgic Nations. May 11, 2017. Accessed on December 08, 2019. http://www.panarmenian.net/rus/details/239481/

The Main Problem for the Armenians in Krasnodar is Identity Preservation, Says the Head of the Community. June 08, 2012. Accessed on June 13, 2017. http://www.PanArmenian.net/arm/news/110953/.

Panorama.am, *The Number of Tourists Visiting Armenia Increased by 10.5% in 2018*. Accessed on February 19, 2021. https://www.panorama.am/en/news/2019/02/08/tourists/2070280

Panossian, Razmig. *The Past as Nation: Three Dimensions of Armenian Identity*. Geopolitics 7(2). January 2002.

Panossian, Razmig. *Between Ambivalence and Intrusion: Politics and Identity in Armenia-Diaspora Relations*. Diaspora: A Journal of Transnational Studies. University of Toronto Press. Volume 7. Number 2. Fall 1998.

Papastergiadis, Nikos. *Why Multiculturalism Makes People So Angry and Sad*. Space. Place and Culture. 2013. 1-25.

Parliament of New South Wales, *Members: Gradys Berejiklian*. Accessed on June 15, 2017. https://www.parliament.nsw.gov.au/members/Pages/member-details.aspx?pk=21.

Payaslian, Simon. *The History of Armenia: From the Origins to the Present*. Palgrave Macmillan. 2007.

Petrosyan, David, *Armenian Community in Iran*, AB Publishing House, Sweden. Accessed on June 13, 2017. http://www.ca-c.org/journal/15-1998/st_10_-petrosjan.shtml.

Plaza, Sonia and Ratha, Dilip. *Diaspora for Development in Africa*. World Bank Publications. 2011.

PoliAtlas, A Look at the Political Map of the World, *Country Profile: Armenia*. Accessed on June 28, 2017. https://poliatlas.com/2015/11/30/country-profile-armenia/.

Population Australia. Accessed on April 15, 2018. http://www.population.net.au.

Post Magazine, A relic of the Raj - Kolkata's iconic Fairlawn Hotel changes hands http://www.scmp.com/magazines/post-magazine/travel/article/2136410/relic-raj-kolkatas-iconic-fairlawn-hotel-changes. Accessed on January 10, 2018.

Prolades.com Latin American Socio-Religious Studies Program, *The Armenian Community in the Los Angeles Area*, 2007. Accessed on June 13, 2017. http://www.prolades.com/glama/la5co07/armenian_community.htm.

President of the Republic of Armenia official website, *Nagorno Karabakh Republic: History and Current Reality*. Accessed on June 29, 2017. http://www.president.am/en/Artsakh-nkr/.

Presidential Library of Russian Federation (official website). *The Treaty of Turkmenchay Between Russia and Iran Signed*. Accessed on June 25, 2017. http://www.prlib.ru/en-us/history/Pages/Item.aspx?itemid=433 .

Radio Liberty/Radio Free Europe

Armenian PM 'Allowed to Retain Post In 2018'. Accessed on June 26, 2017. https://www.azatutyun.am/a/28311226.html.

Nikol Pashinyan. *The U.S. Senate Resolution Is Important and Historic*. Accessed on December 15, 2019. https://www.youtube.com/watch?v=Y55Gi6mufSY.

Radio Poland, *President Marks 650 Years of Armenian Community in Poland*. Accessed on June 8, 2017. http://www.thenews.pl/1/9/Artykul/300263,President-marks-650-years-of-Armenian-community-in-Poland.

Ragazzi, Francesco. *A Comparative Analysis of Diaspora Policies*. Political Geography 41 (2014) 74-89.

Rajan, S. Irudaya. *India Migration Report 2014: Diaspora and Development*. Volume 5. Routledge. 2014.

Rangan Datta, *Armenian Churches of West Bengal*. Accessed on June 25, 2017. https://rangandatta.wordpress.com/2013/06/26/armenian-churches-of-west-bengal/.

Refworld, *Law of the Republic of Armenia on the Citizenship of the Republic of Armenia*. Accessed on January 10, 2018. http://www.refworld.org/pdfid/51b770884.pdf.

RepatArmenia, *Armenia: The Power of the Diaspora*. Accessed on June 25, 2017. http://repatarmenia.org/en/engage/inspiration/a/armenia-the-power-of-the-diaspora.

Reuters (Irish, John and Rose, Michel). *France Accuses Turkey of Sending Syrian Jihadists to Nagorno-Karabakh*. Accessed on March 16, 2021. https://www.reuters.com/article/us-armenia-azerbaijan-putin-macron-idUSKBN26L3SB

Rios, Michael and Adv, Naomi. *Geographies of Diaspora: A Review*. UC Davis Centre for Regional Change. 2012.

Rodinson, Maxime. *Israel: A Colonial-Settler State?* Monad Press. 1973.

Rogobete, Silviu E. *The Interplay of Ethnic and Religious Identities in Europe: A Possible Mapping of a Complex Territory*. Europolis. 6/2009.

Said, Edward. *Orientalism*. Penguin Books. 25th anniversary edition. 1995.

Sanjian, Ara. *The Armenian Contribution to the Allied Victory in the Second World War*. Paper presented at the 60th Anniversary of the Victory over Fascism in the Second World War. The University of Balamand. April 19, 2005.

Santos, Amanda Proenca and Contreras, Rodolfo. *The World's First Christian Country?* BBC Travel. Accessed on June 25, 2017. http://www.bbc.com/travel/story/20170330-the-worlds-first-christian-country.

Sarkisian O. L. (et al). *Problems of National Identity under Globalization*. Russian-Armenian University Press. 2014.

Savage, Victor R. *The Idea of Singapore: What Recipes for Success and Challenges for the Future*. The Horizon – A Journal of Social Sciences. 1/2012. Volume III. January 2012.

Seferian, Nareg. *The Armenian Island of Venice*, World News, 21.03.2017. Accessed on June 29, 2017. http://www.euronews.com/2017/03/21/the-armenian-island-of-venice.

Seth, Mesrovb Jacob. *Armenians in India: from the Earliest Times to the Present Day*. Luzac and Co. London. 1897. Reprint by Forgotten Books. 2012.

Shoghakat TV of the Armenian Apostilic Church, *About Us*. Accessed on June 8, 2017. http://www.shoghakat.am/en/site/about.

Sideway, James and Grundy-Warr, Carl. *The Place of the Nation-State*, In Daniels, Peter, Bradshaw, Michael, Shaw, Denis, and Sidaway, James. *An Introduction to Human Geography: Issues for the 21st Century*. 3rd edition. Pearson Prentice Hall. 2008.

Simonyan, Hripsimeh. *This is Armenia: The Land of Ours*. Tigran Mets Publishing. Yerevan. 2009.

Sinatti G. and Horst C. *Migrants as Agents of Development: Diaspora Engagement Discourse and Practice*. Ethnicities. Vol. 15. Issue 1 (2015). pp. 134-152.

Skrbis, Zlatko. *Long-Distance Nationalism*. Ashgate. 1999.

Smith, Anthony D. *National Identity*. University of Nevada Press. 1991.

Smith, Anthony D. *National Identity and the Idea of European Unity*. International Affairs. 68, 1, 1992.

Smith, Anthony D. *Culture, Community and Territory: The Politics of Ethnicity and Nationalism*. Workshop on Ethnicity and International Relations. The Royal Institute of International Affairs. 23-24 November 1995.

Smith, Anthony D. *When is a Nation?* Geopolitics. Volume 7. 2002 – Issue 2.

Sökefeld, Martin and Schwalgin, Susanne. *Institutions and Their Agents in Diaspora: A Comparison of Armenians in Athens and Alevis in Germany*. Transnational Communities Programme. Transcomm.ox.ac.uk. The 6th European Association of Social Anthropologists Conference. Krakau. 26-29 July, 2000.

Soja, Edward W. *Postmodern Geographies: The Reassertion of Space in Critical Social Theory*. Verso. 1989.

Srapionyan, Serzh. *The 'Ari Tun' Program Became a Viable Programme Over the Years* (interview). Hayern Aysor periodical. Ministry of Diaspora of the Republic of Armenia. 27/04/2017. Accessed on June 9, 2017. http://hayernaysor.am/en/archives/244055.

Steffens, Liliana. *Armenia Tourism, on the Rise, Chair of State Tourism Committee Says*, Argophilia Travel News. Accessed on June 25, 2017. http://www.argophilia.com/news/armenia-tourism-rise/217794/.

Stevens, Stan. *Fieldwork as Commitment*. Geographical Review. Vol. 91. No.1/2. Doing Fieldwork (Jan. – Apr., 2001). pp. 66-73.

Stewart, Frances. *Religion versus Ethnicity as a Source of Mobilisation: Are There Differences?* University of Sussex. 2009.

Suny, Ronald G. *Armenia, Azerbaijan and Georgia: Country Studies*. DIANE Publishing. 1996.

Suny, Ronald G. *They Can Live in a Desert But Nowhere Else: a History of the Armenian Genocide*. Princeton University Press. 2015.

TaTever – Wings of Tatev, official website. Accessed on June 25, 2017. https://www.tatever.am/en.

Tejirian, Eleanor and Simon, Reeva Spector. *Conflict, Conquest and Conversion: Two Thousand Years of Christian Missions in the Middle East*. Columbia University Press. 2012.

The Armenian Apostolic Church of St. Mary, Melbourne. Accessed on June 25, 2017. http://www.armenianchurchmelb.com.au/History.aspx.

The Armenian Church

Gevorkian Seminary. Accessed on January 10, 2018. https://www.armenian-church.org/index.jsp?sid=1&id=16850&pid=16849&lng=en.

Mother See of Holy Etchmiadzin. Accessed on January 10, 2018. https://www.armenianchurch.org/index.jsp?lng=en.

The Armenian Weekly. *Remembering Bash Aparan and Building a Green Sustainable Armenia*. June 9, 2017. Accessed on June 30, 2017. http://armenian-weekly.com/2017/06/09/remembering-bash-aparan/.

The Atlantic. *The Ancient Ghost City of Ani*. Accessed on June 25, 2017. https://www.theatlantic.com/photo/2014/01/the-ancient-ghost-city-of-ani/100668/.

The Australian, *The Last Armenians of Old Calcutta*. May 14, 2016. Accessed on March 30, 2018. https://www.theaustralian.com.au/life/travel/the-last-arme-nians-of-old-calcutta/news-story/728a832b860d54c5c5e7c29b6f71301f.

The CIA World Factbook

Armenia. Accessed on June 13, 2017. https://www.cia.gov/library/publications/the-world-factbook/geos/print_am.html.

Country Comparison. Population. Accessed on January 10, 2018. https://www.cia.gov/library/publications/the-world-factbook/rankorder/2119rank.html#am.

Lebanon. Accessed on June 13, 2017. https://www.cia.gov/library/publications/the-world-factbook/geos/le.html.

Turkey. Accessed on June 25, 2017. https://www.cia.gov/library/publications/the-world-factbook/geos/tu.html.

The Economist, *Nagorno-Karabakh's War: A Frozen Conflict Explodes*. Accessed on June 25, 2017. http://www.economist.com/news/europe/21696563-after-fac-ing-decades-armenia-and-azerbaijan-start-shooting-frozen-conflict-explodes.

The Guardian

The Syrian Refugee Restaurateurs Spicing Up Armenian Cuisine. Accessed on July 16, 2017. https://www.theguardian.com/world/2016/mar/07/the-syrian-refu-gee-restaurateurs-spicing-up-armenian-cuisine.

What Happened at Gallipoli? April 24, 2015. Accessed on June 15, 2017. https://www.theguardian.com/news/2015/apr/24/gallipoli-what-happened-military-disaster-legacy.

The Istana, *Toast by President Tony Tan Keng Yam at the State Dinner in Honour of the President of the Republic of Armenia His Excellency Serzh Sargsyan at the Istana Banquet Hall on 28 March 2012 at 7:30pm.* Accessed on March 29, 2018. http://www.istana.gov.sg/the-president/former-presidents/dr-tony-tan-keng-yam/speeches/toast-president-tony-tan-keng-yam-the-state-dinner-he-serzh-sargsyan-president-the-republic-armenia.

The National Geographic. *Armenian and the Armenians.* Volume XXVIII. No. 4. October, 1915.

The New York Times. *Senate Passes Resolution Recognizing Armenian Genocide, in Defiance of Trump.* Accessed on December 15, 2019. https://www.nytimes.com/2019/12/12/us/politics/senate-armenian-genocide.html.

The REUT Institute. *Engaging the Israeli Diaspora: Toronto as a Case Study.* Tamuz5773. June, 2013.

The Straight Times, Newspaper SG, *Armenia Ship Arrives in Singapore,* June 12, 2011. Accessed on June 01, 2017. http://eresources.nlb.gov.sg/newspapers/digitised/issue/straitstimes20110612-1.

The Zoryan Institute. Accessed on June 9, 2017. http://zoryaninstitute.org/about-us/#about-zoryan.

Thrift, Nigel. *Space: The Fundamental Stuff of Human* Geography. In Holloway, Sarah L., Rice, Stephen P., and Valentine, Gill. *Key Concepts in Geography.* SAGE. 2003.

Tölölyan, Khachig. *Diaspora Studies: Past, Present and Promise.* Oxford Diasporas Programme. Working Paper Series 2011. No. 55.

Tölölyan, Khachig. *Elites and Institutions in the Armenian Transnation,* Diaspora: A Journal of Transnational Studies. University of Toronto Press. Volume 9. Number 1 Spring 2000.

TravelTip map generation. Accessed on May 01, 2017. www.traveltip.org.

Tuan, Yi-Fu. *Space and Place: The Perspective of Experience.* University of Minnesota Press. 7th edition. 2011.

United Nations, *Population in 1999 and 2000: All Countries.* Accessed on June 25, 2017. http://www.un.org/popin/popdiv/pop1999-00.pdf .

United Nations: Armenia, *UNICEF Calls for Proposal: Background and Context.* Accessed on June 16, 2017. http://www.un.am/hy/vacancy/74.

United Nations Refugee Agency – Refworld. Accessed June 15, 2017. http://www.refworld.org/pdfid/51b770884.pdf.

U.S. Commission on Security and Cooperation in Europe. *Report on the Armenian Referendum for Independence.* Washington, D. C. October 01, 1991.

Uzelac, Gordana. *When Is the Nation? Constituent Elements and Processes.* Geopolitics. 7:2. 2002.

Vardanyan, Ruben and Alekyan, Nune. *At the Crossroads: History, Civilisations, Ideas.* 2018.

Vardanyan, Vahagn. *An Open Letter (to several Armenian organisations).* 168.am Newspaper. Accessed on November 13, 2019. https://en.168.am/2016/10/17/11289.html.

Vardanyan, Vahagn. *Attracting Investments in Armenia Assumes a Logical Sequence* (in Armenian), 168Finance. Accessed on September 24, 2019. https://168.am/2019/03/03/1089166.html.

Vardanyan, Vahagn. *Development Philosophy of a Small Nation-State: Singapore's Case* (in Armenian). Economics Scientific, v. 1, pp. 40-58, Jun. 2019.

Vardanyan, Vahagn. *Homeland and Diaspora: Connection Through Spaces.* Култура/Culture. Vol. 6. 14/2016. pp. 75-84.

Vardanyan, Vahagn. *What Can the Amount Collected by Hayastan All-Armenian Fund Tell Us?* Aravot.am. Accessed on March 07, 2021. https://www.aravoten.am/2020/11/06/269696/?fbclid=IwAR3QJfSdpXg_BL6G5ROs7Sp1-nAX152B5JsNKUxvu4bFADejkaILxV2Foxnk.

Vardanyan, Vahagn. *What Is Armenia's Future Path?* (in Armenian) Aravot.am. Accessed on March 06, 2021. https://www.aravot.am/2021/02/27/1174320/?fbclid=IwAR3C_OwVvqgsza0_JSVSk-OIwJVHJGee7lrcCjcEIrNWiwsUN-VEIkMIqIf0.

Walker, Christopher J. *Armenia: A Very Brief History.* MIA Publishers. Yerevan. 2014.

Warren, Adrien. *Desperately Seeking Refuge: From Syria to Armenia,* Eastbook.eu project. 12 August 2013. Accessed on June 13, 2017. http://www.eastbook.eu/en/2013/08/12/desperately-seeking-refuge-the-syrian-armenian-humanitarian-crisis/.

Webner, Pnina. *Complex Diasporas.* in Knott, Kim and McLoughlin, Sean (editors). *Diasporas: Concepts, Intersections, Identities.* Zed Books. London-New York. 2010.

Wise, Amanda. *Exile and Return Among the East Timorese.* University of Pennsylvania Press. 2006.

Whelan, Yvonne. *(Inter)national Naming: Heritage, Conflict and Diaspora.* ACME: An International E-Journal for Critical Geographies. 2011. 10(1). pp. 7-12.

World Heritage Encyclopedia, *Kessab.* Accessed on June 9, 2017. http://cn.worldheritage.org/articles/Kessab.

WorldPopulationReview.com. Accessed on June 11, 2017.

Armenia Population 2017. http://worldpopulationreview.com/countries/armenia-ation/

Cairo Population 2017. http://worldpopulationreview.com/world-cities/cairo-population/

Georgia Population 2017. http://worldpopulationreview.com/countries/ukraine-population/

Marseille Population 2017. http://worldpopulationreview.com/world-cities/marseille-population/

Moscow Population 2017. http://worldpopulationreview.com/world-cities/moscow-population/

New York City Population 2017. http://worldpopulationreview.com/us-cities/new-york-city-population/

Population of Cities in Iran. http://worldpopulationreview.com/countries/iran-population/cities/

Population of Cities in Lebanon. http://worldpopulationreview.com/countries/lebanon-population/cities/

Sao Paolo Population 2017. http://worldpopulationreview.com/world-cities/saopaulo-population/

Syria Population 2017. http://worldpopulationreview.com/countries/syria-population/

Tehran Population 2017. http://worldpopulationreview.com/world-cities/tehran-population/

Ukraine Population 2017. http://worldpopulationreview.com/countries/ukraine-population/

Uruguay Population 2017. http://worldpopulationreview.com/countries/uruguay-population/

Yeoh, Brenda S.A. and Willis, Katie (editors). *State/Nation/Transnation.* Routledge. 2004.

Zohry, Ayman. *Armenians in Egypt.* XXV IUSSP International Population Conference. International Union for the Scientific Study of Population. American University in Cairo. 2005.

Zolian, Mikael, *Remembering and Demanding: How Armenia and the Diaspora are Approaching the Centennial of the Armenian Genocide.* In Heinrich Böll Stiftung. Accessed on January 10, 2018. https://ge.boell.org/en/2015/04/22/remembering-and-demanding-how-armenia-and-diaspora-are-approaching-centennial-armenian.